A Phonetics Workbook
for Students

Building a Foundation
for Transcription

Heidi M. Harbers

Illinois State University

Boston   Columbus   Indianapolis   New York   San Francisco   Upper Saddle River
Amsterdam   Cape Town   Dubai   London   Madrid   Milan   Munich   Paris   Montreal   Toronto
Delhi   Mexico City   São Paulo   Sydney   Hong Kong   Seoul   Singapore   Taipei   Tokyo

Executive Editor & Publisher, Professional and Career: Stephen D. Dragin
Editorial Assistant: Michelle Hochberg
Marketing Manager: Joanna Sabella
Production Editor: Karen Mason
Production Coordination and Electronic Composition: Shylaja Gattupalli/
    Jouve India Private Limited
Text Design and Illustrations: Jouve India Private Limited
Cover Designer: Jennifer Hart

Text Credits: p. 71: From EDWARDS. Applied Phonetics, 3/E. © 2003 Delmar Learning, a part of Cengage Learning, Inc. Reproduced by permission. www.cengage.com/permissions. p. 80, Figure 10.1, from Bauman-Waengler, Jacqueline. *Articulatory and Phonological Impairments: A Clinical Focus*, 3RD Ed., © 2008. Reprinted and Electronically reproduced by permission of Pearson Education, Inc., Upper Saddle River, New Jersey. pp. 106–107: From Shriberg, Lawrence D.; Kent, Raymond D.; *Clinical Phonetics*, 3/e © 2003. Reprinted and Electronically reproduced by permission of Pearson Education, Inc., Upper Saddle River, New Jersey.

PEARSON

ISBN 10: 0-13-282558-9
ISBN 13: 978-0-13-282558-0

To my parents

Contents

List of Exercises

Contents of Audio CD

41 Tracks; Total play time 56 minutes, 42 seconds

Track	Contents	Time
1	Transcription practice set 1: *Front/back monophthongs in isolation*	1:24
2	Transcription practice set 2: *Front/back monophthongs in CV/VC syllables*	1:26
3	Transcription practice set 3: *Front/back monophthongs in CV/VC syllables*	1:25
4	Transcription practice set 4: *All monophthongs in CVC syllables*	1:26
5	Transcription practice set 5: *Phonemic diphthongs in simple syllables*	1:28
6	Transcription practice set 6: *All monophthongs and phonemic diphthongs in simple syllables*	1:24
7	Transcription practice set 7: *Controlled /r/ diphthongs in simple syllables*	1:28
8	Transcription practice set 8: *All vowels in simple syllables*	1:23
9	Transcription practice set 9: *Stop-plosives in simple syllables*	1:22
10	Transcription practice set 10: *Fricatives/affricates in simple syllables*	1:25
11	Transcription practice set 11: *All obstruents in simple syllables*	1:22
12	Transcription practice set 12: *All sonorants in simple syllables*	1:20
13	Transcription practice set 13: *Prevocalic sequences*	1:19
14	Transcription practice set 14: *Postvocalic sequences*	1:19
15	Transcription practice set 15: *Pre- and postvocalic sequences*	1:23
16	Examples of coarticulation	1:00
17	Examples of alveolar flap/tap	:37
18	Examples of glottal stop for intervocalic /t/	:28
19	Examples of /l/ productions	1:15
20	Examples of velar nasal with and without /g/	:41
21	Introduction to stress: Vowels in stressed and unstressed syllables	1:26
22	Compound words	:31
23	Stress patterns in nouns and verbs	1:04
24	Sample sentences with nouns and verbs	:49
25	Exercise 22-A	1:57
26	Exercise 22-E	1:14
27	Exercise 22-F	:47
28	Exercise 22-G	:41
29	Exercise 22-H	:51
30	Exercise 22-I	:40
31	Exercise 22-J	1:29
32	Exercise 22-K	2:39
33	Exercise 22-L	1:29
34	Exercise 22-N	1:53
35	Exercise 22-P	:52
36	Exercise 22-R	1:43
37	Reduction of vowels to schwa in unstressed syllables	1:32
38	Exercise 22-S	2:15
39	Exercise 22-U	1:35
40	Exercise 22-V	1:24
41	Exercise 22-W	4:33

Preface

About This Workbook

If 10 professors who taught the undergraduate phonetics courses at their respective universities came together, each of them would approach the acquisition of phonetics and subsequent transcription skills differently. I recall my own phonetics course, taken more than 30 years ago, taught by a professor in broadcasting (although I was majoring in communication disorders). We spent 50 minutes, three times per week, transcribing words spoken by the professor. *Pianissimo* is one such word that has not left my memory bank!

My background in language and phonology, and my research in phonological awareness and early literacy skills, have informed the way I teach my own phonetics course. I treat learning the International Phonetic Alphabet (IPA) in much the same way as children learn to read. Awareness of sounds needs to be addressed prior to learning which symbols are used to represent those sounds. Additionally, conventions of the written symbol system need attention. Because the foundation for the IPA is sounds, it is imperative that the nuances in the pronunciation of sounds also are emphasized.

The primary focus of this workbook is to *prepare* students to be able to transcribe speech phonetically by increasing their awareness and knowledge about the English sound system, their knowledge of how individual sounds are formed, and their understanding of how sounds combine to form words. This workbook presents an active learning tool for individuals studying articulatory phonetics and English pronunciation skills. Its goal is to provide a "sound" foundation from which transcription skills can develop. This workbook is not the "typical" phonetics workbook. Using this workbook will provide students with a sufficient foundation needed to learn to attend to sounds in words so that learning and applying a new symbol system will be a successful experience for them. Because one of its goals is to provide a sound foundation from which transcription can build, this workbook slows down the learning process so that students have an opportunity to develop the skills and strategies they need before they are required to use them.

In order to learn and use the IPA for transcribing speech, students must attend to the sound structure of the language. Becoming aware of the sounds of English phonology can be challenging because a typical student has not paid attention to individual sounds since mastering reading and spelling. Although we hear language on a daily basis in the form of conversation, television programs, music, etc., and encounter print on a daily basis by reading, texting,

etc., we give minimal attention to the particular sounds in the overall message because our ability to process speech and print is very rapid and automatic. This automaticity, however, can disrupt adult students from attending to the sound system of their language as they are faced with the task of learning a symbol system that is based solely on what sounds are heard. Since becoming competent in literacy, we have learned to bypass the auditory channel and solely focus our attention on the visual forms of words. Van Riper and Smith (1979) refer to this as being "eye-minded" rather than "ear-minded." For adult students, who are about to learn about the English sound system and acquire a new symbol system (IPA), attention needs to shift back to the auditory and kinesthetic characteristics of those sounds (i.e., return to being ear-minded). Learning to apply the IPA when transcribing speech will eventually require a balance of being both ear-minded and eye minded.

I have learned a great deal from my students over the past 15 years. My students have taught me that they need repeated exposure to the symbols in order to use them accurately and efficiently. Some students encounter difficulty isolating sounds and matching them to a new symbol. Without a solid foundation, these students encounter difficulty with subsequent transcription skills and clinical application remains problematic. Other students seem to be able to match sounds to the IPA symbols with ease, yet they do not always have a solid understanding of articulatory phonetics for efficient and effective application in clinical situations. In order to be able to accurately transcribe the speech of others, students need to learn about how sounds are formed, how those sounds change in different contexts, what symbols represent those sounds, and what rules guide the use of those symbols.

Because of these issues, this workbook is based on a "meta" approach to learning. Meta skills require that conscious attention be given to a specific entity apart from understanding the meaning. To be meta requires knowledge to become explicit, rather than implicit. Becoming explicitly aware of the phonological structure of our language is a cognitive task and one that requires focused attention, active learning, a great deal of practice, and a fair amount of reflection. Additionally, increasing awareness of the orthographic system is needed in order to effectively shift our attention to the sounds on which that system is based. The content in this workbook is presented in such a way that students have to think about sounds in an explicit manner. Information is presented in order to create cognitive dissonance in students so that they are encouraged to make sense from what is presented to them. My goal is to have the individuals who use this workbook *think* about the sounds of the English language as they never have in the past. My primary aim throughout this workbook is to design exercises for students to become reacquainted with the English sound system through discovery. As they complete the exercises, I would like for them to experience "ah-ha" moments as they make sense of the phonological system of English.

Explanation of Organizational Framework

The overall presentation of information is deliberate, explicit, and systematic to promote successful learning. The first challenge it presents to students is to think about sounds in the face of orthography (Unit 1). It then introduces the vowels (Unit 2) and consonants (Unit 3) of the English phonology system. Pronunciation information, including allophonic, dialectal, and accent variations, are included within each of these units. Lastly, the topics of broad transcription and word stress are introduced (Unit 4). Most published texts provide these three levels (i.e., awareness, IPA symbols and articulatory phonetics information, transcription) simultaneously, despite the fact that most students do not learn these skills in that way. Most instructors supplement existing phonetics workbooks with additional practice material to insure student learning. It is the aim of this workbook to systematically lead students through each level *separately* so they are able to learn new information on a firmer foundation.

The chapters within each unit lay the foundation, provide the pertinent content, and then provide ample practice for students to adequately learn the specifics and meet the established goals. The exercises build upon each other so that each student can learn solidly by taking from what they have previously learned and applying the knowledge to new material. This systematic approach to learning provides a layering of information to scaffold student learning. Along with a variety of practice exercises, questions are posed to students to encourage them to think about their sound system and reflect upon specific areas. The final chapter in each unit provides a review of terms (Units 1–3), a focus on pronunciation (Units 2 and 3), and additional practice that elaborates and extends previous exercises.

The first unit focuses on phonological awareness (i.e., awareness of syllables, onsets, rimes, and sounds) as well as orthographic knowledge (i.e., knowledge about how spoken language is represented in print) and introduces students to basic terminology. It briefly presents the concepts of phonology, phonemes, allophones, coarticulation, assimilation, dialects, and accents and alerts students to the impact these concepts may have on pronunciation and perception. This unit lays the foundation for the information and exercises that will be introduced in Units 2 and 3.

The focus then moves to the production of individual sounds (articulatory phonetics) and the IPA symbols that represent them. The second unit focuses on the vowel system of the English language. Vowels are presented first because, in my experience, students are challenged more by vowels than consonants. Because the symbols for 16 consonant sounds are the same in the IPA and the Roman alphabet, students can immediately be exposed to the vowel symbols in the context of words. Unit 2 provides exercises for the learner to focus on the specific characteristics that help to distinguish vowels from each other. It details the individual vowels in the vowel system: 14 monophthongs (Chapters 6, 7, and 9), diphthongs (Chapter 10), and rhotic/controlled-r diphthongs and triphthongs (Chapter 11). Understanding the specific vowel characteristics within the context of the vowel quadrilateral is emphasized in the exercises presented in Chapter 8 so that students understand the classification of monophthongs and come to view the vowel quadrilateral as a useful tool in future clinical decision making.

Unit 3 concentrates on the 25 consonant sounds in the English language. How consonants are classified is addressed first, and the introduction of voicing, place, and manner of articulation is introduced through experiential sorting exercises (Chapter 13). The six manner classes serve as the organizational framework when individual sounds are described and detailed (Chapters 14–19). Each chapter presents the sounds within a specific manner class, along with their characteristics. Once students learn the characteristics of each sound, they will be able to compare and contrast sounds with each other. For speech–language pathology students, this will serve as a foundation for understanding development, phonological patterns and processes, and articulation errors. Included in each chapter in this unit is pronunciation information (in the form of allowable differences) that will help students understand their own and others' sound production in words. This will be followed by exercises to practice the information for consonant singletons. Students will be asked to (1) "read" phonetic symbols to create a familiar word, (2) translate the sounds in a word into phonetic symbols, (3) use an "equation" of phonetic information to make words, and (4) write a phonetic equation for presented words. The consonant sounds in each manner class will then be introduced in the context of consonant sequences. Two familiar exercises (reading phonetic symbols to make words and writing a word in phonetic symbols) will assist students in focusing on the consonant sounds in sequences. Additional exercises are included in the final chapter to provide additional exposure to sounds that are frequently problematic for students.

Up until this point in the workbook, individual sounds in single-syllable words were emphasized using broad phonemic transcription. Unit 4 discusses phonetic transcription and the role it plays in clinical application. Specific rules when transcribing consonants and vowels are presented. The role of stress in pronunciation and transcription is introduced and elaborated. Exercises in reading phonetic symbols as well as in transcribing words into symbols are included to achieve the automaticity required for clinical application. This unit serves as the basis for transcription exercises that occur next in the training of speech–language pathologists; that is, word productions are presented live or via tape presentation, and students translate what they hear into phonetic symbols. Practicing transcription in this way is outside the scope of this workbook.

The supplemental audio CD that accompanies this workbook serves several purposes. Fifteen practice transcription sets are provided to assist the retrieval of the IPA symbols upon hearing a nonsense syllable. Five tracks are provided that demonstrate pronunciation notes. Half of the content of the CD provides auditory models of content and exercises from Chapter 22: Stress. Although listening to the CD is not required to complete the exercises in Chapter 22, it will be helpful to students because stress is difficult to detect when listening to one's own speech.

Most of the pronunciations used in this book reflect the author's Midwestern (central Illinois) dialect. When transcribing a word that is not presented orally, your pronunciation patterns may differ. Be assured that differences are not errors. Based on your own dialect, how you pronounce specific sounds (especially vowels) may be different from those presented in the exercises. Please check with your instructor for explanations of differences.

New! CourseSmart eTextbook Available

CourseSmart is an exciting new choice for students looking to save money. As an alternative to purchasing the printed textbook, students can purchase an electronic version of the same content. With a CourseSmart eTextbook, students can search the text, make notes online, print out reading assignments that incorporate lecture notes, and bookmark important passages for later review. For more information, or to purchase access to the CourseSmart eTextbook, visit www.coursesmart.com.

Van Riper, C., & Smith, D. (1979). *An introduction to General American phonetics*. Prospect Heights, IL: Waveland Press.

Acknowledgments

The exercises for this workbook grew out teaching CSD 215, "Clinical Phonetics" at Illinois State University. I thank the approximately 100 students each year who challenge me to do my best work. I am grateful to my past teaching assistants Beth Maher, Renee Moore, Kandace Davis, and Melissa Griffin who helped me creatively find ways for students to learn and practice the symbols needed for transcription. A special thank you goes to my present teaching assistant, Ashley Ciecko, who was a constant in assisting me when this workbook was taking shape over the past several semesters. Gratitude also goes to Sarah Huey, Christi Patterson, Maggie O'Shea, and Jessica Uhlir, who assisted in providing their viewpoints and ideas as well as researching specific areas. Thanks to the Pearson reviewers, Jean Andruski, Wayne State University; Raymond Dalfonso, Kutztown University; and Laureen O'Hanlon, California State University of Sacramento. I am grateful to Elizabeth Harbers Warden and Clare Maksimovich who knew nothing about phonetics but were careful proofreaders. A special thank you also goes to Aaron Paolucci who recorded and produced the audio CD and Connie de Veer, Mark de Veer, Gwen de Veer, and Jeb Burris for their voices. This workbook would not have been possible without the efforts of the Pearson "team." Many thanks to Steve Dragin and Karen Mason for their leadership and support, and Carrie Fox and Shylaja Gattupalli and their teams for their work with the final production.

To the Student About to Embark on This Sound Journey

I hope these exercises increase your awareness of how complex and amazing speech sound perception and production can be. Because this workbook is about sounds, it is important for you to listen and feel your own pronunciations and listen and watch how others produce their sounds in words, phrases, and sentences. The sounds in the words used in the exercises, especially the vowel sounds, may not reflect your own pronunciation. There is a great deal of variability in how the vowels, and sometimes the consonants, in words are produced. Be patient with yourself as you learn to train your mind to focus on sounds. May your travels be filled with many insights into what most speakers take for granted!

UNIT
1 *Laying the Foundation*

Read the following groups of words aloud:

fear	gear	wear
meat	sweat	great
tough	cough	dough
perk	cork	work
chef	shoe	sure
who	whoa	white

While reading these words, you soon realize that the spellings you *see* do not always reflect the sounds you *hear*.

As a student about to learn the International Phonetic Alphabet (IPA), you must think *more* about the *sounds* in the words you use than about their spellings. To do this, you need to become reacquainted with the sounds of the English language. Van Riper and Smith (1979) refer to this as becoming "ear-minded" rather than "eye-minded."

The goals for the first unit include:

- To reacquaint you with the sound make-up of words in the English language

- To assist you in differentiating between the sounds you hear and the letters you see when looking at a word

- To introduce you to basic terminology that will be used throughout the workbook

- To provide you with exercises to improve your attention to sounds in words in order to prepare you to learn a new symbol system—the IPA

- To introduce you to the concept of coarticulation and how it influences your perception and production of sounds in words and connected speech

- To introduce you to the concept of dialects and accents and how these influence your perception and production of sounds

Thinking About the English Phonology System: Syllables and Sounds

Phonology refers to the sound system of a language. The phonological system of a language consists of (1) the group of specific sounds used in that language, (2) the permissible variations of those sounds when produced, and (3) the particular rules for combining those sounds.

Two groups of sounds make up a phonology system: consonants and vowels. **Consonants** are speech sounds produced as a result of air moving through the vocal tract encountering some constriction or obstruction. The **articulators** (i.e., lips, front teeth, lower jaw, tongue, or the velum) close the vocal tract in some way by interfering with, obstructing, or modifying the outgoing breath stream to produce these types of sounds. As a result, consonants are referred to as *closed* sounds. The consonants in a word can be by themselves (**singleton**) or in a series (**sequence**). An example of a word with consonant singletons is *bat*; an example of a word with consonant sequences is *stops*. When consonants are in a sequence, each consonant sound retains its identity during pronunciation. Sequences can occur within a syllable (**cluster**) or across syllables. Both sequences in the earlier example of *stops* can be referred to as a cluster; however, the sequences in the words *basket* and *husband* fall across syllables.

Vowels are speech sounds produced as a result of air moving through a relatively *open* vocal tract. Although movement of the articulators (i.e., lips, tongue, and jaw) changes the shape of the mouth, producing different vowel sounds, the breath stream remains unimpeded. Vowels contain the most acoustic energy and therefore are perceived as stronger sounds (as compared with consonants).

Consonants and vowels serve different functions in our sound system. Both contribute to the clearness and intelligibility of speech. Because they are the most prominent, vowels carry the intonation and prosody of our language. Consonants act as dividing units, assisting in creating boundaries in words. Think about talking while yawning or saying something with a pen in your mouth. Depending on the context, the listener may still understand your message because of the intonation. What is lacking, however, is the finer distinctions and clarity made by the consonants.

The Syllable

A **syllable** is a unit of pronunciation consisting of a vowel sound alone or a vowel sound with the consonants that precede or follow it. There is only one vowel sound in a syllable. When adjacent vowels are produced as separate sounds, separate syllables are formed (e.g., *helium*, *rodeo*). An exception to this definition is when a consonant can serve as the nucleus of a syllable. Only three consonants (i.e., m, n, and l) can serve this role. This special circumstance will be explained in Unit 4.

Parts of a Syllable

Vowels

Vowels are essential to syllable formation. A syllable must contain a vowel sound. Each vowel serves as the **nucleus** of the syllable. Because a vowel sound has the strongest acoustic energy, they are often referred to as the **peak** of the syllable.

Vowel = peak/nucleus

EXERCISE 1-A: COUNTING SYLLABLES

Say each word aloud and count the number of syllables you hear in the following words. Write the correct number of the line that follows each word.

happy	_____	catastrophe	_____	sequential	_____
alphabet	_____	alligator	_____	boys	_____
retroactive	_____	appropriate	_____	introduce	_____
imagination	_____	ditches	_____	oncoming	_____
psychological	_____	include	_____	overwhelming	_____
grounded	_____	computer	_____	spindle	_____
unspeakable	_____	spilled	_____	unilateral	_____

Return to your answers. The number of syllables = the number of vowel *sounds* you hear in each word. Think of 20 more words. Say each word aloud and count the number of syllables in each.

SOMETHING TO CONSIDER **Pronunciation Variance**	There are many words that may be pronounced with different syllable counts. Consider the following words: *every*, *boundary*, *usually*. Can you say them two different ways? Think of other words that can be pronounced with different syllable counts.

Consonants

Because the vowel sound is the nucleus of the syllable, consonants are described by their relationship to the vowel. **Prevocalic consonants** (singleton or sequence) are those consonants that come before the vowel. **Postvocalic consonants** (singleton or sequence) are those consonants that come after the vowel. These two terms refer to the consonant placement within a syllable. When the *word* (rather than the syllable) is the unit of pronunciation, the term **intervocalic** may be included. Intervocalic consonants (singletons or sequences) are those consonants that are between vowels in a word with two or more syllables.

EXERCISE 1-B: DISTINGUISHING CONSONANTS IN A WORD IN REFERENCE TO THE VOWEL SOUND

Say each word aloud. Classify the consonant sounds in each word in terms of their relationship to the vowel.

Word	*Prevocalic Consonants*	*Intervocalic Consonants*	*Postvocalic Consonants*
me			
up			
not			
vase			
skip			
bend			
helps			
wagon			
basket			
consonants			

REMINDER

Consonants within a syllable unit: *Onsets* are *prevocalic* consonants; *codas* are *postvocalic*.

Singleton: consonant sound by itself

Sequence: two or more adjacent consonant sounds; each consonant sound retains its identity during pronunciation.

Although the vowel is essential to syllable formation, consonants are not necessary. When consonants are present in a syllable, they are defined by their relationship to the vowel nucleus. The consonant(s) that precede the vowel in a syllable is/are termed the **onset**; the consonant(s) that follow the vowel in a syllable is/are termed the **coda**. Remember, consonant sounds can be alone before or after a vowel (**singleton**), or two or more consonant sounds can be adjacent to each other before or after a vowel (**sequence**).

EXERCISE 1-C: FOCUS ON CONSONANTS: IDENTIFYING ONSETS AND CODAS

Say each of the following words aloud. Identify which consonant sounds/letters make up the onset and which sounds/letters make up the coda. Be careful—not all of the words will have an onset; not all of the words will have a coda. Remember to focus on the *sounds* you hear when you pronounce each word rather than the letters you see. Try not to be tricked by the spelling!

goat   onset _____   coda _____

path   onset _____   coda _____

snake   onset _____   coda _____

try   onset _____   coda _____

word   onset _____   coda _____

bulb   onset _____   coda _____

eight   onset _____   coda _____

rips   onset _____   coda _____

frost   onset _____   coda _____

book   onset _____   coda _____

own   onset _____   coda _____

thread   onset _____   coda _____

left   onset _____   coda _____

if   onset _____   coda _____

be   onset _____   coda _____

EXERCISE 1-D: FINDING WORDS WITH THE SAME CODA

Read the words in each row aloud; focus on the ending consonant sounds. Find the two words in the row with the same coda. Cross out the word that does not share the same coda with the other two. Remember to focus on the *sounds* you hear when you pronounce each word rather than the letters you see.

picks	fox	cups
noise	nose	voice
bathe	mouth	bath
comb	tub	some
eyes	less	cheese
cape	help	deep
feud	mud	hoped
beige	vague	dog
sponge	wrong	arrange
slept	hoped	robbed
laugh	stove	leaf
licorice	mustache	research
box	hunks	sphinx
talked	strict	tagged
whisk	wax	flask

EXERCISE 1-E: FINDING WORDS WITH THE SAME ONSET

Read the words in each row aloud; focus on the beginning consonant sounds. Find the two words in the row with the same onset. Cross out the word that does not share the same onset with the other two. Remember to focus on the *sounds* you hear when you pronounce each word rather than the letters you see.

the	thaw	thumb
chorus	chore	kite
honor	horse	who

sure	sauce	shot
cube	cool	cure
there	this	think
suede	square	sweat
one	own	world
cheese	chef	chief
join	gel	girl
quick	chase	choir
king	court	cent
squirt	skirt	scoop
ooze	you	use
Xerox	zoo	ski

SOMETHING TO CONSIDER

Which statement(s) is/are true?

Every syllable has a vowel.

Every syllable has a coda.

Every syllable has an onset.

For each false statement, provide a word as evidence to support your decision.

LET'S REVIEW: SYLLABLE PARTS

Nucleus/peak: the vowel
Onset: all consonants (singleton or sequence) that come before the vowel
Coda: all consonants (singleton or sequence) that come after the vowel

➔ An additional syllable component is called the **rime**. This is the part of the syllable that includes the vowel (nucleus/peak) and the consonants that follow it (coda).

Rime of the syllable = nucleus/peak (vowel) + coda.

The following diagram shows a syllable tree for a consonant + vowel + consonant (CVC) syllable.

The following diagram shows a syllable tree for a consonant + consonant + vowel + consonant (CCVC) syllable.

EXERCISE 1-F: CREATING SYLLABLE TREES

Create a syllable tree for each of the following words.

            hat   cups   spoon

REMEMBER
Onsets and codas can contain consonant singletons or sequences. Syllables do not need to have an onset or a coda, but they *must* contain a vowel.

Did you know? We use the *rime* to rhyme. As children, we first *hear* rhymes, and then later, we are introduced to groups of rhyming words (word families) in order to learn similarities in spelling patterns. Teachers use the term *phonogram* to refer to the written representation of the rime. By using phonograms, children are introduced to word families (e.g., "-ap" is the phonogram in the words *cap, gap, nap, map, tap*).

EXERCISE 1-G: FINDING WORDS THAT RHYME

Find the words that rhyme in each group by crossing out the word/s that do not share the same rime. Remember to focus on the *sounds* you hear when you pronounce each word rather than the letters you see. Write the phonogram on the line.

rug	bug	mug	~~wig~~	hug	___-ug___	bell	well	all	will	yell	_____
back	bank	sack	lake	track	_____	cry	fly	boy	by	my	_____
made	paid	brand	race	grade	_____	care	hair	near	pear	store	_____
rose	does	buzz	us	was	_____	on	some	done	won	bun	_____
fur	blur	stir	four	here	_____	dog	hog	frog	log	lock	_____

EXERCISE 1-H: IDENTIFYING SYLLABLE PARTS

Identify the syllable parts in each of the following words. Write the letters that match the sounds that comprise each syllable part.

Word	Vowel Nucleus/Peak	Onset	Coda	Rime
bats	a	b	ts	ats
soup	ou	s	p	oup
knot	_____	_____	_____	_____
look	_____	_____	_____	_____
moist	_____	_____	_____	_____
sound	_____	_____	_____	_____
laugh	_____	_____	_____	_____
frown	_____	_____	_____	_____
joy	_____	_____	_____	_____
gift	_____	_____	_____	_____

EXERCISE 1-H: IDENTIFYING SYLLABLE PARTS (*continued*)

Word	Vowel Nucleus/Peak	Onset	Coda	Rime
odd	_____	_____	_____	_____
one	_____	_____	_____	_____
twice	_____	_____	_____	_____
sky	_____	_____	_____	_____
nest	_____	_____	_____	_____

Now, provide your own one-syllable words and identify their syllable parts.

Word	Vowel Nucleus/Peak	Onset	Coda	Rime
_____	_____	_____	_____	_____
_____	_____	_____	_____	_____
_____	_____	_____	_____	_____
_____	_____	_____	_____	_____
_____	_____	_____	_____	_____
_____	_____	_____	_____	_____

Types of Syllables

One way to classify syllables is by the presence or absence of the coda. Note: V = vowel; C = consonant.

Open syllables refer to any syllable that ends with a vowel sound; no coda is present.

Examples: I/eye = V; me = CV; know = CV

Closed syllables refer to any syllable ending with a consonant sound/s; these syllables have a coda.

Examples: I'm = VC; meat = CVC; nose = CVC

SOMETHING TO CONSIDER	*Use the definitions of vowels and consonants to help you differentiate between these types of syllables.*
	Vowels are produced with a relatively open vocal tract, whereas consonants are produced with some degree of closure. If a vowel sound is the last sound in a syllable, the vocal tract is open; if a consonant sound is the last sound in a syllable, the vocal tract is closed (to varying degrees).
	Ends with a vowel → open syllable
	Ends with a consonant → closed syllable

EXERCISE 1-I: DETERMINING SYLLABLE TYPE: OPEN VERSUS CLOSED

Determine the type of syllable shape for each of the following monosyllabic words. Remember to focus on the *last sound* you hear when you pronounce each word rather than the letters you see. Use C for a closed syllable (coda is present; word/syllable ends in a consonant) or O for an open syllable (coda is absent; word/syllable ends in a vowel).

sit	_____	hope	_____	can	_____
off	_____	pick	_____	eye	_____
buzz	_____	twig	_____	am	_____
call	_____	row	_____	wash	_____
tray	_____	grass	_____	knew	_____
sing	_____	cough	_____	though	_____

Another way to view syllables is by the type of consonants contained within them. Recall that consonants can be in singleton form (i.e., one consonant sound next to a vowel), or they can be in a sequence (two or more consonant sounds adjacent to one another with each sound being produced). Note: V = vowel; C = consonant.

Simple syllable: A syllable that contains no consonants or only singleton consonants

Examples: eye = V; my = CV; I'm = VC; mine = CVC

Complex syllable: A syllable that contains at least one sequence

Examples: ask = VCC; spy = CCV; spice = CCVC; sprint = CCCVCC

SOMETHING TO CONSIDER	*Use what you know about consonant singletons and sequences to help you differentiate between these types of syllables.*
	In terms of production, a single consonant is easier to produce (i.e., simple) than a sequence (i.e., complex).
	Contains consonants singletons → simple syllable
	Contains consonant sequences → complex syllable

EXERCISE 1-J: DETERMINING SYLLABLE TYPE: SIMPLE VERSUS COMPLEX

In this exercise, you are to do three things. First, after saying the word aloud in order to hear all the sounds, represent each sound with a *V* (for each vowel) and *C* (for each consonant). Second, circle all sequences, wherever they may be in the word. Third, determine whether the syllable is simple or complex.

skip	CCVC →	CC VC	Simple	(Complex)
comb	_____		Simple	Complex
truck	_____		Simple	Complex
town	_____		Simple	Complex
most	_____		Simple	Complex
slip	_____		Simple	Complex
lamps	_____		Simple	Complex
this	_____		Simple	Complex
sign	_____		Simple	Complex

Phonology and Phonetics

Earlier, you were introduced to the term **phonology** as referring to the sound system of a language consisting of the sounds of a given language, all their variations, and the rules for combining those sounds.

When a speech sound (or **phone**) is used to differentiate meaning in words, it is referred to as a **phoneme**. This is the smallest unit that distinguishes words from each other. Consider the word pairs "key-pea" and "top-stop." Each pair of words differs by one sound (referred to as a **minimal pair**). That one sound (phoneme) is used to signal a meaning difference. In the first word pair, "key-pea", it is the "k" and "p" sounds; in the second word pair, "top-stop", it is the "s." When we change a phoneme in a word, we change its meaning.

We also do not produce a given sound in the same way all the time. An **allophone** or **allophonic variation** of a sound are the variant pronunciations of a particular phoneme. Allophones of a phoneme are a set of similar sounds that occur in different phonetic contexts but do not change the meaning of a word (Ladefoged, 1993). Each phoneme may have one or more different ways of pronunciation. Consider the sound represented by the letter "t" in the following words: *two, stew, it, better, button*, and *baton.* A "t" phoneme is present in each of these words; however, because of the different sound environments, the sound is produced differently. You may have noticed that the puffs of air (i.e., aspiration) used in each production differed, especially when producing the words *two, stew, and it.* Additionally, when the phoneme "t" is between two vowels, it is produced differently. You most likely produced a different "t" phoneme in the three words *better, button,* and *baton.* Allophones are different ways of producing a specific sound, but they are not considered phonemes because they do not change the meaning of a word.

Phonotactic constraints refer to the allowable combinations of sounds in a particular language. In the English language, "s" can be paired with a "p", "t", or "k" (but not a b, d, or g) to create a prevocalic cluster (e.g., *spy, star, ski*). We also have prevocalic clusters of "pl" and "bl", and "cl" and "gl", but not the prevocalic clusters "tl" or "dl." The phoneme represented by the letters ng is only present in the intervocalic and postvocalic positions of words. Three English consonant sounds (i.e., h, w, y) can only be present in the prevocalic and intervocalic positions in words—never as a coda. These "rules" define what sound combinations may or may not occur in a given language. Even if you knew all the speech sounds present in a language, you would still need to know the *phonotactic constraints* operating within it in order to make words. A language's phonotactic constraints can challenge a second language learner. Consider the "vr" combination in French. How many Americans actually pronounce the word *Louvre* correctly?

Phonetics is an area that focuses on how speech sounds are produced. **Articulatory phonetics** is a branch of phonetics that examines the production features of speech sounds and categorizes/classifies them according to specific parameters in the effort to describe how sounds are formed. **Articulation** refers to the actions of the speech organs (i.e., lips, teeth, tongue, jaw) in the production of speech sounds.

Focus on the location of your tongue tip when producing the "t" and "d" sounds in the following pairs of words: *tip-trip, dug-drug, tack-track, dive-drive.* You may have noticed that your tongue tip moved more posterior in the second word of each pair. In the second word, you were anticipating the location of the "r" sound, which is produced in the center of your mouth, whereas the "t" and "d" sounds are produced farther forward.

When we produce sounds in words, we rarely produce each sound "perfectly." We also do not produce a given sound in the same way all the time. There is not enough time for the articulators to produce each phoneme in its intended isolated form. Within a word, one sound flows seamlessly into the next. You were already introduced to the term **allophonic variation** (i.e., the different pronunciations of a phoneme). While completing the exercises in this chapter, you may have noticed that your production of certain sounds was not constant and that the sounds in certain words confused you.

Coarticulation refers to the process that occurs as we produce sounds together in syllables, words, phrases, and sentences. During production of these sound units, individual phonemes overlap each other during production. Producing sounds in words, phrases, and sentences occurs very rapidly, and coarticulation is a time-efficient way to ease the demands of production.

Coarticulation can easily be noticed when it occurs across word boundaries. Focus on your production of the final sound in the word *horse*. For this sound, your tongue tip is forward in the mouth, somewhere behind your teeth. Now focus on what happens to the final sound in *horse* when you produce it as the first part of the compound word *"horseshoe."* We typically do not pronounce both intervocalic sounds (i.e., "s" and "sh"); rather, we prolong the vowel and produce the "sh" and not the "s." Did you feel your tongue tip at all? This is coarticulation, an overlapping of speech sounds during articulation.

Try another example. Say the word *"kept."* This word has a postvocalic sequence, and you probably noticed your lips coming together for the *p* and then opening again so that your tongue tip tapped behind your teeth to produce the *t*. Now say the same word in the two-word phrase *"kept quiet"* or *"kept busy."* Did you notice that you did not produce the final sound in the sequence "pt"? You more than likely omitted this sound because you were already anticipating production of the next sound.

Now say the following words:

like   would   go   you   to

When you pronounced each word separately and distinctly, you probably noticed producing fairly clearly the "d" sound at the end of word "would" and the long "u" sound in the word "to." But we do not speak with spaces between our words.

Now say the following question:

Would you like to go?

Did you produce the "j" sound between the first two words? Because of the rapid movements of our speech and the resulting overlapping of our articulatory movements when we move from one sound to another, *"would you"* turns into *"wood-joo"* or *"woodja"*. The word "to" may have lost its distinct vowel sound and may have been pronounced as *"tuh"*, so instead of *"to go"*, a speaker says *"tuhgo."*

Try these words:

his   what's   name

Now say the following question:

What's his name?

What changes did you notice when there were no spaces between the words? Say it again, but faster. Did you notice additional changes?

Here's another set of words to try separately:

she   know   does

And now together:

Does she know?

Track 16

Listen to additional
examples of coarticulation

We do not talk with spaces between our words; sounds run together. As a result, we sometimes produce sounds differently (allophones), omit the sounds entirely, or change them to be more like the sounds in the immediate environment. This latter situation refers to the concept of **assimilation.**

Read the following words out loud and listen to the vowel sound: *add-and, bed-bend, lib-limb, lawn-long.* The second word in the pair included a consonant sound immediately after the vowel that is produced through the nose (i.e., n, m, ng). Although the vowel sounds are the same in the words in each pair, the vowel sound in the second word sounded more nasal than the vowel sound in the first word, which did not have such a consonant. Now say the word *input.* What was the second sound you produced? Was it the sound "n" or the sound "m"? Say the word again but divide it into syllables (in – put). The sound for "n" was clearly produced, but it changed to resemble the sound for "m" when you produced the syllables as one word.

Assimilation is defined as the changes that a sound undergoes when influenced by its sound environment. It is often the direct result of *coarticulation.* A particular sound may influence a sound directly next to it, a sound that comes after it, or a sound that comes before it. The sound changes that you previously identified in the questions "Would you like to go?" and "Does she know?" illustrate this concept of *assimilation.* Sounds in words changed because of the influence of neighboring sounds when the words were produced in a sentence or question.

Be mindful of these concepts in the next two units as you learn how individual sounds are produced, classified, and categorized. We will return to these concepts after you learn about individual sound production.

Dialects and Accents

Another important concept that influences how we perceive and produce sounds in our language is **dialect**, defined by Wolfram (1991) as any variety of a language that is shared by a group of speakers. American English has many dialects, most noticeably identified by geography. Along with regional differences, variety in how we use language can be created by social or economic differences. Dialects can encompass differences in sound preferences, vocabulary, and/or grammar.

Although many of us use the terms *dialect* and **accent** interchangeably, they refer to different, but related, concepts. We use the term *accent* to describe the specific way individuals *pronounce* words based on a national or regional tendency (e.g., an Australian accent; a Southern accent). An accent also refers to the influence of sounds from one's first language when producing a second language. You may have heard of the phrase "accented English" when describing an individual's English pronunciation when English is his/her second (or third) language.

No two people produce sounds and speech the same way. An **idiolect** is the uniqueness of our speech caused by our vocal tract anatomy as well as our personal experiences (e.g., travel, education) (Owens, 2008). An individual's idiolect is composed of distinct language characteristics, including rate of speech, stress and intonation patterns, and vocal quality, as well as use of vocabulary and pronunciations. Consider your own life journey so far. What influences (geographical, social, educational) have factored into you speaking the way you do?

Words that may reflect dialectal differences in their pronunciation are the following: *aunt*, *caramel*, *pajamas*, *mirror*, *greasy*, *route*, *pecan*, *syrup*, *wash*, *lawyer*, *coupon*, *crayon*, *salmon*, *idea*, *scared*, and *orange*. Ask your classmates and/or friends to pronounce these words. Do they sound the same across all speakers? What other words can you add to this list?

We all have a speech history. Although I was raised in a small rural community in central Illinois, I lived more than 9 years in Milwaukee, Wisconsin, and another 3 years in St. Paul, Minnesota. When I first began my academic career in northwest Pennsylvania, everyone thought that I was from Wisconsin or Minnesota rather than Illinois, primarily because of my vowels. (I also discovered quite a difference when teaching vowel sounds during my first semester!) Within my own family, the way I produce my vowel sounds is quite distinct because of the influence of where I have lived as compared with where my siblings have lived. Most of the individuals from my hometown community "warsh" their clothes. Consider your own speech history. Where have you lived? What distinct pronunciations are reflective of your experiences?

We are often not aware of our dialect use. I recently spoke to a group of speech–language pathologists. After my presentation, a member of the audience approached me and asked where I was from because she explained that she had not heard anyone pronounce the word *especially* the way I had since moving to Illinois from Pennsylvania. I was not aware of how I pronounced the word, which, I was told, was "*ekspecially*." This was news to me!

Sound production and perception are influenced by dialects and accents. In Units 2 and 3, dialectal variations and language influences will be noted as you are introduced to each vowel and consonant sound in the English language. Your own dialect may influence how you pronounce words in the upcoming units that introduce you to the sounds of English and the symbols associated with those sounds. The goal of this workbook is to prepare you for transcribing other people's speech. Once you become familiar with individual sounds in words, you will be able to hear (and see) these sounds when produced by others far easier than trying to perceive your own sound production. Be patient with yourself, and seek out your instructor for further explanation.

2 *English Orthography*

Some of the exercises in the previous chapter may have been challenging for you. Have you figured out why you were sometimes confused when paying attention to sounds in words? One reason for your confusion is the difference between the *sounds* in English and the *spelling* of English. Most of your early education in reading and spelling moved you away from focusing on sounds to automatically deciphering visual patterns. Think about it. When was the last time you sounded out a word when listening to someone talk to you, when talking to someone, when reading, when writing? The challenges posed by the English language are well-documented.

Consider the following:

- **Different letters may represent the same sound.**

  The words *to, two, too, through, threw, clue, shoe,* and *Sioux* all share the same vowel sound.

  > One sound → 8 different spellings

  The words *share, hair, there, pear,* and *heir* all share the same vowel sound ("air").

  > One sound → 5 different spellings

  The words *cap, key, chorus, hockey, khaki, bouquet,* and *walk* all have the "k" sound.

  > One sound → 7 different spellings

  Your turn: Write as many words as you can think of with different spellings for the sound "f."

  _____ _____ _____ _____

  _____ _____ _____ _____

  _____ _____ _____ _____

- **The same letter represents different sounds.**

  The letter "u" is used seven times in the following sentence: *Surely, busy students bury thugs and then buy furs.* Each "u" is pronounced differently.
  The letter "s" in the words <u>s</u>ee, wa<u>s</u>, <u>s</u>ugar, and plea<u>s</u>ure is pronounced differently (i.e., as "s" sound, "z" sound, "sh" sound, and "zh" sound, respectively).
  The letter "a" in the words m<u>a</u>t, c<u>a</u>ke, c<u>a</u>ll, <u>a</u>ny, and sof<u>a</u> represents five different sounds.

In the word *reentered* there are four e's, each having a different pronunciation (including one that is silent).

- **Combinations of letters may represent one sound.**

In the English language, two letters can stand for one sound (either a consonant or vowel). These are termed **digraphs**. Consonant digraphs tend to be two-grapheme combinations that create a new sound (rather than the sound represented by one of the letters).

Consonant digraphs include <u>sh</u>irt, <u>ph</u>one, <u>th</u>e, chee<u>k</u>, <u>thing</u>, and cou<u>gh</u>.
Vowel digraphs include r<u>ai</u>d, r<u>ea</u>d, and r<u>oa</u>d.

- **Combinations of letters may represent a string of sounds.**

When focusing on the sounds in a word, it is important to pronounce the word so you can hear and feel when a consonant sequence is present. Remember, a sequence refers to two or more adjacent consonant sounds; each consonant sound retains its identity during pronunciation. These also are referred to as *clusters* and/or *blends*.

- **Letters in a word may represent no sound.**

The words *bom<u>b</u>, cak<u>e</u>, <u>p</u>neumonia, s<u>c</u>ience, <u>k</u>nee, gnat, thou<u>gh</u>, de<u>b</u>t*, and *recei<u>p</u>t* all contain "silent" letters. In fact, most letters of the English alphabet can serve as silent letters, given the variety of English spelling patterns.

Your turn: Think of some words that have the same letters (e.g., *numb* and *number*) but differ in the pronunciation of those letters (some may have silent letters or digraphs rather than consonant sequences). Circle the words that contain a sequence/cluster.

_____   _____   _____   _____

_____   _____   _____   _____

_____   _____   _____   _____

Spelling patterns are based on:

- **How the word sounds**

The first words that children are taught to spell contain short vowels and predictable patterns of consonants. The word "s*it*" is much easier to spell for a young child than the word "one" or "was".

- **How the word is used** (see next example)

- **The meaning of the word**

Think of "there", "their", and "they're". All are **homonyms** (words that sound the same but are spelled differently), but their spellings are dictated by their meaning and function in a phrase or sentence.

- **The origin of the word**

Words containing a *y* as a vowel are from Greek roots (e.g., s*y*stem, st*y*le), as are words that use *ph* to spell the "f" sound (e.g., <u>ph</u>one, gra<u>ph</u>).

Words containing "soft" g and c are from Latin roots (e.g., <u>c</u>ity, <u>g</u>iant)

Words in which the letters "ch" are produced "sh" come from French (e.g., <u>ch</u>ef, <u>ch</u>ic) as are words that end in "que" (e.g., bouti<u>que</u>, mysti<u>que</u>).

Because English orthography reflects both sound and meaning, it is described as a **morphophonemic** language. *Morphophonemics* refers to the changes in pronunciation (phonemic) that occur when bound morphemes are added to a word. Consider the example of the past tense suffix *–ed*. How this suffix is pronounced is determined by the final sound of the verb to which it is attached. For example, this suffix is pronounced as a "t" sound in *"jumped"* but as a "d" sound in *"jogged"*. Another morphophonemic change is reflected in the vowel sounds in the adjectives *sane* and *brief* when the suffix –ity is attached to each word to form a noun (i.e., sanity, brevity). Not only is the vowel sound changed in *brief-brevity*, but the final sound in *brief* changes as well. These principles will be useful to you in understanding transcription and stress in Unit 4.

Although our alphabet system is based on sounds, the relationship is a complicated one. Terms that refer to sounds used in words differ from terms used to refer to letters used in words. These are presented to you in Table 2.1.

TABLE 2.1 Terms to Know, Understand, and Differentiate

Sounds of English	Spellings of English
Phonology	**Orthography**
The sound system of a language. Includes sounds and their variations and rules for combining those sounds.	A language's writing (spelling) system. Includes symbol–sound associations and rules for combining those symbols.
Phonological awareness	**Orthographic awareness**
Umbrella term for an individual's ability to attend to the sound structure of the language apart from meaning	What an individual knows about a language's writing system
Phonemic awareness	
An individual's awareness and understanding of individual sounds in a word	
Phoneme	**Grapheme**
The smallest sound unit that distinguishes words from each other	A letter or group of letters used to represent one sound
Allophone/allophonic variation	**Allograph**
The different pronunciations of a given sound based on the surrounding contexts	The different spellings for each sound in our language
Consonant sequence	**Consonant digraph**
Two or more consonant sounds produced next to each other in a word	Two letters that represent a single phoneme. A grapheme of two letters.
Cluster	Most common include *sh, th, ch, ph, –gh, –ng*.
Sequence within a syllable	

EXERCISE 2-A: FINDING CONSONANT SEQUENCES AND DIGRAPHS

Write the letters that represent the sequence and/or digraph on the lines that follow each word. To be successful, you will need to do more than just look for two or more consonant graphemes next to each other in a word. To determine whether a sequence or digraph is present, remember to focus on the *sounds* you hear and feel when you pronounce each word rather than the letters you see. Note: Because all of these words are one syllable, the consonant sequence can be considered a *cluster*.

Helpful hint: When two or more consonant graphemes are next to each other in a word, how many sounds do you hear? If two or more sounds are heard, you have a sequence. If only one sound is heard, you have a digraph or a word with silent letters.

Find the consonant sequences and digraphs in the words below.

Word	*Sequence/Cluster*	*Digraph*
blush	bl	sh
the		
chains		
swing		
throat		
chilled		
scold		
through		
shrink		
rough		
scratch		
mix		
walked		

Word	Sequence/Cluster	Digraph
thumb	_____	_____
phone	_____	_____
slither	_____	_____
quick	_____	_____

This exercise may have been fraught with more errors than you expected. Orthography is limited when we discuss sounds. Did you identify the letter "x" as the sound sequence of /k/+/s/? The letters "qu" as the sound sequence of /k/+/w/? Did you notice that many sounds are part of a final sequence with t, d, and/or s and z? When the suffix –ed or –s is attached to a one-syllable word that ends in a consonant, a sequence (two or more consonant sounds next to each other in a word) is created. Did you discover that some consonant digraphs can also be a part of sequence, usually combined with "r" (e.g., _shrink_, _throat_)?

Do you know? In the English language, how many **phonemes** (not graphemes) can be in an initial sequence/cluster? How many **phonemes** (not graphemes) can be in a final sequence/cluster? Provide examples to substantiate your guess.

What Do You Think?	All sounds are represented in more than one way. Which spellings are more consistent and predictable? The spellings for consonants or vowels?

The connection between sounds and symbols in orthography is complex. More than 250 graphemes are used to spell the sounds in the English phonological system (Moats, 1995). Tables 2.2 and 2.3 present the allographs for consonants and vowels, respectively. This information will be useful to you as you pay more attention to sounds than letters.

Orthography inquiry The graphemes g and c have a "hard" sound as well as a "soft" sound. Do you know the spelling rule for when these two sounds have a "soft" pronunciation?

Did you notice? Short vowel sounds (except for the short "u" sound) have fewer allographs than long vowel sounds.

Did you know? Although dialects/accents can affect both consonant and vowels, vowels and diphthongs are most affected.

TABLE 2.2   Spellings (Allographs) for Singleton Consonants

Sound	Prevocalic (Syllable Initial) Spellings	Intervocalic (Word Medial) Spellings	Postvocalic (Syllable Final) Spellings
"p"	*p*en	a*p*art, ha*pp*y	cu*p*
"b"	*b*at	ha*b*it, ri*bb*on	mo*b*, e*bb*
"t"	*t*ie, *pt*erodactyl, *th*yme	ci*t*y, o*tt*er, si*ght*ing	ca*t*, mi*tt*, dou*bt*, recei*pt*, mi*ght*, back*ed*, ya*cht*
"d"	*d*oor	e*d*it, la*dd*er	ai*d*, o*dd*, mo*wed*, coul*d*
"k"	*k*ey, *c*an, *ch*orus, *kh*aki, *qu*iche	wa*k*en, ba*c*on, ho*ck*ey, e*ch*o, bou*qu*et, la*cqu*er, o*cc*ur, tal*k*ing	ne*ck*, wal*k*, atti*c*, a*che*, stoma*ch*, pla*que*
"g"	*g*o, *gh*ost	a*g*ain, ji*gg*le, a*gh*ast	ru*g*, va*gue*
"w"	*w*as, *wh*en*, *o*ne, q*u*it	flo*w*er, no*wh*ere	
"y"	*u*se, *y*et, *Eu*rope, *ew*e, g*y*ro	lo*y*al, fig*u*re, on*i*on, tort*ill*a	
"m"	*m*e	li*m*it, ha*mm*er	a*m*, co*mb*, hy*mn*, paradi*gm*
"n"	*n*o, *kn*ee, *gn*aw, *pn*eumonia	ho*n*or, pe*nn*y	i*n*, si*gn*
"ng"		si*ng*er	ba*ng*
"h"	*h*e, *wh*ole	be*h*ave	
"f"	*f*ar, *ph*one	wa*f*er, mu*ff*in, tou*gh*en, hy*ph*en	o*ff*, che*f*, cou*gh*, hal*f*
"v"	*v*an	ha*v*en	ha*ve*, o*f*
"s"	*s*ee, *c*ent, *sc*ene, *ps*ychic, *sw*ord	ma*s*on, mi*ss*ile, a*sc*end, thi*s*tle, fau*c*et	ga*s*, gra*ss*, ba*se*, sau*ce*
"z"	*z*oo, *X*erox, *cz*ar	thou*s*and, do*z*en, pu*zz*le	qui*z*, bu*zz*, a*s*, chee*se*, fro*ze*
"th" (mouth)	*th*in	no*th*ing	mou*th*
"th" (mother)	*th*at	mo*th*er	ba*the*
"sh"	*sh*oe, *s*ugar, *ch*ef	fi*sh*ing, con*sc*ience, ten*si*on, o*ce*an, a*ss*ure, fa*ci*al, mo*ti*on, ma*ch*ine	pu*sh*
"zh"		trea*s*ure, vi*si*on	bei*ge*
"ch"	*ch*op	ri*ch*er, pi*tch*er, fu*t*ure	mu*ch*, wa*tch*
"j"	*j*eep, *g*ym	e*j*ect, a*g*ent, ga*dg*et, e*d*ucate, exa*gg*erate, ad*j*ust	ca*ge*, e*dge*
"r"	*r*est, *wr*ite, *rh*yme	wea*r*y, ca*rr*y	r**
"l"	*l*oud, *ll*ama	fee*l*ing, ba*ll*oon	ee*l*, bi*ll*, smi*le*, ai*sle*,

*Most of us produce the "wh" in *when, what,* and **where** as "w" rather than "wh."

**When *r* comes after a vowel, it functions as a vowel in the word. This is termed a *rhotic* or controlled *r* diphthong and is discussed in the diphthong section.

What Do You Think?	**LET'S RETURN TO A QUESTION POSED TO YOU EARLIER**
	All sounds are represented in more than one way. Which spellings are more consistent and predictable? The spellings for consonants or vowels?
	When looking at Tables 2.2 and 2.3, there seems to be more variation in the spellings for vowel sounds. Spellings for consonants tend to be clearer than vowels because consonant sounds are not affected by stress patterns.
	Consider how the vowel sounds change in the word pairs *deep–depth* and *know–knowledge.*

TABLE 2.3 Spellings for Vowel Sounds

Vowel Sound	Possible Spellings
Short *a*	c*a*n l*au*gh h*a*v*e*
Long *a*	b*a*s*e* *a*pron *ai*m p*ay* *ei*ght h*ey* gr*ea*t d*e*but
Short *e*	*e*lf d*ea*d *a*ny
Long *e*	h*e* b*ee*p *e*v*e* *ea*ch l*ea*ve g*ee*se k*ey* ch*ie*f ch*i*c l*ei*sure
Short *i*	*i*f m*y*th
Long *i*	ch*i*ld b*i*k*e* d*ie* s*igh* b*y* d*ye* t*y*p*e* g*uy* h*ei*ght g*ui*de
Short *o*	*o*dd sw*a*mp g*e*nre
Long *o*	b*o*n*e* g*o*es b*oa*t *ow*n m*o*st d*ough* s*ou*l b*eau*
Short *u* (one-syllable words)	*u*s wh*a*t t*o*n bl*oo*d d*oe*s r*ou*gh n*o*n*e*
Long *u*	*u*nit r*u*l*e* m*oo*n *oo*z*e* wh*o* m*o*v*e* sh*oe* s*ou*p d*ew* tr*ue* s*ui*t sl*eu*th b*eau*ty
"aw"	l*aw*ful *au*tumn *a*ll b*o*ss *ou*ght
"oy"	b*oy* t*oi*l
"ow"	h*ow* *ou*ch b*ough*
short *oo*	p*u*t, b*oo*k, c*ou*ld
Controlled *r* vowels (vowel + *r*)	
"er"	p*urr* n*ur*se v*er*b b*ir*d w*ere* sh*ir*t w*or*d *ear*ly j*our*ney
"ear"	*ear* h*ere* ch*eer* p*ier*
"air"	*air* h*are* p*ear* th*eir* wh*ere*
"ar"	c*ar* g*uar*d biz*arre* mem*oir*
"or"	*or* *ore* *oar* d*oor* f*our* w*ar*d
"oor"	s*ure* t*our* p*oor*
"eye" + "er"	f*ire*
"ow" + "er"	*our*

Remember, a **phoneme** is a sound that creates differences in meaning. The **International Phonetic Alphabet (IPA)** is a universal alphabet that represents all phonemes in the world's languages. Unlike our English orthographic system, whereby 26 symbols are used to represent more than 40 sounds (and is often quite confusing), there is a *one-to-one relationship* between a phonetic symbol and the sound it represents. The phonetic alphabet is a tool that will assist you in recording the speech you hear. **Phonetic transcription** is a sound-by-sound interpretation/recording of speech using the symbols in the IPA.

You will learn the symbols of the IPA in Units 2 and 3, along with the characteristics of each sound in English. You then will be given guidelines in Unit 4 that will assist you in becoming adept at transcription.

3 *Paying Attention to Sounds*

After experiencing the activities in Chapter 2, you realize the challenges in attending to the sounds in a word while looking at the spellings of that word. The focus of this chapter is to present exercises to encourage you to pay attention to the sounds despite the presence of orthography that offers no assistance to you. Strategies are provided that will help you to focus on the sounds you hear in production and not the letters you see. These activities are presented to help you attend to sounds—something you have not attended to since becoming an automatic reader/speller.

WORDS OF ADVICE

- Learning phonetics requires you to pay attention to sounds. It is important for you to say words aloud. Tune into what you hear and avoid relying on what you see!

- Say the words *as naturally as possible*. Students learning phonetics have a tendency to over-pronounce. Doing so will result in transcribing sounds that are not present—especially vowels.

- Listen to others' speech. Eventually, you will be transcribing another person's speech, not your own. It is important for you, as a future transcriber, to tune into the productions of others.

EXERCISE 3-A: COUNTING SOUNDS IN WORDS

Pronounce each word in the following groups and determine how many sounds are in each. To help you focus your attention on sounds, here are two strategies to try:

1. Draw a box around the graphemes you see that comprise each sound you hear.

   w o n __3__   t w o __2__   ch ur ch __3__

2. Using a *C* for consonant and *V* for vowel, change each word into a combination of Cs and Vs.

   cut = consonant + vowel + consonant   CVC   __3__
   sigh = consonant + vowel   CV   __2__

GROUP #1

wild ____   put ____   fist ____   has ____   elf ____   cabin ____

stem ____   trip ____   log ____   busy ____   wag ____   grand ____

wasp ____   jump ____   gift ____

Did you notice? In each of the previous words, each sound was represented by one letter. Number of letters = number of sounds. When there were two consonant letters next to each other, they comprised a sequence—each sound retained its identity in production.

GROUP #2

could ____   hymn ____   scene ____   listen ____   who ____

debt ____   knock ____   answer ____   thyme ____   walk ____

gnaw ____   known ____   castle ____   lamb ____   calf ____

might ____   wrote ____   align ____

Did you notice? At least one consonant sound in each word was represented by more than one grapheme. Number of consonant graphemes > number of sounds. Each word had at least one silent letter. Were you tricked by any of them?

GROUP #3

laugh ____   month ____   whole ____   with ____   phone ____

wish ____   chord ____   thigh ____   tough ____   swing ____

though ____   thing ____   showed ____   chime ____   choose ____

Did you notice? In each of the previous words, at least one consonant sound was represented by two graphemes. Each word contained a consonant digraph.

GROUP #4

Consonant sequences, digraphs, and silent letters—be careful!

thumb ____   six ____   branch ____   shrink ____   chalk ____   thought ____

threw ____   fright ____   should ____   ghost ____   soften ____   nation ____

autumn ____   pseudo ____   bridge ____   honest ____   breathe ____   catcher ____

EXERCISE 3-A: COUNTING SOUNDS IN WORDS (*continued*)

Did you notice? *After checking your answers, return to any errors. Where did you make your mistakes?*

GROUP #5

Let's turn to vowels. Continue to count the number of sounds in each word.

meant ____	obey ____	aim ____	said ____	plaid ____	blood ____
guide ____	mauve ____	cruised ____	niece ____	weigh ____	you've ____
snow ____	young ____	crowd ____	coins ____	joy ____	mouse ____

Did you notice? In each of the previous words, the vowel sounds were represented by more than one grapheme. Number of vowel graphemes > number of sounds. These are examples of vowel digraphs and vowel diphthongs.

CHALLENGE GROUP

Pronounce each word out loud, paying attention to the sounds you hear. Write the number of sounds in each word on the line.

mix	_____	quote	_____	cute	_____
music	_____	exit	_____	view	_____
quipped	_____	amusing	_____	anguish	_____

Did you notice? Did you identify the letter "x" as a sequence /k/ + /s/ and the letters "qu" as the sequence /k/ + /w/? Did you find the consonant blends containing the "y" and "w" sounds even though the letter *y* or *w* was not evident in the word?

Once you learn the phonetic alphabet, counting sounds in words such as these will be much easier because there is a one-to-one relationship between the phonetic symbol and the sound it represents.

EXERCISE 3-B: MAKING COMPARISONS: NUMBERS OF SOUNDS IN WORDS

Read each pair of words aloud. Pay attention to the sounds you pronounced and not the letters you see. Identify the number of sounds you hear in each word; then make a comparison between the pair. If the two words have the same number of sounds, put an equal sign (=) on the line between them. If the first word has more sounds than the second word, write a greater than sign (>) on the line; if the first word has fewer sounds than the second word, write a less than sign (<) on the line between the words.

Helpful hint: Translate each word into a C & V combination (suggestion given to you in Exercise 3A) before making your final decision.

Word 1		Word 2	Word 1		Word 2
cat	=	dog	bees	_____	eyes
CVC (3)		CVC (3)	all	_____	ox
nose	>	know	hear	_____	here
CVC		CV	adult	_____	away
stop	_____	ship	bouquet	_____	mother
jog	_____	badge	night	_____	weight
back	_____	milk	who	_____	how
ouch	_____	itch	came	_____	crane
toad	_____	toe	missed	_____	mist

EXERCISE 3-C: COUNTING SOUNDS: FIND THE ERRORS

Review my answers that identify the number of sounds in each word. After drawing a box around the graphemes that represent each sound, as well as changing the sounds to Cs and Vs, judge the accuracy of my answers. If incorrect, please provide the correct response.

Word	My Answer	Draw a Box Around the Graphemes That Represent Each Sound	Change Sounds to Cs & Vs	Your Answer
thread	5	th r ea d	C C V C	4
pill	4	p i l l	_____	_____

EXERCISE 3-C: COUNTING SOUNDS: FIND THE ERRORS (*continued*)

Word	My Answer	*Draw a Box Around the Graphemes That Represent Each Sound*	*Change Sounds to Cs & Vs*	*Your Answer*
speech	5	s p e e c h	_____	_____
ships	5	s h i p s	_____	_____
pocket	6	p o c k e t	_____	_____
foolish	5	f o o l i s h	_____	_____
blurred	4	b l u r r e d	_____	_____
itch	3	i t c h	_____	_____
squirt	4	s q u i r t	_____	_____
highlights	6	h i g h l i g h t s	_____	_____
eight	3	e i g h t	_____	_____
honest	5	h o n e s t	_____	_____
thought	4	t h o u g h t	_____	_____
trophy	5	t r o p h y	_____	_____
stayed	5	s t a y e d	_____	_____

4 *Term Review and Practice*

The goals for the first unit included:

- Reacquainting you with the sound make-up of words in the English language.
- Assisting you in differentiating between the sounds you hear and the letters you see when looking at a word.
- Introducing you to basic terminology that will be used throughout the workbook.
- Providing you with exercises to improve your attention to sounds in words in order to prepare you to learn a new symbol system—the IPA.
- Introducing you to the concept of coarticulation and how it influences your perception and production of sounds in words and connected speech.
- Introducing you to the concept of dialects and accents and how these influence your perception and production of sounds.

By completing the exercises in this chapter, you will:

- Continue to increase your awareness of the sound structure of our language.
- Review key terms.
- Establish connections between related concepts.

TERMS

The following terms were introduced in Chapters 1 through 3. Not only is it important for you to understand what each term means, but it is also important for you to understand how the terms are connected to each other. Create a concept map to assist you in understanding how the terms are related to each other.

accent	dialect	phoneme
allograph	digraphs	phonemic awareness
allophone/allophonic variation	grapheme	phonetics
	idiolect	phonogram
articulation	intervocalic consonants	phonological awareness
articulators		
articulatory phonetics	minimal pair	phonology
assimilation	morphophonemic	phonotactic constraints

closed syllable	nucleus	postvocalic consonants
cluster	onset	prevocalic consonants
consonant sequence	open syllable	rime
coarticulation	orthographic awareness	simple syllable
coda	orthography	singleton
complex syllable	peak	syllable
consonants	phone	vowels

EXERCISE 4-A: SORTING WORDS BY NUMBER OF SYLLABLES

Sort the following words by their number of syllables. Write each word in the appropriate column based on the number of syllables. Remember, the number of vowel sounds you hear equals the number of syllables in the word.

marvelous	retrospective	rhythm	communism	organization
kilometer	quintuplet	anthropology	mathematician	intrusion
community	legislature	maneuver	addition	reliable
denominator	abbreviated	athlete	procrastination	settlement
commotion	presidential	recreation	crisis	asymmetrical
atmosphere	conversation	another	principle	accident
belong	excused	preview	collection	
accompany	companion	spectacular	contamination	

2	3	4	5	6
	marvelous			

2	3	4	5	6

EXERCISE 4-B: MANIPULATING ONSETS AND CODAS

1) Identify the onset and coda for each of the following words. Reminder: Onsets are prevocalic consonant singletons or sequences; codas are postvocalic consonant singletons or sequences. 2) Determine what happens when you transpose the onset and coda. If the onset or coda is a sequence, keep the sound order of the sequence intact when you transpose the intrasyllabic units. Does it make a permissible word in English (does it violate phonotactic constraints)? Remember to focus on the sounds you hear and not the letters you see.

Word	*Onset*	*Coda*	*New Word*	*Permissible?*
ace	_____	ce	say	Yes No
dock	_____	_____	_____	Yes No
sing	_____	_____	_____	Yes No
beige	_____	_____	_____	Yes No
step	_____	_____	_____	Yes No
tubs	_____	_____	_____	Yes No
jumped	_____	_____	_____	Yes No
grass	_____	_____	_____	Yes No
mask	_____	_____	_____	Yes No
toads	_____	_____	_____	Yes No
wagged	_____	_____	_____	Yes No
twice	_____	_____	_____	Yes No
land	_____	_____	_____	Yes No

EXERCISE 4-B: MANIPULATING ONSETS AND CODAS (*continued*)

Word	*Onset*	*Coda*	*New Word*	*Permissible?*

Create 5 more examples and share them with your neighbor. Compare your answers.

_____	_____	_____	_____	Yes No
_____	_____	_____	_____	Yes No
_____	_____	_____	_____	Yes No
_____	_____	_____	_____	Yes No
_____	_____	_____	_____	Yes No

EXERCISE 4-C: COUNTING SOUNDS IN WORDS

Determine how many sounds are in the following words. Write the number of sounds on the line.

Helpful hint: To help you focus your attention on sounds, you may want to draw a box around the graphemes you see that comprise each sound you hear. This will help focus your attention. Example: blue: b l ue = 3

food _____	ought _____	cute _____
store _____	queen _____	water _____
chew _____	calf _____	tense _____
which _____	church _____	sugar _____
sure _____	fang _____	thank _____
box _____	socks _____	might _____
loose _____	known _____	track _____
lose _____	mother _____	birthday _____
rowboat _____	cough _____	thick _____

EXERCISE 4-D: MAKING MORE COMPARISONS: NUMBER OF SOUNDS IN WORDS

Just as you did in Exercise 3-B, read each pair of words aloud and attend to the sounds you pronounced (and not the letters you see). Compare the number of sounds in each word. If the two words have the same number of sounds, put an equal sign (=) on the line between them. If the first word has more sounds than the second word, write a greater than sign (>) on the line; if the first word has fewer sounds than the second word, write a less than sign (<) on the line between the words. Use the strategy of translating each word into a C & V combination to assist you.

Word 1		*Word 2*
rose	=	road
CVC		CVC
comb	_____	itch
align	_____	aghast
guys	_____	guide
fright	_____	friend
quote	_____	quit
rhymes	_____	shrimp
there	_____	once
coughed	_____	glasses
chrome	_____	charge
brown	_____	brain
glisten	_____	ocean
tighter	_____	brother

EXERCISE 4-E: REVERSING SOUNDS IN WORDS

For the following words, reverse the sounds in the word to create a new word.
Example: knife → fine. Remember: Think sounds, not letters.

sick	_____	nose	_____	enough	_____
foe	_____	chip	_____	nuts	_____
ice	_____	scope	_____	light	_____
Knicks	_____	peace	_____	gave	_____
might	_____	knack	_____	teach	_____

EXERCISE 4-F: SORTING WORDS BY NUMBER OF SOUNDS

Sort the following words by the *number of sounds* contained in each. Be careful of the "hidden" sounds. Pay attention to sounds rather than spellings. Use your strategies to assist you.

silver	saw	graph	knee	slow	sunk
stinks	scram	cheese	works	shrimp	change
flood	frozen	row	chew	cute	lost
spokes	mix	though	quest	joy	house
swimming	clay	half	twig	charge	clasp
crept	voiced	numbered	fumes	quota	mixed
banana	machine	dictate	thy	threw	sixth

2	3	4	5	6
			s i l v er	

2	3	4	5	6

EXERCISE 4-G: APPLYING TERMS: FINDING WORDS

Read the statements carefully. Circle all that apply.

Which of the following words do not have a **coda**?

how   far   bus   mink   joy   blow

Which of the following words do not have an **onset**?

who   all   honor   own   oh   what

Which of the following words contain a **sequence**?

sheep   cups   scene   catch   quick   tossed

Which of the following words contain a **consonant digraph**?

dishes   chief   limb   small   moth   known

Which of the following single syllable words are **simple syllables**?

comb   bread   pitch   play   ice   shoes

Which of the following single syllable words are **complex syllables**?

sheep   cups   scene   catch   quick   tossed

Which of the following words have three or **fewer phonemes**?

know   play   who   hour   eye   where

EXERCISE 4-H: APPLYING SYLLABLE TERMS: WHAT'S ON THE LINE?

Use a term used for a *specific part* of a syllable to describe the following underlined items.

b<u>oa</u>ts	st<u>o</u>p	str<u>ing</u>	_____
b<u>oa</u>ts	st<u>o</u>p	str<u>ing</u>	_____
b<u>oa</u>ts	s<u>to</u>p	<u>s</u>tring	_____
boa<u>ts</u>	st<u>o</u>p	stri<u>ng</u>	_____

EXERCISE 4-I: SYLLABLE TALK: MATCHING TERMS WITH DEFINITIONS

You were introduced to several terms used to describe the different types of syllables or the consonant in a syllable (in relation to the vowel sound). Write the correct term on the line next to its definition/description.

A syllable without a coda   _____

A syllable with at least one consonant sequence   _____

A consonant that follows a vowel in a syllable   _____

A syllable with only a vowel or a combination of
singleton consonants and a vowel   _____

A consonant that is between two vowels in a *word*   _____

A syllable that ends in at least one consonant   _____

A consonant that comes before a vowel in a syllable   _____

EXERCISE 4-J: TRUE–FALSE

Check your understanding of concepts by completing this true–false section.

True   False   There are more sounds than phonetic symbols.

True   False   The phonological system of a language consists not only of the specific sounds
                   used in that language, but also the rules for combining those sounds.

True	False	There can be only one vowel sound in a syllable.
True	False	There are fewer graphemes than phonemes in the English language.
True	False	A syllable onset refers to a postvocalic consonant.
True	False	A consonant sequence refers to two graphemes that represent one sound.
True	False	There are more allographs for the sound /f/ than for /h/.
True	False	A syllable coda can be a consonant singleton or sequence.
True	False	When consonants are in a sequence, each consonant sound retains its identity during pronunciation.
True	False	All syllables contain a vowel.
True	False	Phonetics refers to the overlapping process of sounds when produced in words, phrases, or sentences.
True	False	Consonants are produced as a result of air moving through a relatively *open* vocal tract.
True	False	All syllables contain a coda.
True	False	Coarticulation may occur because of time; because connected speech occurs so rapidly, there is not enough time to hit the "targets" of each sound.
True	False	An accent refers to the influence of one's first language on the pronunciation of sounds of one's second language.
True	False	When sounds are modified during coarticulation, assimilation may result.

EXERCISE 4-K: IDENTIFY THE TERM

Read the definition and write the correct term on the line provided.

_____ Two or more consonant sounds produced next to each other in a word

_____ Another name for an alphabet letter

_____ The sound system of a language

_____ The **nucleus** of the syllable; also the peak

_____ The term that refers to one's distinct way of speaking

_____ Refers to all the possible different letter sequences that can be used to represent a sound

EXERCISE 4-K: IDENTIFY THE TERM (*continued*)

_____   The allowable combinations of sounds in a particular language. For example, *st*, *sp*, and *sk* are allowable prevocalic consonant sequences, whereas *sd*, *sb*, and *sg* are not.

_____   A unit of pronunciation consisting of a vowel sound alone or a vowel sound with the consonants that precede or follow it

_____   The study of the production and perception of speech sounds; concerns itself with classifying sounds by how they are produced

_____   A sound that creates a difference in meaning

_____   The variant pronunciations of a particular phoneme

_____   Speech sounds produced as a result of air moving through the vocal tract encountering some constriction or obstruction

_____   A variety of a language that is produced by a group of speakers

_____   Two graphemes representing one sound

_____   Subunit of a syllable that contains the *nucleus/peak* and *coda*

UNIT
2
The Vowel System

Your goals for Unit 2 include the following:

- To learn the types of vowels comprising the English vowel system
- To know the characteristics of all vowel sounds
- To understand how vowels are classified using the vowel quadrilateral as the reference point
- To learn the phonetic symbol for each vowel sound
- To learn the characteristics of each monophthong
- To learn the basic characteristics of the diphthongs
- To be introduced to the role word stress plays on central vowels
- To perform exercises to improve attention to vowel sounds in words
- To understand dialectal variations/accent influences on vowel sounds

5 *Overview*

EXERCISE 5-A: TUNING INTO THE VOWEL SOUNDS IN WORDS

1. Read each group of words aloud, listening for the vowel sound in each word.
2. Find the word that has a different vowel sound from the group and cross that word out.
3. Re-read the group of remaining words. They should all share the same vowel sound.
4. Think of another word that shares that same vowel sound and write it in the space provided.

eight	that	shade	change	_____
cough	tough	but	rough	_____
patch	zap	calf	calm	_____
schwa	talk	odd	tock	_____
jeans	quiche	chief	health	_____
sign	build	buy	wild	_____
limb	kind	quilt	gym	_____
bowl	down	cow	howl	_____
squad	squat	gauze	cot	_____
full	hood	food	push	_____
cheer	here	heard	weird	_____
talk	moss	most	ought	_____
whose	cool	juice	won't	_____
mouth	shout	ground	soup	_____
cork	word	shore	forge	_____
loose	few	cook	do	_____
joy	found	boys	voice	_____
though	thought	growth	known	_____

yes	deep	etch	dense	_____
toss	most	comb	sold	_____
stare	fair	star	bear	_____
wolf	would	wool	wound (noun)	_____
said	late	guess	friend	_____
laugh	quack	went	plaid	_____
glow	moan	how	own	_____
length	bread	bend	thank	_____
wound (verb)	brown	own	chow	_____
worst	swirl	hers	born	_____
flood	food	rub	does	_____
bead	pick	big	ding	_____
if	quiz	hymn	length	_____
quartz	storm	corpse	worm	_____
warm	sharp	chart	yarn	_____
wound (noun)	south	moon	womb	_____

Time to check your answers! *Without* looking at the key, return to the beginning of the exercise and say the four remaining words aloud. Their vowel sounds should sound the same.

REMINDERS
• It is important for you to say words aloud. Tune into what you hear with your ears and feel in your mouth. Spellings can be very deceiving!
• Say the words *as naturally as possible*. Overdoing the pronunciation will result in distorting the sounds you are trying to detect.
• Listen to others' speech. Eventually, you will be transcribing another person's speech, not your own. It is important for you, as a future transcriber, to tune into the productions of others.

Characteristics of Vowel Sounds

Vowels are produced with a relatively *open* vocal tract. The airstream from the vocal folds traveling to the lips encounters no significant obstruction. All vowel sounds are *voiced*; they are produced with vocal fold vibration. Vowel sounds contain the most acoustic energy; recall that they serve as the syllable *peak*. Their function in our language is an important one: They serve as the nucleus of a syllable.

Vowel sounds are produced by movements of the tongue, jaw, and lips. Each time you move one or all of these articulators, the shape of the oral cavity changes, and a new sound is created.

Vowels can be classified in four ways:

1. Tongue height
2. Tongue advancement/position in the mouth
3. Tongue tension
4. Lip rounding

> *Tongue height* refers to the level of the tongue in the oral cavity when the sound is produced. Tongue height is related to jaw opening. When the tongue is high in the oral cavity, the jaw is nearly closed. As the tongue lowers in the mouth, the jaw opens. The tongue height of vowels can be *high*, *mid*, or *low*.

FOCUS ON TONGUE HEIGHT

Tongue height is easy to determine because you can see the gradations in your mouth (where the tongue is in your oral cavity) as you produce vowels differing in tongue height. Say the following pairs of words, focusing on the vowel sound. Do you feel a difference in tongue height? Look in a mirror. Do you see a difference in jaw opening?

These vowels go from high to mid to low: heat → hate → hat
These vowels go from low to mid to high: ah → oh → boo

Take a guess: Order the following groups of words from highest in the mouth to lowest (greater jaw opening).

Group 1		Group 2		Group 3	
hand	_____	hope	_____	bait	_____
hit	_____	hop	_____	beat	_____
hen	_____	hoop	_____	bat	_____

> *Tongue advancement/position in the mouth* refers to the position of the tongue within the oral cavity during vowel articulation and which part of the tongue is primarily involved. The tongue advancement/position of vowels can be *front*, *central*, or *back*.

FOCUS ON TONGUE ADVANCEMENT/POSITION

Tongue advancement is difficult to describe, feel, and see. Say the following pairs of words, focusing on the vowel sound. Do you feel a difference in the position of the tongue in your mouth? Look in a mirror. Do you see a difference in tongue position?

Column 1	*Column 2*
who – he	hate – hut
hoe – hay	pit – put
hah – had	sheet – shoot
oh – uh	shack – shock

The movement in the pairs of words in Column 1 went from posterior to anterior (i.e., began in the back and moved to the middle of the mouth or the front of the mouth). The movement in the pairs of words in Column 2 was the reverse. The vowel sound in the first word was positioned in the front of the mouth; the vowel sound in the second word was positioned in the middle or back of the mouth.

Tongue tension refers to the amount of muscle tension used to produce a particular vowel sound. Vowels can be *tense* or *lax*. Tense vowels are longer in duration.

FOCUS ON TONGUE TENSION

Circle the words that you think are tense; that is, those words that have a vowel sound that seems longer in duration and requires more muscle tension.

heat	hit	hate	hen	hat
odd	ought	oat	hook	who

Lip rounding refers to whether or not the lips are rounded during production. Vowels can be *rounded* or *unrounded*. Unrounded vowels may be referred to as retracted or spread; these terms describe the lip positioning. For our purposes, we will focus on whether the lips are rounded or not during production.

FOCUS ON LIP ROUNDING

Lip rounding should be fairly easy to detect. Say the following pairs of words out loud. Circle the word that has the rounded vowel. Look in the mirror to help you, if needed.

nose – knees   shoot – shot   tack – took   tock – talk   on – in

odd – ought   it – oat   hood – hid   he – her   he – who

Types of Vowels

The English vowel system consists of two types of vowels: monophthongs and diphthongs. **Monophthongs** are considered "pure" vowels. Their production is qualitatively the same from beginning to end. There is minimal movement of the articulators during production so that the sound produced is steady. Each of the 14 monophthongs can be classified by the four descriptors of tongue advancement, tongue height, tongue tension, and lip rounding and occupies a specific place on the **vowel quadrilateral**. This is a figure that represents the tongue position inside the oral cavity. You will learn about each of these vowel sounds in Chapters 6, 7, and 9.

Diphthongs refer to another type of vowel sound that is created by a rapid blending of two (di) separate vowels sounds that create one sound. Because of the movements in the articulators, the quality of a diphthong changes. The quality change resembles a gliding movement. Say the sound "ah". Now say the word "eye". Both are one sound; however, when producing "ah", the articulators did not move during sound production, creating a stable sound quality (i.e., monophthong), whereas when producing "eye", the mouth began to open and then glided to a more closed position, creating a change in sound quality (i.e., diphthong). Although diphthongs are created by blending two different vowel sounds together, they are still considered one sound. As a preview for what you will be introduced to in Chapter 10, say the following pairs of words: ah/eye, ah/ow, aw/oy. The first word in each pair is a monophthong; the second word in each pair is a diphthong.

Another type of diphthong is created when "r" follows a vowel in the same syllable (i.e., postvocalic). When this happens, a **rhotic diphthong**, or controlled-r diphthong, is created. Sometimes this type of vowel is termed an "r-colored vowel". You hear it in the words "part", "hear", "fair", "core", and "sure". These sounds will be explained to you in Chapter 11.

The Vowel Quadrilateral

The IPA vowel chart is a diagram that shows how the vowels are produced within the oral cavity. Tongue height and tongue advancement are the two characteristics that are clearly depicted. Figure 5.1 shows this vowel quadrilateral situated in the mouth.

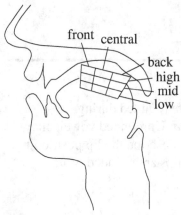

front central
back
high
mid
low

Figure 5.1

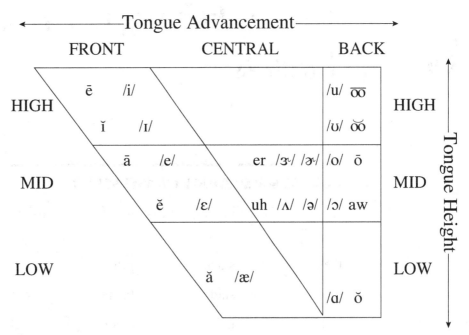

Figure 5.2

In the next chapters, you will be shown the tongue height and advancement of each vowel sound as produced in the mouth.

Figure 5.2 presents an overview of the 14 monophthongs situated in the vowel quadrilateral that will be introduced to you in the next several chapters. Each sound is presented in orthographic and phonetic (in / /) symbols. As you can see, new symbols need to be learned!

As you begin to be introduced to the sounds in American English, the website http://www.uiowa.edu/~acadtech/phonetics/ serves as a useful tool for students learning how sounds are produced, as it presents animated production of each sound in English (as well as in German and Spanish).

Monophthongs: Front Vowels

EXERCISE 6-A: SORTING BY VOWEL SOUND

Organize the following words into five groups according to their vowel sounds.

they	stand	prince	let	key
guess	said	beige	ease	fill
head	he's	chief	help	that
change	big	will	gaze	his
each	have	black	green	hand
laugh	claim	bend	bridge	lay

Vowel #1	*Vowel #2*	*Vowel #3*	*Vowel #4*	*Vowel #5*

The words you have just sorted contain the five front vowel sounds. These vowels are produced with the tongue positioned more forward in the mouth. The front of the tongue is the most involved in the production of each vowel. Each of these sounds will be introduced to you in the same way. The phonetic symbol will be located in the upper left-hand corner of the box. Directly under this new symbol will be the orthographic symbol that is used in the dictionary. A picture showing tongue advancement and height using the vowel quadrilateral situated in the oral cavity will be included. Next to the new symbol will be the four articulatory descriptors of the vowel sound according to the dimensions introduced earlier (i.e., tongue height, tongue advancement/position, tongue tension, lip rounding). Also included in each box is a space to write a key word that will assist you in associating the vowel sound with the IPA symbol. This information will be followed by two exercises: (1) "reading" phonetic symbols to create a familiar word, and (2) translating the sounds in a word into phonetic symbols.

/i/	Tongue height	HIGH
ē	Tongue position	FRONT
	Degree of tongue tension	TENSE
	Degree of lip rounding	UNROUNDED
	Key word _____	

EXERCISE 6-B: DECODING PHONETIC SYMBOLS: WORDS WITH /i/

Read each of the following phonetic symbols and blend them together to make a word. Write the word that is created in orthography. Note: The phonetic symbol for the consonants in these words will look familiar to you. The symbols for the consonant sounds are the same as those used in the alphabet.

/it/ _____   /bif/ _____   /wik/ _____   /stil/ _____   /mi/ _____

/pis/ _____   /kiz/ _____   /pliz/ _____   /iz/ _____   /bin/ _____

/ski/ _____   /sniz/ _____   /hi/ _____   /pli/ _____   /bist/ _____

/spik/ _____   /ni/ _____   /fri/ _____   /grin/ _____   /blid/ _____

EXERCISE 6-C: WRITING WORDS IN PHONETIC SYMBOLS: WORDS WITH /i/

Write the following words in phonetic symbols. All of these words contain the high front tense unrounded vowel /i/. The symbols for the consonant sounds are the same as those used in the alphabet.

east _____   geese _____   he's _____   steam _____   beep _____

leaf _____   niece _____   street _____   zeal _____   tease _____

brief _____   freak _____   heave _____   keep _____   need _____

grease _____

/ɪ/	Tongue height	HIGH
ĭ	Tongue position	FRONT
	Degree of tongue tension	LAX
	Degree of lip rounding	UNROUNDED
	Key word _____	

EXERCISE 6-D: DECODING PHONETIC SYMBOLS: WORDS WITH /ɪ/

Read each of the following phonetic symbols and blend them together to make a word. Write the word that is created in orthography. Note: The phonetic symbol for the consonants in these words will look familiar to you. The symbols for the consonant sounds are the same as those used in the alphabet.

/ɪn/ _____   /wɪt/ _____   /rɪb/ _____   /kwɪk/ _____   /ɪz/ _____

/stɪk/ _____   /mɪlk/ _____   /spɪl/ _____   /dɪg/ _____   /sɪks/ _____

/grɪn/ _____   /lɪft/ _____   /fɪl/ _____   /trɪp/ _____   /klɪf/ _____

/swɪm/ _____   /hɪz/ _____   /gɪv/ _____   /tɪpt/ _____   /rɪns/ _____

EXERCISE 6-E: WRITING WORDS IN PHONETIC SYMBOLS: WORDS WITH /ɪ/

Write the following words in phonetic symbols. All of these words contain the high front lax unrounded vowel /ɪ/. The symbols for the consonant sounds are the same as those used in the alphabet.

dim _____   build _____   film _____   skipped _____   fizz _____

rip _____   slim _____   splint _____   kiss _____   sick _____

strip _____   gift _____   pig _____   wilt _____   limb _____

trimmed _____

/e/	Tongue height	MID
ā	Tongue position	FRONT
	Degree of tongue tension	TENSE
	Degree of lip rounding	UNROUNDED
	Key word _____	

EXERCISE 6-F: DECODING PHONETIC SYMBOLS: WORDS WITH /e/

Pronounce the sound represented by each of the following phonetic symbols and blend them together to make a word. Write the word that is created in orthography. Note: The phonetic symbol for the consonants in these words will look familiar to you. The symbols for the consonant sounds are the same as those used in the alphabet.

/he/ _____   /med/ _____   /kes/ _____   /stret/ _____   /em/ _____

/nel/ _____   /fent/ _____   /ples/ _____   /bek/ _____   /rest/ _____

/kle/ _____   /swed/ _____   /det/ _____   /test/ _____   /sem/ _____

/kwek/ _____   /kep/ _____   /rez/ _____   /gren/ _____   /bled/ _____

EXERCISE 6-G: WRITING WORDS IN PHONETIC SYMBOLS: WORDS WITH /e/

Write the following words in phonetic symbols. All of these words contain the mid front tense unrounded vowel /e/. The symbols for the consonant sounds are the same as those used in the alphabet.

ate _____   lay _____   wave _____   traced _____   fake _____

paid _____   praise _____   grapes _____   face _____   paste _____

flame _____   snake _____   game _____   paint _____   trade _____

sleigh _____

/ɛ/	Tongue height	MID
ĕ	Tongue position	FRONT
	Degree of tongue tension	LAX
	Degree of lip rounding	UNROUNDED
	Key word _____	

EXERCISE 6-H: DECODING PHONETIC SYMBOLS: WORDS WITH /ɛ/

Read each of the following phonetic symbols and blend them together to make a word. Write the word that is created in orthography. Note: The phonetic symbol for the consonants in these words will look familiar to you. The symbols for the consonant sounds are the same as those used in the alphabet.

/ɛnd/ _____   /nɛk/ _____   /sɛnd/ _____   /sɛns/ _____   /ɛg/ _____

/dɛnt/ _____   /fɛl/ _____   /gɛst/ _____   /bɛl/ _____   /bɛst/ _____

/stɛm/ _____   /wɛpt/ _____   /hɛn/ _____   /lɛs/ _____   /fɛns/ _____

/spɛk/ _____   /gɛs/ _____   /hɛd/ _____   /nɛlt/ _____   /blɛd/ _____

EXERCISE 6-I: WRITING WORDS IN PHONETIC SYMBOLS: WORDS WITH /ɛ/

Write the following words in phonetic symbols. All of these words contain the mid front lax unrounded vowel /ɛ/. The symbols for the consonant sounds are the same as those used in the alphabet.

elf _____   get _____   tense _____   beg _____   debt _____

lend _____   spread _____   spent _____   desk _____   kept _____

friend _____   stepped _____   belt _____   tell _____   meant _____

cent _____

/æ/	Tongue height	LOW
ă	Tongue position	FRONT
	Degree of tongue tension	LAX
	Degree of lip rounding	UNROUNDED
	Key word _____	

EXERCISE 6-J: DECODING PHONETIC SYMBOLS: WORDS WITH /æ/

Read each of the following phonetic symbols and blend them together to make a word. Write the word that is created in orthography. Note: The phonetic symbol for the consonants in these words will look familiar to you. The symbols for the consonant sounds are the same as those used in the alphabet.

/æt/ _____   /bæk/ _____   /hænd/ _____   /træns/ _____   /mæp/ _____

/pæs/ _____   /kræb/ _____   /læm/ _____   /hæt/ _____   /kænt/ _____

/dæns/ _____   /snæp/ _____   /fæn/ _____   /plæd/ _____   /læst/ _____

/hæf/ _____   /næg/ _____   /fækt/ _____   /krækt/ _____   /wæks/ _____

EXERCISE 6-K: WRITING WORDS IN PHONETIC SYMBOLS: WORDS WITH /æ/

Write the following words in phonetic symbols. All of these words contain the low front lax unrounded vowel /æ/. The symbols for the consonant sounds are the same as those used in the alphabet.

bag _____   act _____   has _____   glad _____   add _____

gas _____   calf _____   staff _____   band _____   have _____

laugh _____   plan _____   damp _____   fast _____   van _____

flag _____

7 *Monophthongs: Back Vowels*

EXERCISE 7-A: SORTING BY VOWEL SOUND

Organize the following words into five groups according to their vowel sounds.

flew	mom	no	could	pull
toe	ought	room	group	wood
show	foot	dog	shoot	all
spa	lock	drop	caught	mold
fruit	claw	hot	road	oak
long	true	put	cot	shook

Vowel #1	*Vowel #2*	*Vowel #3*	*Vowel #4*	*Vowel #5*

The next five vowels to be introduced to you are the back vowels. For these vowel sounds, the tongue is positioned in the back of your mouth with the back of the tongue being the most active in production. Each of these vowel sounds will be introduced to you in the same way you were introduced to the front vowels. The phonetic symbol will be located in the upper left-hand corner of the box. Directly under this new symbol will be the orthographic symbol that is used in the dictionary. A picture showing tongue advancement and height using the vowel quadrilateral situated in the oral cavity will be included. Next to the new symbol will be the four articulatory descriptors of the vowel sound according to the dimensions introduced earlier (i.e., tongue height, tongue advancement/position, tongue tension, lip rounding). Also included in each box is a space to write a key word that will assist you in associating the vowel sound with the IPA symbol. This information will be followed by two exercises: (1) "reading" phonetic symbols to create a familiar word, and (2) translating the sounds in a word into phonetic symbols.

/u/	Tongue height	HIGH
ū	Tongue position	BACK
	Degree of tongue tension	TENSE
	Degree of lip rounding	ROUNDED
	Key word _____	

EXERCISE 7-B: DECODING PHONETIC SYMBOLS: WORDS WITH /u/

Read each of the following phonetic symbols and blend them together to make a word. Write the word that is created in orthography. Note: The phonetic symbol for the consonants in these words will look familiar to you. All symbols for consonant sounds are true to the sounds that are associated with the alphabet letter.

/tun/ _____   /sup/ _____   /tub/ _____   /klu/ _____   /plum/ _____

/muv/ _____   /bum/ _____   /gus/ _____   /kluz/ _____   /snuz/ _____

/zu/ _____   /lup/ _____   /ful/ _____   /grups/ _____   /spun/ _____

/hu/ _____   /blu/ _____   /gru/ _____   /skul/ _____   /pruv/ _____

EXERCISE 7-C: WRITING WORDS IN PHONETIC SYMBOLS: WORDS WITH /u/

Write the following words in phonetic symbols. All of these words contain the high back tense rounded vowel /u/. The symbols for the consonant sounds are the same as those used in the alphabet.

boot _____   room _____   goose _____   stoop _____

ooze _____   suit _____   two _____   spool _____

moose _____   soup _____   true _____   flute _____

food _____   soon _____   new _____   broom _____

/ʊ/	Tongue height	HIGH
ŏŏ	Tongue position	BACK
	Degree of tongue tension	LAX
	Degree of lip rounding	ROUNDED
	Key word _____	

EXERCISE 7-D: DECODING PHONETIC SYMBOLS: WORDS WITH /ʊ/

Read each of the following phonetic symbols and blend them together to make a word. Write the word that is created in orthography. Note: The phonetic symbol for the consonants in these words will look familiar to you. All symbols for consonant sounds are true to the sounds that are associated with the alphabet letter.

/fʊt/ _____   /wʊlf/ _____   /wʊdz/_____   /pʊt/ _____   /lʊk/ _____

/gʊd/ _____   /fʊl/ _____   /kʊks/ _____   /hʊd/ _____   /stʊd/ _____

/kʊd/ _____   /wʊd/ _____   /bʊk/ _____   /kʊkt/ _____   /brʊks/_____

/rʊk/ _____

EXERCISE 7-E: WRITING WORDS IN PHONETIC SYMBOLS: WORDS WITH /ʊ/

Write the following words in phonetic symbols. All of these words contain the high back lax rounded vowel /ʊ/. The symbols for the consonant sounds are the same as those used in the alphabet.

hook _____   bull _____   crook _____

pull _____   brook _____   books _____

took _____   would _____   cook _____

hoods _____   wool _____   looked _____

/o/	Tongue height	MID
ō	Tongue position	BACK
	Degree of tongue tension	TENSE
	Degree of lip rounding	ROUNDED
	Key word _____	

EXERCISE 7-F: DECODING PHONETIC SYMBOLS: WORDS WITH /o/

Read each of the following phonetic symbols and blend them together to make a word. Write the word that is created in orthography. Note: The phonetic symbol for the consonants in these words will look familiar to you. All symbols for consonant sounds are true to the sounds that are associated with the alphabet letter.

/on/ _____   /kom/ _____   /wok/ _____   /tost/ _____

/fom/ _____   /poz/ _____   /kloz/ _____   /rod/ _____

/bolz/ _____   /bon/ _____   /hol/ _____   /spok/ _____

/hop/ _____   /kold/ _____   /bost/ _____   /kwot/ _____

/zon/ _____   /roz/ _____   /krom/ _____   /glob/ _____

EXERCISE 7-G: WRITING WORDS IN PHONETIC SYMBOLS: WORDS WITH /o/

Write the following words in phonetic symbols. All of these words contain the mid back tense rounded vowel /o/. The symbols for the consonant sounds are the same as those used in the alphabet.

boat _____   goes _____   robe _____   grown _____

fold _____   loaf _____   nose _____   stove _____

home _____   froze _____   roll _____   phone _____

hose _____   goal _____   glow _____   crow _____

/ɔ/	Tongue height	MID
"aw"	Tongue position	BACK
	Degree of tongue tension	LAX
	Degree of lip rounding	ROUNDED
	Key word _____	

EXERCISE 7-H: DECODING PHONETIC SYMBOLS: WORDS WITH /ɔ/

Read each of the following phonetic symbols and blend them together to make a word. Write the word that is created in orthography. Note: The phonetic symbol for the consonants in these words will look familiar to you. All symbols for consonant sounds are true to the sounds that are associated with the alphabet letter.

/rɔt/ _____ /gɔz/ _____ /kɔzd/ _____ /stɔk/ _____

/ɔf/ _____ /sɔft/ _____ /kɔf/ _____ /flɔz/ _____

/bɔld/ _____ /dɔg/ _____ /tɔl/ _____ /sɔlt/ _____

/fɔl/ _____ /pɔ/ _____ /bɔs/ _____ /fɔls/ _____

/lɔn/ _____ /drɔ/ _____ /kɔt _____ /brɔt/ _____

EXERCISE 7-I: WRITING WORDS IN PHONETIC SYMBOLS: WORDS WITH /ɔ/

Write the following words in phonetic symbols. All of these words contain the mid back lax rounded vowel /ɔ/. The symbols for the consonant sounds are the same as those used in the alphabet.

all _____ lost _____ pawn _____ straw _____

dawn _____ hawk _____ call _____ broad _____

fought _____ gone _____ called _____ fault _____

haunt _____ pause _____ fraud _____ scald _____

/ɑ/	Tongue height	LOW
ŏ	Tongue position	BACK
	Degree of tongue tension	LAX
	Degree of lip rounding	UNROUNDED
	Key word _____	

EXERCISE 7-J: DECODING PHONETIC SYMBOLS: WORDS WITH /ɑ/

Read each of the following phonetic symbols and blend them together to make a word. Write the word that is created in orthography. Note: The phonetic symbol for the consonants in these words will look familiar to you. All symbols for consonant sounds are true to the sounds that are associated with the alphabet letter.

/dat/ _____   /gab/ _____   /rak/ _____   /baks/ _____

/mab/ _____   /spa/ _____   /spat/ _____   /pram/ _____

/ad/ _____   /gat/ _____   /drap/ _____   /stamp/ _____

/hap/ _____   /plap/ _____   /drapt/ _____   /klak/ _____

/nad/ _____   /mam/ _____   /skwad/ _____   /bland/ _____

EXERCISE 7-K: WRITING WORDS IN PHONETIC SYMBOLS: WORDS WITH /ɑ/

Write the following words in phonetic symbols. All of these words contain the high front tense unrounded vowel /ɑ/. The symbols for the consonant sounds are the same as those used in the alphabet.

bond _____   tops _____   knocks _____   stopped _____

hot _____   wasp _____   swamp _____   swap _____

pop _____   slob _____   clocks _____   plot _____

knot _____   stock _____   hopped _____   fox _____

Monophthongs: Front and Back

A Focus on Pronunciation

Purpose:

- To focus your attention on vowel sounds in words
- To help you discriminate between vowel sounds
- To increase your awareness in terms of allophones and sound contexts
- To increase your awareness in terms of the impact of coarticulation

Tongue Height

Difference Between /ɪ/ and /æ/ (High vs. Low)

Both are front, unrounded, lax. *The difference between these two sounds is tongue height.*

> sit/sat   big/bag   tin/tan   miss/mass

Tongue height difference should be obvious as you watch a speaker say these word pairs.

Difference Between /ɪ/ and /ɛ/ (High vs. Mid)

Both are front, unrounded, lax. *The difference between these two sounds is tongue height.*

> pin/pen   big/beg   bill/bell   pit/pet
> since/sense   mist/messed   mint/meant   wrist/rest

Look at someone else saying these words. Do you see a difference in mouth opening?

Tongue Tension

Difference Between /i/ and /ɪ/

Both are high, front, unrounded. *The difference between these two sounds is tongue tension.*

> heap/hip   beat/bit   seek/sick   lead/lid
> pick/peak   he's/his   leak/lick   heat/hit

Did you notice that even when you say the words naturally, tense vowels are longer than lax?

Difference Between /u/ and /ʊ/

Both are high, back, rounded. *The difference between these two sounds is tongue tension.*

could /cooed   wooed /would   shoe/should   took/tooth

Difference Between /o/ and /ɔ/

Both are mid, back, rounded. *The difference between these two sounds is tongue tension.*

know/gnaw	sew/saw	low/law	coat/caught	choke/chalk
boat/bought	bowl/ball	woke/walk	sold/salt	owed/Aud.

Allophonic Variations

An **allophone** is the variant pronunciation of a particular phoneme. Allophones of a phoneme are a set of similar sounds that occur in different phonetic contexts but do not change the meaning of a word (Ladefoged, 1993). In this section, pay attention to how the vowel sound changes as the environment changes.

Read the groups of syllables. The vowel sounds stays the same, although it is influenced by the type of consonant that follows it.

at – an	ab – am	ag – ang
it – in	ib – im	ig – ing
et – en	eb – em	eg – eng

Read the following groups of words across. The vowel sound is the same across the words, although it is affected by the consonant (where it is produced in the mouth and the voicing) that follows it.

Vowel					
/æ/	bat	bad	ban	bang	bank
	rat	rad	ran	rang	rank
	sat	sad	sand	sang	sank
/ɪ/	kit	kid	kin	king	kink
	pit		pin	ping	pink
			thin	thing	think
/ɔ/	sought	sawed		song	

VOWELS BEFORE A POSTVOCALIC /l/

Read the following pairs of words. What did you notice about how the post-vocalic /l/ influences the vowel sounds in each pairing? What did you see? Hear? Feel?

seal – sill	spool – pull	roll – all
coal – call	wheel – will	sale – sell
bail – bell	bowl – ball	pool – pull
she'll – shell	steel – still	ale – yell
eel – ill	roll – all	fool – full

In each pair, the vowels differ by tension (first word has a tense vowel; second word has a lax vowel). Did you notice that when a tense vowel precedes a postvocalic /l/, you may have added an additional vowel before it? This probably did not occur when saying the second word in each pairing. Why do you think this happened?

Say the following pairs of words in each column, focusing on the vowel. What did you notice? What differences did you hear? What differences did you feel?

Column A	Column B	Column C
bee – beat	beat – bead	bee – bead
owe – oat	oat – owed	owe – owed
boo – boot	boot – booed	boo – booed
A – ate	ate – aid	A – aid
hi – height	height – hide	hi – hide

Read the following pairs of words, focusing on the vowel. Both words in each pair contain the same vowel. *Is there any difference in how you say the vowel in the two words?*

fat – vat	thigh – thy	punt – bunt	tock – dock
sip – zip	cheap – jeep	fine – vine	peep – beep

* * * * * * *

Now try these pairings. Remember to pay attention to the vowel. *Is there any difference in how you say the vowel in the two words?*

cop – cob	right – ride	bet – bed	pick – pig
grace – graze	fuss – fuzz	rough – of	etch – edge

Based on the Above Exercises....   Which consonant influences the vowel the most: prevocalic or postvocalic?

Practice

EXERCISE 8-A: COMMON BONDS

Given the following sets of symbols, explain (by using one or more of the four ways to classify monophthongs) how they are alike. What is their common bond? Be sure to refer to the vowel quadrilateral.

/i/	/u/	/ʊ/	all are high vowels
/ɛ/	/ʊ/	/ɑ/	_____
/e/	/o/	/ɔ/	_____
/u/	/o/	/ɔ/	_____
/æ/	/ɑ/	/ɔ/	_____
/ɛ/	/ɔ/	/ʊ/	_____
/ʊ/	/o/	/u/	_____
/i/	/e/	/u/	_____
/æ/	/ɪ/	/ɛ/	_____
/ɪ/	/ʊ/	/i/	_____
/ʊ/	/ɔ/	/ɑ/	_____

EXERCISE 8-B: IDENTIFY THE VOWEL

Write the correct phonetic symbol for the following descriptions of sounds.

Mid front tense unrounded	_____	Mid back tense rounded	_____
High front tense unrounded	_____	Low back lax unrounded	_____
Mid front lax unrounded	_____	High back lax rounded	_____
Mid back lax rounded	_____	High back tense rounded	_____
Low front lax unrounded	_____	High front lax unrounded	_____

EXERCISE 8-C: WORKING WITH THE VOWEL QUADRILATERAL

The purpose of this exercise is to assist you in learning the front and back monophthongs on the vowel quadrilateral and their relationship to each other. Please refer to the vowel quadrilateral as you progress through each step.

Remember: You need to know four things about each monophthong: tongue height, tongue advancement, tongue tension, and lip rounding.

Make a word out of the following information	*Symbol*	*Word*
"b" + high back tense rounded vowel + "t"	/_____/	_____

→ *Next, change the tongue advancement and the degree of lip rounding.*

high _____ tense _____   /_____/   _____

→ *Next, change the tongue tension.*

high _____   /_____/   _____

→ *Next, change the tongue height to the next closest level.*

_____   /_____/   _____

→ *Next, change the tongue advancement and the degree of lip rounding.*

_____   /_____/   _____

→ *Next, change the tongue tension.*

_____   /_____/   _____

→ *Next, change the tongue advancement and the degree of lip rounding.*

_____   /_____/   _____

→ *Next, change tongue tension as well as the tongue height to the lowest level.*

_____   /_____/   _____

EXERCISE 8-D: IDENTIFYING THE VOWEL CHANGES

Read the following table, focusing on the vowel sound in each word. The first line provides the information for the /ʊ/ in took. Each subsequen t word will change the vowel in some way. The completed table shows you the change(s) that occurred in vowel characteristics each time the vowel changes. Complete the second column by writing the correct vowel symbol for each word.

Word	Vowel Symbol	Tongue Height	Tongue Advancement	Tongue Tension	Lip Rounding
took	/ʊ/	high	back	lax	rounded
talk	_____	√ (mid)	back	lax	rounded
tock	_____	√ (low)	back	lax	√ (unrounded)
tack	_____	low	√ (front)	lax	unrounded
take	_____	√ (mid)	front	√ (tense)	unrounded
tick	_____	√ (high)	front	√ (lax)	unrounded

Begin with the first word. Write the vowel symbol and all words that describe its characteristics. For each subsequent word, place a check (√) in the column of the specific change that occurred in vowel production. Write what changed next to each check mark.

Word	Vowel Symbol	Tongue Height	Tongue Advancement	Tongue Tension	Lip Rounding
lad	_____	_____	_____	_____	_____
lead (verb)	_____	_____	_____	_____	_____
lead (noun)	_____	_____	_____	_____	_____
load	_____	_____	_____	_____	_____
lid	_____	_____	_____	_____	_____
laid	_____	_____	_____	_____	_____

Word	Vowel Symbol	Tongue Height	Tongue Advancement	Tongue Tension	Lip Rounding
hope	_____	_____	_____	_____	_____
hip	_____	_____	_____	_____	_____
hop	_____	_____	_____	_____	_____
hoop	_____	_____	_____	_____	_____
heap	_____	_____	_____	_____	_____

EXERCISE 8-D: IDENTIFYING THE VOWEL CHANGES (*continued*)

Word	Vowel Symbol	Tongue Height	Tongue Advancement	Tongue Tension	Lip Rounding
bought	_____	_____	_____	_____	_____
boat	_____	_____	_____	_____	_____
bat	_____	_____	_____	_____	_____
bait	_____	_____	_____	_____	_____
bit	_____	_____	_____	_____	_____
boot	_____	_____	_____	_____	_____
bet	_____	_____	_____	_____	_____
beet	_____	_____	_____	_____	_____

EXERCISE 8-E: VOWEL CLASSIFICATION PRACTICE: CREATING WORDS

A monophthong is described in each line. After you write the symbol for the monophthong on the short line, create real words by blending together the phoneme descriptions provided. Write the word on the line provided (in orthography).

"sh" + high back tense rounded	/u/	shoe
"s" + mid front tense unrounded	_____	_____
"h" + high back tense rounded	_____	_____
High front lax unrounded + "t"	_____	_____
Mid back lax rounded + "f"	_____	_____
High front tense unrounded + "z"	_____	_____
Mid back tense rounded + "n"	_____	_____
Low back lax unrounded + "k" + "s"	_____	_____
"l" + high back tense rounded + "p"	_____	_____
"b" + mid back lax rounded + "s"	_____	_____
"p" + high front tense unrounded + "s"	_____	_____

"ch" + mid back lax rounded + "k"   _____   _____

"j" + low front lax unrounded + "m"   _____   _____

"w" + high front lax unrounded + "g"   _____   _____

"h" + high back lax rounded + "d"   _____   _____

"r" + high front tense unrounded + "ch"   _____   _____

"b" + mid front tense unrounded + "zh"   _____   _____

"t" + high back tense rounded + "th"   _____   _____

"sh" + high back lax rounded + "d"   _____   _____

"k" + mid back lax rounded + "z"   _____   _____

"w" + low back lax unrounded + "ch"   _____   _____

"th" + "r" + mid back tense rounded   _____   _____

"p" + mid front tense unrounded + "s" + "t"   _____   _____

"p" + mid back tense rounded + "s" + "t"   _____   _____

"r" + high front lax unrounded + "s" + "k"   _____   _____

"s" + mid front lax unrounded + "n" + "s"   _____   _____

EXERCISE 8-F: IDENTIFYING THE VOWEL IN WORDS

The following groups (vertical) of words share the same consonant "skeleton" but differ by vowel sounds. Write the correct vowel sound for each word on the line provided.

rook _____	plaid _____	soup _____	John _____
rack _____	plod _____	sop _____	gin _____
wreck _____	played _____	sip _____	June _____
wreak _____	pled _____	seep _____	jean _____
rake _____	plead _____	soap _____	Jane _____

EXERCISE 8-F: IDENTIFYING THE VOWEL IN WORDS (*continued*)

teal _____	cap _____	sit _____	flew _____
tall _____	cape _____	soot _____	flowed _____
tail _____	cope _____	seat _____	flee _____
till _____	coop _____	sat _____	flawed _____
tool _____	keep _____	suit _____	fled _____

EXERCISE 8-G: READING IPA SYMBOLS

Words are presented to you in phonetic symbols. Note: Sixteen symbols for consonant sounds are already known to you, as they are the same symbol in orthography. Decode each set of symbols and write the resulting word on the line.

/zu/ _____	/pik/ _____	/læm/ _____
/tɔs/ _____	/læf/ _____	/gʊd/ _____
/fud/ _____	/nɑk/ _____	/hɪz/ _____
/wæg/ _____	/wet/ _____	/lon/ _____
/mun/ _____	/dɛf/ _____	/tep/ _____
/pɛg/ _____	/gɪv/ _____	/pʊt/ _____
/hom/ _____	/lɔg/ _____	/kon/ _____
/bɛts/ _____	/bruz/ _____	/fɛns/ _____
/plænt/ _____	/rost/ _____	/ples/ _____
/brum/ _____	/stræp/ _____	/fist/ _____

Track 1, 2, 3

Practice transcribing
front and back
monophthongs in simple
syllables (V, CV, VC)

Pronunciation Notes: Dialectal Variations

Is There a Difference Between the /ɔ/ and /ɑ/ Sounds in Your Dialect?

An interesting website for you to discover is the map presented on the following page: http://www.ling.upenn.edu/phono_atlas/ICSLP4.html#Heading2. This map is part of the Phonological Atlas of North America (Labov, 1996) and shows in which regions of the country speakers differentiate between these two back vowels. Labov describes regions that do not differentiate between these sounds as those areas of the country where a sound merger has taken place. This map provides information regarding the locales that produce these two sounds the same or similar as well as those areas that produce them as two distinct vowel sounds.

According to these data, Standard American dialects that do differentiate between these two sounds (i.e., speakers who produce the word *cot* differently than *caught*) include heavily populated areas in the North, North Midland/Upper Midwest, most of the South, and the mid-Atlantic States. Those areas in the country where there is not such a clear demarcation include portions of Northeastern New England, the Western Pennsylvania region including eastern Ohio, portions of West Virginia, and northern Kentucky. Speakers in upper Minnesota, as well as in the western part of the United States, appear to produce these sounds very similarly.

If your dialect does differentiate between these two vowel sounds, the following exercises may be useful.

Both sounds are produced back and lax. /ɔ/ is a mid vowel produced with rounded lips. /ɑ/ is a low vowel produced with no lip rounding. *The difference between these two sounds is tongue height and lip rounding.*

aw – aahhh	raw – rah	Aud. – odd	boss – box
mall – mob	saw – sod	talk – tock	drop – drawn

Read the following groups of words. Decide which monophthong is shared by each word in the group. Did you pronounce the vowel the same in all words in each group? Remember, many speakers may not be able to distinguish the difference between these two vowel sounds because the production of these sounds has merged in their specific dialect.

/ɔ/ or /ɑ/	talk	walk	chalk	stalk
/ɔ/ or /ɑ/	gob	bob	mob	rob
/ɔ/ or /ɑ/	ball	call	fall	hall
/ɔ/ or /ɑ/	knock	dock	sock	rock
/ɔ/ or /ɑ/	nod	odd	pod	cod
/ɔ/ or /ɑ/	jaw	gnaw	saw	paw
/ɔ/ or /ɑ/	fog	log	dog	hog
/ɔ/ or /ɑ/	hot	cot	not	pot
/ɔ/ or /ɑ/	mop	hop	drop	chop
/ɔ/ or /ɑ/	loss	toss	sauce	cross

Below are some, but definitely, not all, of the variations (dialectal and based on accented English) that occur with the front and back vowel sounds in American English. Not included are variations that occur in English spoken elsewhere in the word.

Key to dialect abbreviations:

GA   General American English
SA   Southern American English
AA   African American English

- **/i/ becomes /ɪ/ (laxing)**

  In a few words, especially ending in /k/ (e.g., *creek* is pronounced as /krɪk/) in General American English (GA) (Edwards, 1992)

  In words before a final /l/ sound (e.g., *meal* is pronounced as /mɪl/; *really* is pronounced as /rɪlɪ/) in Southern American English (SA) and African American English (AA) (Bauman-Waengler, 2008; Bernthal, 2008; Small, 2005)

- **/ɪ/ becomes /ɛ/**

  In words before /l/ (e.g., *milk* is pronounced /mɛlk/) in GA (Edwards, 1992)

  In words before "ng" (e.g, *thing* is pronounced "theng") in SA and AA) (Bernthal, 2008; Edwards, 1992; Mendoza-Denton, 2001)

- **/ɪ/ becomes /i/ or /iɪ/**

  In SA, there is a tendency to tense the high front vowel before "sh" (e.g., *fish* is pronounced "feesh") or combine the tense vowel with the lax (e.g., *fish* is pronounced "feeish") (Bauman-Waengler, 2008; Bernthal, 2008; Edwards, 1992; Labov, 1997).

  For non-native speakers, there is a tendency to overuse /i/ when the lax high front vowel /ɪ/ is required (Edwards, 1992). Examples include Arabic-influenced English (Roseberry-McKibbin, 2002), Spanish-influenced English (Roseberry-McKibbin, 2002; Owens, 2008), and Asian-influenced English (Bauman-Waengler, 2008; Owens, 2008). In Asian-influenced English, you may notice both a lengthening (i.e., /ɪ/ becomes /i/) and shortening (e.g., /i/ becomes /ɪ/) in different words.

- **/ɛ/ becomes /e/ (tensing)**

  Tensing before the "g", "k", "sh", and "zh" sounds (e.g., *leg* is pronounced /leg/; *fresh* is pronounced "frāsh"; *treasure* is pronounced "trāsure") in GA and SA (Bauman-Waengler, 2008; Bernthal, 2008; Edwards, 1992; Labov, 1997). In SA, you may also notice a blending of two vowel sounds /eɪ/ (e.g., *leg* is pronounced as /leɪg/) (Bernthal, 2008; Edwards, 1992; Mendoza-Denton, 2001). Tensing is also observed in AA before a /d/ sound (e.g., *head* is pronounced as /hed/) (Edwards, 1992).

- **/ɛ/ becomes /ɪ/**

  This sound change tends to occur before a nasal sound ("n", "m", "ng") and is common in GA, SA, and AA dialects (e.g., *pen* is pronounced /pɪn/) (Bauman-Waengler, 2008; Edwards, 1992; Small, 2005).

For non-native speakers, /ɛ/ tends to be problematic (Edwards, 1992) and may be replaced with several other sounds (i.e., /e/, æ/, /ɑ/, or /ʌ/). The lax quality of the /ɛ/ may also be tensed in Spanish-Influenced English, especially preceding nasals (e.g., *friend* is pronounced as "frānd") (Bauman-Waengler, 2008).

- **/e/ becomes /ɛ/**

In AA, this sound change tends to occur before /k/ (e.g., *snake* is pronounced as /snɛk/) (Edwards, 1992) and /l/ (e.g., *bale* is pronounced as /bɛl/) (Bauman-Waengler, 2008). This sound change is noted in particular words in GA (Edwards, 1992). An example of this is pronouncing the word *naked* as /nɛkɪd/.

- **/æ/ becomes /ɑ/**

In Eastern American English (EA), this shifting from front to back may occur in any context but is especially noted before the sounds "f", "s", "th", and "n" sequences (e.g., *half* is pronounced /hɑf/; *can't* is pronounced /kɑnt/) (Bernthal, 2008; Edwards, 1992).

- **/æ/ becomes /æɪ/ or /eɪ/**

In SA, in any context, the vowel /ɪ/ is added (e.g., *half* is pronounced as /hæɪf/). Before a nasal sound, this vowel sound tends to be raised and tensend (e.g., *can't* is pronounced /keɪnt/) (Bauman-Waengler, 2008; Edwards, 1992; Labov, 1997).

- **/æ/ tensing and elongation**

Speakers with a New York City dialect tend to produce this sound longer (Bauman-Waengler, 2008; Labov, 1997; Mendoza-Denton, 2001).
/æ/ is not a common sound in the languages of the world and for non-native speakers may be substituted with the low back vowel /ɑ/, another lax vowel /ɛ/, or a central vowel.

- **/u/ becomes /ʊ/**

In GA and EA, a laxing of this vowel may occur (e.g., *roof* and *hoof* may be pronounced /rʊf/ and /hʊf/; *root* may be pronounced /rʊt/) (Bernthal, 2008; Edwards, 1992).

- **/u/ becomes /ʊ + ə/**

In GA and SA, there is a laxing and adding of a vowel in words ending with /l/ (e.g., *pool* is pronounced /pʊəl/). Note: /ə/ is the /uh/ sound (Edwards, 1992).

- **/u/ produced more anterior**

Individuals speaking with a western dialect tend to produce this sound more forward in the mouth (Bauman-Waengler, 2008; Labov, 1997).

- **/u/ produced as "you"**

The addition of a "y" sound before the vowel may be observed in speakers of SA and EA, especially after the certain sounds (i.e., "t", "d", "n"). Speakers of EA also include this sound after the "s", "z", and "th" sounds.

Tune may be pronounced as "tyoun," *news* as "nyous," *super* as "syouper" (Bernthal, 2008; Edwards, 1992; Mendoza-Denton, 2001). Speakers of GA would use /u/ (Edwards, 1992).

- **/ʊ/ becomes /u/**

  In GA, a tensing of this vowel, especially before the "sh" or "ch" sounds, may occur (e.g., *bush* is pronounced "boosh") (Edwards, 1992). Similar to all tense-lax vowel pairings, non-native speakers show the tendency to tense the vowel, thus substituting /u/ for /ʊ/ (Edwards, 1992). This is commonly heard in Spanish-influenced and Asian-influenced English.

- **/o/**

  According to Edwards (1992), no significant dialect variations have been reported for this sound.

- **/ɔ/**

  Speakers with a New York City dialect tend to produce this sound with some nasality and more lip rounding than speakers in other parts of the country (Edwards, 1992).

- **/ɔ/ and /ɑ/**

  Many speakers of the same regional dialect often interchange the /ɔ/ and /a/ sounds. This results in words such as *caught* and *cot* produced as homonyms. In EA and SA, these two sounds have merged into an intermediate vowel (Bauman-Waengler, 2008; Labov, 1997). Individuals speaking with a northern or southern dialect tend to reduce the lip rounding in this vowel and produce it as /ɑ/ (Bernthal, 2008; Labov, 1997; Bauman-Waengler, 2008).

CHAPTER

9

Central Vowels

Two additional monophthongs are needed to complete the vowel quadrilateral. Central vowels (the sounds "uh" and "er") are produced at a point midway between the front and back vowels and between high and low vowels. According to Edwards (2003, p. 247), central vowels:

- Do not have clearly defined articulation
- Are not transcribed consistently by phoneticians
- Are difficult for students to discern
- Rely on linguistic stress rather than on purely phonemic (meaning) consideration

But, central vowels:

- Assist in our understanding of linguistic stress (discussed in Chapter 22)
- Occur with great amount of frequency in American English

Although there are two mid-central vowel sounds, each sound can be represented by two symbols. Which symbol to use will be determined by the amount of stress placed on the syllable in which it is located. Because we are focusing on monosyllable words in this unit, the stressed symbol for each sound will be emphasized. Stress will be the focus in Chapter 22 and both the stressed and unstressed symbols for each central vowel will be used in that chapter.

The central vowel sounds will be introduced to you in the same way as you were introduced to the front and back monophthongs. The phonetic symbol will be located in the upper left-hand corner of the box. Directly under this new symbol will be the orthographic symbol that is used in the dictionary. A picture showing tongue advancement and height using the vowel quadrilateral situated in the oral cavity will be included. Next to the new symbol will be the four articulatory descriptors of the vowel sound according to the dimensions introduced earlier (i.e., tongue height, tongue advancement/position, tongue tension, lip rounding). Also included in each box is a space to write a key word that will assist you in associating the vowel sound with the IPA symbol. This information will be followed by two exercises: (1) "reading" phonetic symbols to create a familiar word, and (2) translating the sounds in a word into phonetic symbols.

Symbols for the Mid-Central Vowels in Stressed Syllables

This symbol, for what you might recognize as the short "u" sound, will be used in one-syllable words and in the stressed syllable in multisyllable words. In the exercises in this chapter, you will only use the stressed symbol.

71

/ʌ/	Tongue height	MID
ŭ	Tongue position	CENTRAL
	Degree of tongue tension	LAX
	Degree of lip rounding	UNROUNDED
	Key word _____	

EXERCISE 9-A: DECODING PHONETIC SYMBOLS: WORDS WITH /ʌ/

Read each of the following phonetic symbols and blend them together to make a word. Write the word that is created in orthography. Note: The phonetic symbol for the consonant sounds in these words will look familiar to you. All symbols for consonants are true to the sounds that are associated with that specific alphabet letter.

/dʌn/ _____   /lʌk/ _____   /bʌg/ _____

/mʌd/ _____   /stʌd/ _____   /kʌps/ _____

/pʌk/ _____   /tʌn/ _____   /ʌs/ _____

/stʌf/ _____   /plʌm/ _____   /drʌm/ _____

/klʌk/ _____   /sʌm/ _____   /lʌvd/ _____

/hʌnt/ _____   /mʌg/ _____   /pʌls/ _____

EXERCISE 9-B: WRITING WORDS IN PHONETIC SYMBOLS: WORDS WITH /ʌ/

Write the following words in phonetic symbols. All of these words contain the /ʌ/ sound. The symbols for the consonant sounds are the same as those used in the alphabet.

bus _____   of _____   none _____

pup _____   won _____   dump _____

plus _____   stuck _____   come _____

fuzz _____   dust _____   gulf _____

lump _____   punt _____   rough _____

/ɝ/	Tongue height	MID
"er"	Tongue position	CENTRAL
	Degree of tongue tension	TENSE
	Degree of lip rounding	ROUNDED
	Key word _____	

This symbol will be used in one-syllable words that have a clear "er" sound (e.g., _bird_) and in the stressed syllable in multisyllable words (e.g., _bursting_, _certain_, _assure_, _alternative_).

EXERCISE 9-C: DECODING PHONETIC SYMBOLS: WORDS WITH /ɝ/

Read each of the following phonetic symbols and blend them together to make a word. Write the word that is created in orthography. Note: The phonetic symbol for the consonant sounds in these words will look familiar to you. All symbols for consonants are true to the sounds that are associated with that specific alphabet letter.

/dɝt/ _____   /gɝl/ _____   /lɝn/ _____

/wɝm/ _____   /stɝ/ _____   /kɝb/ _____

/pɝk/ _____   /tɝn/ _____   /sɝv/ _____

/skɝt/ _____   /ɝn/ _____   /bɝd/ _____

/vɝb/ _____   /hɝt/ _____   /sɝ/ _____

/fɝst/ _____   /kɝs/ _____   /nɝd/ _____

EXERCISE 9-D: WRITING WORDS IN PHONETIC SYMBOLS: WORDS WITH /ɝ/

Write the following words in phonetic symbols. All of these words contain the central vowel /ɝ/. The symbols for the consonant sounds are the same as those used in the alphabet.

burn _____   her _____   work _____

slurp _____   clerk _____   purse _____

EXERCISE 9-D: WRITING WORDS IN PHONETIC SYMBOLS: WORDS WITH /ɝ/ (*continued*)

nurse _____   herb _____   burp _____

heard _____   burst _____   turf _____

swirl _____   term _____   world _____

Symbols for the Mid-Central Vowels in Unstressed Syllables

When the "uh" sound is produced in an unstressed syllable, we will use another symbol, called the *schwa* (described below). You will learn in Unit 4 that the schwa is the most common vowel in the English language due to the prevalence of vowel reduction in multisyllable words. The schwa is the vowel to which all other vowels reduce when they occur in unstressed syllables.

/ə/	Tongue height	MID
ŭ	Tongue position	CENTRAL
	Degree of tongue tension	LAX
	Degree of lip rounding	UNROUNDED
	Key word _____	

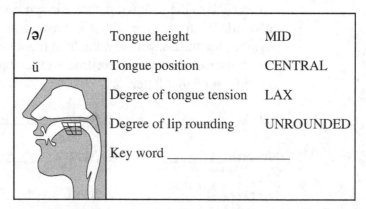

When the "*er*" sound is produced in an unstressed syllable, we will use another symbol, called the "*schwar*" (described below). The /ɚ/ sound occurs with greater frequency in American English speech than its stressed counterpart /ɝ/. Think of all the comparative words ending with the inflectional suffix –*er* (e.g., *colder*), as well as changing a verb to a noun by adding the derivational suffix –*er* (e.g., *teacher*, *actor*, *starter*, *watcher*).

/ɚ/	Tongue height	MID
"er"	Tongue position	CENTRAL
	Degree of tongue tension	LAX
	Degree of lip rounding	ROUNDED
	Key word _____	

We will explore more with these sounds and how stress determines their presence when we focus on transcription in Unit 4.

REMEMBER

/ɝ/ and /ɚ/ are the symbols for the "er" sound.

/ʌ/ and /ə/ are the symbols for the "uh" sound.

	"er"	"uh"
Stressed syllables	/ɝ/	/ʌ/
Unstressed syllables	/ɚ/	/ə/

Track 4

Practice transcribing all monophthongs in CVC syllables

CHALLENGE EXERCISE 9-E: TWO-SYLLABLE WORDS WITH CENTRAL VOWELS

Try to figure out the following words by reading the phonetic symbols. Each word contains two central vowels, requiring a stressed and unstressed symbol to be used.

/mɝdɚ/ _____   /sɝkəs/ _____

/hʌndrəd/ _____   /pʌzəl/ _____

/bɝglɚ/ _____   /əlɝt/ _____

/bʌtən/ _____   /mɝmɚ/ _____

/əbʌv/ _____   /dʌzən/ _____

/fɝnəs/ _____   /ʌndɚ/ _____

How well did you do?

Pronunciation Variation of Central Vowels

Although the /ʌ/ sound is a neutral vowel, speakers with a northern dialect may produce it as /ɔ/ (Bauman-Waengler, 2008; Labov, 1997). Speakers of EA will produce the schwar /ɚ/ for the schwa /ə/ in unstressed syllables, often before a syllable or word that begins with a vowel. This is termed the "intrusive-r" (Bernthal, 2008; Edwards, 1992). Have you ever heard someone on television speak of an "idear"?

In both the /ɝ/ and /ɚ/ sounds, speakers of EA, SA, and those speaking with the New York City dialect will omit the r-coloring (Bauman-Waengler, 2008;

Bernthal, 2008; Edwards, 1992; Goldstein, 2000), resulting in a more neutral vowel. This sound change also is noted in speakers of AA (Bauman-Waengler, 2008; Bernthal, 2008; Edwards, 1992). This same omission of the r-coloring has been reported in speakers of Asian-influenced English (Goldstein, 2000; Roseberry-McKibbin, 2002).

Non-native speakers may substitute the /ɑ/ and /æ/ for the /ʌ/ (Edwards, 1992).

Speakers of Asian-influenced English will insert the schwa between the consonant components of a cluster (termed *epenthesis*) when attempting to produce English clusters (e.g., *ski* will be pronounced /səki/; *blue* will be pronounced /bəlu/). This is prevalent in the Korean language, which does not have consonant clusters within a syllable.

The schwa is also added by these same speakers after certain final consonants (e.g., *beak* /bik/→/bikə/) (Goldstein, 2000).

CHAPTER
10 *Diphthongs*

EXERCISE 10-A: SORTING WORDS WITH DIPHTHONGS

Organize the following words into groups according to their vowel sound. Reminder: Tune into the sound, not the spelling. You should hear three vowel sounds used frequently. There may be some vowel sounds that do not fit in these three groups. Place them in the section below groups A through C.

rhyme	ouch	join	round	wind (verb)
group	enjoy	mine	clue	toys
quite	lounge	choice	eye	laugh
oil	time	caught	doubt	cycle
cow	bridge	buys	voice	key
tile	noise	soy	cloud	height

Group A	*Group B*	*Group C*
_____	_____	_____
_____	_____	_____
_____	_____	_____
_____	_____	_____
_____	_____	_____
_____	_____	_____
_____	_____	_____
_____	_____	_____

EXERCISE 10-A: SORTING WORDS WITH DIPHTHONGS (*continued*)

Group A	*Group B*	*Group C*
_____	_____	_____
_____	_____	_____

Words that do not belong in the above three groups: _____

_____

U p until this point, you have been introduced to monophthongs (mono = one; phthongos = sound). The vowel sounds in the above groups of words may have sounded, and most likely felt, different from the vowel sounds in the previous chapters. The sounds in the above groups of words are called **diphthongs** (di = two; phthongos = sounds).

A Focus on Pronunciation

Say the following pairs of words in front of the mirror or watch and listen as another person says the two words. Watch the articulators that form vowel sounds: tongue, lips, and jaw.

Group 1	*Group 2*	*Group 3*
lot – light	shot – shout	toss – toys
Tom – time	hop – how	saw – soil
hop – hype	fond – found	lawn – loin
blond – blind	dot – doubt	gnaws – noise

What did you see? What did you hear? What did you feel (if you were pronouncing the words)?

The American English phonology system contains a set of vowels that are formed by rapidly blending two monophthongs together to create one sound. The second word in each word pair above contains a diphthong.

A **diphthong** is a rapid blending of two separate vowel sounds within the same syllable. A new vowel sound is created by the gradual movement of the articulators as they transition from one position to the other. A change in quality occurs during the production.

There is no definitive agreement regarding which sounds should be classified as diphthongs or how to transcribe them. We discuss here the five diphthongs that are the most consistent in phonetics books. Three of these sounds represent the vowel sounds in the words in the first exercise you completed. These are the vowel sounds you hear in *eye*, "ow", and "oy". The symbol for each of these sounds is presented in the box that follows.

THE PHONEMIC DIPHTHONGS

/aɪ/   /aʊ/   /ɔɪ/
"eye"   "ow"   "oy"

Each of these sounds is created by beginning at the position of the **on-glide** (first sound component) and ending at the position of the **off-glide** (second sound component).

Say "eye" in front of a mirror. Your jaw begins in an open position (low vowel) and then rapidly moves to a high position for the /ɪ/. A different low vowel sound symbol /a/ is used. This first component is a low central vowel that is often heard in the dialect of individuals residing in the eastern states (e.g., "pahk the cah").

/a/ + /ɪ/ = /aɪ/

Try this again with the vowel sound "ow". Your jaw begins in the position of the same low central vowel (the on-glide) and rapidly moves up and back to the off-glide, the position for the mid-back rounded vowel /ʊ/.

/a/ + /ʊ/ = /aʊ/

The third diphthong, "oy", is a close blending of the vowel sounds /ɔ/ and /ɪ/. Begin in the on-glide position and move rapidly to the off-glide position. Your jaw began in the mid-back rounded position and then rapidly moved to a high front unrounded position to form one sound, /ɔɪ/.

/ɔ/ +/ɪ/ = /ɔɪ/

These three sounds are often termed *phonemic diphthongs*. The presence of each of these sounds reflects a change in meaning (e.g., boy /bɔɪ/, buy /baɪ/, bow [verb] /baʊ/, bee /bi/, boo /bu/, baa /bæ/ or /bɑ/, bay /be/, beau /bo/). Among the series of CV syllables, there is a vowel change. The meaning changes with each different vowel sound.

Characteristics of diphthongs:

- The tongue moves from a lower vowel position (on-glide) to a high vowel position (off-glide). Many textbooks refer to these sounds as *rising* diphthongs.
- A change in quality results due to the change in movement of the articulators. Changes in the mouth will reflect changes in a sound.
- The on-glide (first vowel component) is acoustically more prominent and is longer in duration than the second vowel. The off-glide (second vowel component) is weaker and shorter in duration (MacKay, 1987; Small, 2012).

NON-PHONEMIC DIPHTHONGS

You were introduced to the mid front tense unrounded vowel /e/ in Chapter 6 and the mid back tense rounded vowel /o/ in Chapter 7. In most dialects of American English, these two sounds are most often produced as diphthongs rather than as monophthongs.

When producing these two vowels, you can feel this difference the most when these sounds are in open syllables:

bay   beau

Produce these words both ways:

[be]   [beɪ]   [bo]   [boʊ]

These two sounds are referred to as *non-phonemic diphthongs* because their diphthong production (i.e., [eɪ] and [oʊ]) is not *phonemically* different from the monophthong form (i.e., [e] and [o]). Each of these sounds can be represented by either symbol (i.e., monophthong or diphthong) without a resulting change in meaning. Although *technically* produced as diphthongs, they are commonly transcribed as monophthongs.

The vowel sound in the word *bay* can be transcribed as /be/ or /beɪ/; the vowel sound in the word *beau* can be transcribed as /bo/ or /boʊ/.

PRONUNCIATION NOTE

[e] as a monophthong is rarely used in American English, whereas [o] is most often heard in syllables that receive little or no stress (Mayer, 2004). When we quickly shout "hey" to a friend, you may notice that the diphthong production moves to the steady-state quality of a monophthong. If you listen to Sylvester Stallone as Rocky, you will hear the sound /e/ only as a monophthong.

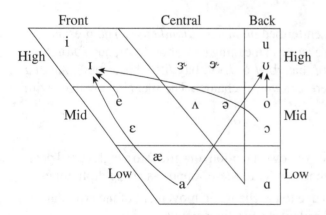

Figure 10.1 Vowel quadrilateral showing rising movement in the formation of diphthongs.

Source: Bauman-Waengler, Jacqueline. Articulatory And Phonological Impairments: A Clinical Focus, 3RD Ed., ©2008. Reprinted and Electronically reproduced by permission of Pearson Education, Inc., Upper Saddle River, New Jersey.

Figure 10.1 displays the rising movement that occurs in the creation of the five diphthongs within the vowel quadrilateral. Notice that the rising movement from the on-glide to the off-glide in the non-phonemic diphthongs (i.e., [eɪ] [oʊ]) covers less distance than the rising movement needed to create the phonemic diphthongs (i.e., [aɪ], [aʊ], [ɔɪ]).

Vowel digraphs (e.g., *r*e*ad*, *d*e*ad*, *bl*oo*d*, *sl*eu*th*) are not diphthongs. Vowel digraphs are combinations of letters that make a single sound (i.e., *c*oa*t*, *p*ai*n*, *b*ee*p*, *st*ea*m*, and *m*oo*n*). Various ways of spelling vowels were presented to you in Table 2.3 in Chapter 2. Whereas vowel digraphs are two-vowel *graphemes* that represent one vowel sound in printed word, a diphthong is one vowel *sound* that is created by rapidly blending two sounds together. Unlike monophthongs, which have a steady-state quality during production (because the move does not move), the gliding movement between the two vowel components (i.e., the on-glide and the off-glide) create a change in quality.

EXERCISE 10-B: IDENTIFYING THE CORRECT SYMBOL FOR DIPHTHONGS

Pronounce each of the following words and circle the correct choice for the vowel sound you hear. The symbols for the three phonemic diphthongs are given. If you hear a vowel sound that is not a phonemic diphthong, circle the last option (i.e., vowel sound not given). In your quest to become "ear-minded," continue to pay attention to the sounds rather than the spellings.

Word	*Choice of Vowel Symbols*			
life	/aɪ/	/aʊ/	/ɔɪ/	vowel sound not given
house	/aɪ/	/aʊ/	/ɔɪ/	vowel sound not given
claim	/aɪ/	/aʊ/	/ɔɪ/	vowel sound not given
loud	/aɪ/	/aʊ/	/ɔɪ/	vowel sound not given
soy	/aɪ/	/aʊ/	/ɔɪ/	vowel sound not given
plaid	/aɪ/	/aʊ/	/ɔɪ/	vowel sound not given
beach	/aɪ/	/aʊ/	/ɔɪ/	vowel sound not given
clown	/aɪ/	/aʊ/	/ɔɪ/	vowel sound not given
void	/aɪ/	/aʊ/	/ɔɪ/	vowel sound not given
head	/aɪ/	/aʊ/	/ɔɪ/	vowel sound not given

EXERCISE 10-C: COUNTING SOUNDS IN WORDS

Read the following words aloud, paying attention to the number of sounds in each word. Focus on the sounds you hear rather than the letters you see. Remember that diphthongs count as one sound in words.

frown _____ shine _____ taupe _____

wife _____ moose _____ sound _____

poise _____ high _____ lounge _____

how _____ joy _____ chai _____

doubt _____ heard _____ voice _____

EXERCISE 10-C: COUNTING SOUNDS IN WORDS (*continued*)

Identify the 12 words that contained diphthongs

_____   _____   _____   _____

_____   _____   _____   _____

_____   _____   _____   _____

EXERCISE 10-D: DECODING PHONETIC SYMBOLS: PHONEMIC DIPHTHONGS

Read each of the following phonetic symbols and blend them together to make a word. Write the word that is created in orthography. Note: The phonetic symbol for the consonant sounds in these words will look familiar to you. All symbols for consonant sounds are true to the sounds that are associated with the alphabet letter.

/bɔɪ/ _____   /waʊ/ _____   /aɪs/ _____

/taɪ/ _____   /vɔɪs/ _____   /naʊ/ _____

/daʊt/ _____   /laɪf/ _____   /laʊd/ _____

/spɔɪl/ _____   /haʊs/ _____   /kɔɪ/ _____

/kaɪt/ _____   /taʊn/ _____   /twaɪs/ _____

/braʊn/ _____   /spaɪn/ _____   /faɪv/ _____

/praɪz/ _____   /aʊl/ _____   /raʊnd/ _____

EXERCISE 10-E: WRITING WORDS IN PHONETIC SYMBOLS: PHONEMIC DIPHTHONGS

Write the following words in phonetic symbols. All of these words contain one of the diphthongs. The symbols for the consonant sounds are the same as those used in the alphabet.

how _____   fry _____   toy _____

sound _____   time _____   noun _____

Track 5, 6

Practice transcribing phonemic diphthongs (5) as well as with all monophthongs (6) in simple syllables

slide _____   foil _____   coin _____

pounce _____   kind _____   down _____

line _____   trout _____   point _____

spice _____   cries _____   proud _____

swipe _____   moist _____   clown _____

Pronunciation

Diphthong reduction is a common occurrence is SA and also is observed in speakers of AA. The on-glide is retained and produced as a monophthong and may be lengthened (Bauman-Waengler, 2008; Bernthal, 2008; Edwards, 1992; Labov, 1997; Mendoza-Denton, 2001). This is commonly noted in the production of /aɪ/ and /ɔɪ/. /aɪ/ will be produced as /a/, and /ɔɪ/ will be produced as /ɔ/ or /o/.

Mayer (2004) describes the Southern/southeastern/southwestern "drawl" as a prolongation of the on-glide that reduces the off-glide to a schwa or a total omission. Another term for this (diphthong becoming a monophthong) is *monophthongization*.

For speakers of EA and SA, the on-glide of the /aʊ/ diphthong tends to be changed to /ɛ/ or /æ/, resulting in a diphthong /ɛʊ/ or /æʊ/.

Speakers of EA tend to produce the /ɔɪ/ with more tension, resulting in the creation of an /oi/ diphthong.

Non-native speakers of English tend to encounter difficulty producing diphthongs. Diphthong reduction to a monophthong is a common occurrence with these speakers.

Rhotic/Controlled /r/ Diphthongs

EXERCISE 11-A: SORTING WORDS BY VOWEL SOUNDS

Organize the following words into groups that contain the same vowel sound. Use the strategies that you have practiced in the previous chapters.

barn	flirt	here	sword	l<u>ar</u>ynx
tired	m<u>er</u>it	pearl	deer	d<u>ai</u>ry
bury	guard	chore	choir	heart
sure	tour	marry	carve	herb
w<u>ear</u>y	pierced	poor	burn	bare
where	wire	charge	hoarse	smeared
four	pure	share	burnt	warm

Group 1	Group 2	Group 3	Group 4	Group 5	Group 6	Group 7	Group 8

In the first unit, you may have been confused in counting sounds in words such as *beard* (three), *pair* (two), and *four* (two). You may have erroneously identified *rt* in the word *art* as a consonant sequence. These errors are common ones in the learning process in which you are currently involved.

In Chapter 10, you were introduced to five diphthongs, a type of vowel that is created by rapidly blending two separate vowel sounds within the same syllable. The resulting sound is one sound that is made by the gradual movement of the articulators as they transition from one position to the other.

In this chapter, you will be introduced to another set of diphthongs that are created when a vowel is combined with the /r/ sound (e.g., *car*, *bear*, *air*). Not all phoneticians agree about how to characterize vowels that precede an /r/ sound. Some do not classify these sounds as diphthongs. Some refer to these sounds as *centering diphthongs* (VanRiper & Smith, 1979). In this workbook, we refer to the vowel + /r/ combination as a **controlled r** or **rhotic diphthong**.

When the /r/ sound follows a vowel and occurs in the same syllable, the vowel anticipates and glides toward the /r/ position and takes on some of its properties. You were introduced to the terms *coarticulation* and *assimilation* in Chapter 1. The /r/ "colors" and modifies the qualities of the vowel that precedes it. As a result, a controlled-r or rhotic diphthong is created by combining certain vowel sounds with the postvocalic /r/.

Read the following pairs of words:

bid	beard
dead	dared
pot	part
caught	court
should	assured
tie	tire
ow!	our

The first word in each pair has that steady, stable quality present in monophthongs (except for *tie* and *ow!*). In each word in the second column, /r/ follows the vowel. The rapid blending of the two sounds (vowel + /r/) combines to form a new sound. Just like the diphthongs described in Chapter 10, each of these sound combinations is considered to be one sound in a word.

SYMBOLS FOR THE RHOTIC/CONTROLLED-/r/ DIPHTHONGS

/ɑɚ/	/ɪɚ/	/ɛɚ/	/ɔɚ/	/ʊɚ/
"ar"	"ear"	"air"	"or"	"ure"

Controlled-r diphthongs all contain a lax monophthong + /ɚ/ sound to form an "r-colored" vowel sound. These symbols are used in all syllables (stressed and unstressed). Because they are diphthongs, they are a rapid blending combination of two vowel sounds to create *one sound*. The lax monophthong is the on-glide (most prominent) and the central vowel (schwar) is the off-glide.

Did you notice that the vowel sound in two of the preceding pairs of words were not monophthongs, but diphthongs (i.e., *tie – tire*, *ow – our*)? When a diphthong combines with the postvocalic /r/, a triphthong is created (still counts as only one sound).

Track 7

Practice transcribing
controlled /r/ diphthongs
in simple syllables

CONTROLLED-/r/TRIPHTHONGS

/aɪɚ/   /aʊɚ/

"ire"   "our"

There is not agreement regarding whether to use the vowel symbol /ɚ/ or the consonant symbol /r/ when representing these sounds. Both are acceptable; just be consistent. Regardless of which symbol you use, this sound functions as a vowel sound in all words.

ALTERNATE SYMBOLS

The /r/ can be used instead of the /ɚ/.

/ɑr/   /ɪr/   /ɛr/   /ɔr/   /ʊr/

/aɪr/   /aʊr/

EXERCISE 11-B: IDENTIFYING THE CORRECT SYMBOL FOR CONTROLLED /r/ DIPHTHONGS

Pronounce each of the following words and isolate the vowel sound. Match the vowel sound you hear with the correct symbol. Circle the correct choice for the vowel sound you hear. The symbols for the controlled-r diphthongs are given. If you hear a vowel sound that is not one of these diphthongs, circle the last option (i.e., "vowel sound not given"). In your quest to become "ear-minded," continue to pay attention to the sounds you hear rather than the spellings you see.

Word			*Choice of Vowel Symbols*			
where	/ɑɚ/	/ɪɚ/	/ɛɚ/	/ɔɚ/	/ʊɚ/	vowel sound not given
heart	/ɑɚ/	/ɪɚ/	/ɛɚ/	/ɔɚ/	/ʊɚ/	vowel sound not given
fierce	/ɑɚ/	/ɪɚ/	/ɛɚ/	/ɔɚ/	/ʊɚ/	vowel sound not given
pear	/ɑɚ/	/ɪɚ/	/ɛɚ/	/ɔɚ/	/ʊɚ/	vowel sound not given
nurse	/ɑɚ/	/ɪɚ/	/ɛɚ/	/ɔɚ/	/ʊɚ/	vowel sound not given
here	/ɑɚ/	/ɪɚ/	/ɛɚ/	/ɔɚ/	/ʊɚ/	vowel sound not given
they're	/ɑɚ/	/ɪɚ/	/ɛɚ/	/ɔɚ/	/ʊɚ/	vowel sound not given
fourth	/ɑɚ/	/ɪɚ/	/ɛɚ/	/ɔɚ/	/ʊɚ/	vowel sound not given
word	/ɑɚ/	/ɪɚ/	/ɛɚ/	/ɔɚ/	/ʊɚ/	vowel sound not given
arch	/ɑɚ/	/ɪɚ/	/ɛɚ/	/ɔɚ/	/ʊɚ/	vowel sound not given

EXERCISE 11-C: DECODING PHONETIC SYMBOLS: CONTROLLED /r/ DIPHTHONGS

Read each of the following phonetic symbols and blend them together to make a word. Write the word that is created in orthography. Note: The phonetic symbol for the consonant sounds in these words will look familiar to you. All symbols for consonant sounds are true to the sounds that are associated with the alphabet letter.

/kɔɚk/ _____   /kaɚt/ _____   /klɪɚ/ _____

/skwɛɚ/ _____   /fɚs/ _____   /faɚs/ _____

/tʊɚz/ _____   /skɛɚd/ _____   /gaɚd/ _____

/dɪɚ/ _____   /sɔɚ/ _____   /glɛɚ/ _____

EXERCISE 11-D: WRITING WORDS IN PHONETIC SYMBOLS: CONTROLLED /r/ DIPHTHONGS

Represent the sounds you hear in each word in phonetic symbols. The symbols for the consonants are the same as those used in the alphabet.

steer _____   store _____   stare _____   star _____

warm _____   beard _____   barn _____   heir _____

rare _____   fork _____   mare _____   park _____

tier _____   arm _____   more _____   hard _____

Pronunciation

Say the following words out loud: *Mary, marry, merry*. For some speakers, these three words sound identical. For others, each word sounds distinct. Still others may make a distinction between only two of the words, pronouncing two of the three in a similar fashion.

Speakers in the Midwestern states, the Great Lakes region, the Midland cities (i.e., Philadelphia, Pittsburgh, Columbus, Cincinnati, Indianapolis, St. Louis, and Kansas City), the West Coast, and Texas produce the controlled-r or rhotic diphthongs.

Speakers from New England, New York City, Southeastern United States (i.e., Virginia, South Carolina), and the South (Alabama, Mississippi, Georgia,

Louisiana) tend to omit the r-coloring in their central vowels /ɚ/, and as a result, the controlled-r diphthongs do not have the rhotic component. In general, New England dialects are referred to as non-rhotic because most speakers of these dialects drop the *r*'s before consonants and at the end of words (Ash, Boberg, & Labov, 1997). For these speakers, the words *bar* and *baa* may sound similar.

Speakers who produce non-rhotic diphthongs may produce the sounds /ɑɚ/, /ɪɚ/, /ɛɚ/, /ɔɚ/, and /ʊɚ/ with a schwa /ə/ instead of a schwar /ɚ/. Speakers from the South tend to lengthen the on-glide (first vowel sound) and omit the schwar (MacKay, 1987).

Speakers in the southeastern part of the country will produce the rhotic-diphthongs with a tense vowel rather than a lax vowel. Speakers who use a tense vowel as the on-glide tend to form two syllables rather than a dipthong (VanRiper & Smith, 1979). Try it yourself: /mɔɚ/ (*more*) versus /moɚ/ (*mower*). Speakers of SA may produce the /ɔɚ/ as /ɑɚ/ (e.g., *for* is pronounced as *far*) (Bauman-Waengler, 2008; Bernthal, 2008; Labov, 2006).

Some speakers of SA and EA will use the vowel /æ/ in two-syllable words that may be produced with a /ɛɚ/ for a Midwesterner (Small, 2005). An example of this would be /kærɪ/ for the word *carry*.

Regional dialects will have an impact on the production of controlled-r diphthongs. Depending on your pronunciation patterns, the word *hair* can be transcribed several ways: /hɛɚ/, /hɛr/, /heɚ/, or /hɛə/. Which transcription best matches your pronunciation?

12 *Term Review and Practice*

Your goals for Unit 2 included:

- Learning the types of vowels comprising the English vowel system.
- Knowing the characteristics of all vowel sounds.
- Understanding how vowels are classified using the vowel quadrilateral as the reference point.
- Learning the phonetic symbol for each vowel sound.
- Learning the characteristics of each monophthong.
- Learning the basic characteristics of the diphthongs.
- Being introduced to the role word stress plays on central vowels.
- Completing exercises to improve attention to vowel sounds in words.
- Understanding dialectal variations/accent influences on vowel sounds.

By completing the exercises in this chapter, you will:

- Continue your journey from being "eye-minded" to "ear-minded."
- Solidify your understanding of the placement of vowels in the vowel quadrilateral.
- Demonstrate your knowledge about the key characteristics of each monophthong.
- Increase your automaticity in reading and writing all vowel symbols.
- Review key terms.
- Establish connections between related concepts.

TERMS

The following terms were introduced in Chapters 5 through 11. Not only is it important for you to understand what each term means, but it is also important for you to understand how the terms are connected to each other. Create a concept map to assist you in understanding how the terms are related to each other.

diphthong	schwa
diphthong reduction	schwar
lip rounding	rhotic diphthong
monophthong	tongue advancement
off-glide	tongue height
on-glide	tongue tension

EXERCISE 12-A: FIND WHAT IS ASKED

Read the following questions carefully. Identify the words that contain what is asked. Hint: Write the vowel symbol above each word before making your selections concerning vowels; use C & V before making decisions about syllables.

Which of the following words contain a **low** vowel?

laugh	loud	shot	rob	of	match

Which of the following words contain a **central** vowel?

blunt	blur	boat	from	way	girl

Which of the following words contain a **back** vowel?

bleed	bloom	blend	book	back	boat

Which of the following words contain a **monophthong**?

piece	price	cat	how	boy	shoe

Which of the following words are considered to have **open** syllables?

car	may	how	eye	shoe	boy

Which of the following words contain a **rounded** vowel?

blue	and	nut	sew	bird	cook

Which of the following words contain a **phonemic diphthong**?

tribe	trip	joy	laugh	now	noise

Which of the following words contain a **lax** vowel?

mean	men	cute	bomb	comb	fig

Which of the following words contain a **mid** vowel?

men	mope	mop	muck	map	make

Which of the following words are considered **closed** syllables?

tribe	trip	joy	own	now	noise

Which of the following words do *not* have an **onset**?

hour	own	how	one	eye	who

Which of the following words have a **coda**?

comb	boy	wow	four	oh	law

Which of the following words contain a **front** vowel?

    mint   back   front   all   piece   new

Which of the following words contain a **tense** vowel?

    late   seen   knot   boat   pull   mat

Which of the following words begin with a **voiced** sound?

    honor   all   eye   eat   law   own

EXERCISE 12-B: COUNTING SOUNDS

Count the number of sounds you hear in the following words. Remember to focus on the sounds you produce and hear rather than the number of graphemes. Diphthongs (phonemic and controlled-r) count as one sound.

feet _____	steak _____	spell _____	shawl _____
plant _____	row _____	ounce _____	chew _____
thought _____	half _____	flood _____	cough _____
noise _____	beige _____	hogs _____	jazz _____
whole _____	gnaw _____	want _____	thank _____

EXERCISE 12-C: COMPARE/CONTRAST PHONETIC CHARACTERISTICS OF VOWELS AND DIPHTHONGS

Using your vowel quadrilateral as a reference, compare and contrast the two sounds in each pair. How are they alike? How are they different? Use *TH* for tongue height, *TA* for tongue advancement, *TT* for tongue tension, and *LR* for lip rounding.

		Similarity	*Difference*
/ɑ/	/æ/	TH, TT, LR	TA
/ʌ/	/o/	_____	_____
/ʊ/	/u/	_____	_____

EXERCISE 12-C: COMPARE/CONTRAST PHONETIC CHARACTERISTICS OF VOWELS AND DIPHTHONGS (*continued*)

		Similarity	*Difference*
/ə/	/ʌ/	_____	_____
/ɛ/	/ɪ/	_____	_____
/i/	/ʊ/	_____	_____
/ɪ/	/æ/	_____	_____
/ɝ/	/ʌ/	_____	_____
/o/	/e/	_____	_____

EXERCISE 12-D: ODD ONE OUT

Read the following groups of words, focusing on the vowel sound. Determine which word does not share the same vowel sound with the others. Cross it out. On the line provided, write the vowel symbol that is shared by the pair that remains.

range	praise	~~laugh~~	/e/
brook	broom	pull	_____
down	ground	grown	_____
tooth	dug	blue	_____
fry	toy	point	_____
wire	bird	word	_____
spies	spice	spin	_____
were	where	stare	_____
left	etch	eight	_____
myth	cry	inch	_____
guard	laugh	quack	_____

large	share	sharp	_____
hearth	earth	nerd	_____
rough	cough	mud	_____
flood	boat	throw	_____
eye	these	she	_____
horn	storm	word	_____
must	put	putt	_____
sell	wheel	men	_____
twice	find	pinned	_____

EXERCISE 12-E: IDENTIFYING THE VOWEL SOUND

Determine the correct vowel symbol for each of the following words. If the correct vowel symbol is not provided, select the last option.

Word	*Choice of Vowel Symbols*			
rough	/ə/	/oʊ/	/ʌ/	correct vowel sound not provided
heard	/ɛɚ/	/ɝ/	/ɪɚ/	correct vowel sound not provided
warn	/ɔr/	/ɑɚ/	/ɝ/	correct vowel sound not provided
gauze	/aʊ/	/aɪ/	/ɔ/	correct vowel sound not provided
coin	/o/	/ɔɪ/	/i/	correct vowel sound not provided
square	/ɪɚ/	/ɑɚ/	/ɛɚ/	correct vowel sound not provided
kind	/ɪ/	/i/	/aɪ/	correct vowel sound not provided
good	/u/	/ʊ/	/o/	correct vowel sound not provided
text	/i/	/ɪ/	/ɛ/	correct vowel sound not provided
ground	/oʊ/	/aʊ/	/o/	correct vowel sound not provided
each	/i/	/ɪ/	/ɛ/	correct vowel sound not provided
weird	/ɛɚ/	/i/	/ɪɚ/	correct vowel sound not provided
shoot	/oʊ/	/ʊ/	/o/	correct vowel sound not provided

EXERCISE 12-E: IDENTIFYING THE VOWEL SOUND (*continued*)

Word			*Choice of Vowel Symbols*	
fin	/i/	/ɪ/	/ɛ/	correct vowel sound not provided
growth	/o/	/aʊ/	/u/	correct vowel sound not provided
shirt	/ɪɚ/	/ɝ/	/ɛɚ/	correct vowel sound not provided

EXERCISE 12-F: VOWEL CHANGE-UP

Identify the phonetic characteristics of the vowel sound in the word in the left column. Put in the order of tongue height (TH), tongue advancement (TA), tongue tension (TT), and lip rounding (LR). The middle column provides information on changing the original vowel sound. Create a new word by changing the specific characteristics. Think about the phonetic characteristics of the new vowel sound. In the last column, include any other characteristic that was altered as a result of the suggested change.

Word	*Characteristics TH, TA, TT, LR*	*Change to*	*New Word*
shoe	*High, back, tense, rounded*	*TA to front/LR*	*she*
ought	_____	TT	_____
pack	_____	TH to mid	_____
cupped	_____	TA to front	_____
cheek	_____	TT	_____
blond	_____	TA front	_____
boat	_____	TT	_____

For the following items, two characteristics will change.

fill	_____	TA back/LR	_____
bowl	_____	TH high/TT	_____
cake	_____	TA back	_____

shut   _____   LR/TT   _____

back   _____   TH high/TA back/LR   _____

EXERCISE 12-G: IDENTIFYING THE VOWEL

The four words across share the same consonant skeleton. Write the correct vowel symbol you hear in each word.

stake	_____	stuck	_____	stock	_____	stack	_____
grinned	_____	grand	_____	ground	_____	grind	_____
pest	_____	post	_____	past	_____	pieced	_____
key	_____	cow	_____	car	_____	core	_____
June	_____	gin	_____	jean	_____	join	_____
took	_____	tuck	_____	tike	_____	tack	_____
note	_____	not	_____	neat	_____	night	_____
wind (noun)	_____	wand	_____	warned	_____	wound (noun)	_____
pout	_____	put	_____	putt	_____	pot	_____
clean	_____	clone	_____	clan	_____	clown	_____
drop	_____	droop	_____	drape	_____	drip	_____
first	_____	feast	_____	fast	_____	fist	_____
least	_____	lust	_____	list	_____	last	_____
grown	_____	green	_____	grain	_____	grin	_____
spike	_____	speck	_____	spark	_____	spook	_____

EXERCISE 12-H: JUDGE THE TRANSCRIPTION

Read each word in orthography and its corresponding transcription. Determine whether or not the vowel symbol is accurate. If it is incorrect, write the correct transcription on the line provided. Reminder: The symbols for the consonants are the same as those used in the alphabet.

Word	Transcription	Is Vowel Transcription Accurate?		If Not, Provide Correct Vowel Transcription
knit	/nɪt/	Yes	No	_____
claim	/klem/	Yes	No	_____
beard	/bɛɚd/	Yes	No	_____
peak	/pik/	Yes	No	_____
verb	/vɛɚb/	Yes	No	_____
gum	/gum/	Yes	No	_____
flight	/flaɪt/	Yes	No	_____
house	/hoʊs/	Yes	No	_____
high	/hi/	Yes	No	_____
dark	/daɚk/	Yes	No	_____
home	/hom/	Yes	No	_____
test	/test/	Yes	No	_____
who	/ho/	Yes	No	_____

EXERCISE 12-I: WHAT'S THE WORD?

Combine the vowel descriptions that follow with the consonant sounds provided to create a word. Write the word in orthography.

	What's the Word?
"l" + mid, front, tense, unrounded + "s"	*lace*
"b" + low, front, lax, unrounded + "j"	*badge*

high, front, lax, unrounded + "ch"	*itch* _____
"h" + high, back, tense, rounded + "z"	_____
"n" + high, front, tense, unrounded	_____
"sh" + high, back, lax, unrounded + "d"	_____
"g" + mid, front, lax, unrounded + "s"	_____
"n" + mid, back, tense, rounded + "z"	_____
"sh" + low, back, lax, unrounded + "p"	_____
"p" + high, front, tense, unrounded + "z"	_____
"r" + mid, back, lax, unrounded	_____
"p" + high, back, lax, rounded + "l"	_____
"d" + mid, front, lax, unrounded + "t"	_____
"l" + low, front, lax, unrounded + "f"	_____
"f" + high, front, lax, unrounded + "sh"	_____
"h" + high, back, tense, rounded + "m"	_____
"j" + high, front, lax, unrounded + "m"	_____
"f" + low, front, lax, unrounded + "n"	_____
"h" + high, back, lax, rounded + "f"	_____
"r" + mid, front, tense, unrounded + "z"	_____
"b" + mid, back, tense, rounded + "l"	_____
"l" + high, back, tense, rounded + "z"	_____
"w" + mid, front, tense, unrounded	_____
"r" + mid, front, lax, unrounded + "d"	_____
"k" + high, back, lax, rounded + "d"	_____
"h" + mid, back, lax, rounded + "l"	_____
"h" + high, front, tense, unrounded + "t"	_____
"p" + low, back, lax, unrounded + "p"	_____
"l" + high, back, tense, rounded + "s"	_____

EXERCISE 12-J: DECODE THE SYMBOLS

Read the following IPA symbols and blend the sounds they represent together to create a word you know.

/lof/ _____   /naɪt/ _____   /wæks/ _____

/blʌd/ _____   /sef/ _____   /gost/ _____

/fæst/ _____   /klɪɚ/ _____   /blɑnd/ _____

/gɪlt/ _____   /nɛlt/ _____   /fɝnz/ _____

/haʊnd/ _____   /prun/ _____   /kɔɪn/ _____

/spɛnd/ _____   /temd/ _____   /slæpt/ _____

/kɔf/ _____   /dɛɚd/ _____   /raɪm/ _____

/wʊl/ _____   /told/ _____   /bruz/ _____

Track 8

Practice transcribing all vowels in simple syllables

UNIT
3
Consonants

Your goals for Unit 3 include the following:

- To understand the ways that consonants can be classified
- To learn the characteristics of each consonant sound
- To learn the phonetic symbol for each consonant sound
- To be able to recognize the similarities and differences across consonant sounds
- To complete exercises to improve attention to consonant sounds in words
- To become aware of the phonetic variations of specific sounds in the context of words
- To increase your awareness of the dialectal variations/accent influences on consonant sounds

13 *Overview*

EXERCISE 13-A: ONSET COMPARISON

Read the following pairs of words. After isolating the *onset* of each word, determine whether their onsets are the same or different. Think: Does the consonant grouping (singleton or sequence) before the vowel contain the same sound(s)? Reminder: Pay attention to the sounds, not the spellings.

phone	far	same	different
sugar	chef	same	different
cake	cell	same	different
judge	gem	same	different
theme	them	same	different
chair	train	same	different
cope	ghost	same	different
tape	cape	same	different
look	lick	same	different
who	hue	same	different
thing	think	same	different
girl	gem	same	different
use	yours	same	different
there	they	same	different
drop	dot	same	different
one	wind	same	different
food	feud	same	different
sip	ship	same	different
me	knee	same	different

EXERCISE 13-B: CODA COMPARISON

Read the following pairs of words. After isolating the *coda* of each word, determine whether their codas are the same or different. Think: Does the consonant grouping (singleton or sequence) after the vowel contain the same sound(s)? Reminder: Pay attention to the sounds, not the spellings.

peas	peace	same	different
cup	mob	same	different
vague	beige	same	different
match	such	same	different
walk	milk	same	different
breath	breathe	same	different
lodge	luge	same	different
calf	buff	same	different
knocks	fox	same	different
cage	edge	same	different
backed	bagged	same	different
bang	bank	same	different
nest	nets	same	different
league	log	same	different
should	yield	same	different
dumb	dub	same	different
rink	thank	same	different
most	coats	same	different

REMINDERS AS YOU PROGRESS THROUGH UNIT 3

- Pay attention to the sounds in a word and not the letters used to spell it. In order to achieve this, you will have to say the word out loud so that you can feel the sound, hear the sound, and see the sound. It may be easier to work with a partner. Listen and watch as your partner pronounces the word.

- Isolate individual sounds in a word in order to pay attention to them, but produce the sounds and words *naturally*.

- Appreciate the influence of the surrounding sound context when producing a word.

Consonants and Vowels

In Chapter 1, you were introduced to the two sounds that make up the English phonology system. In Unit 2, you were introduced to the characteristics of the vowels in our sound system. Unit 3 is about consonants. A comparison between vowel and consonant characteristics is outlined in Table 13.1. Elaboration about the specific characteristics of consonants will follow.

TABLE 13.1 Distinguishing Consonants From Vowels

Vowels	Consonants
Produced with relatively open vocal tract	Produced with some degree of constriction in the vocal tract; varies across manner groups
Airstream from vocal folds to lips encounters no significant obstruction.	Airstream encounters some constriction from vocal folds to lips or nostrils.
All vowels are voiced (have vocal fold vibration).	Consonants are produced with and without vocal fold vibration. Some are voiced; some are voiceless.
Different vowels are created by movements of lips, tongue, and jaw. Classified by: Tongue height	Different consonants are created by changes in voicing, how airstream travels, where obstruction takes place. Classified by:
Position of tongue in mouth	Voicing
Amount of tongue tension	Place
Degree of lip rounding	Manner
Contains the most acoustic energy resulting in louder sounds (sonority*); serves as syllable peak.	Sounds are acoustically less intense
	Varies in amount of sonority
Functions as syllable nucleus	

*__Sonority__ (defined): characteristic of a sound that refers to its loudness relative to other sounds similar in length, stress, and pitch (Ladefoged, 2006). All vowels and certain consonants are considered to be sonorants.

Classification of Consonants

Each consonant sound is classified in three ways.

1. Voicing
2. Place of articulation
3. Manner of articulation

Some consonants may differ by as little as one characteristic; others may differ by all three.

Voicing

The voicing of a consonant sound is determined by whether or not the vocal folds are vibrating during production. Put the palm of your hand across the front of your neck. Hiss like a snake (sssssssssss) and then buzz like a bee (zzzzzzzzzzz). You should be able to feel vibration in only one of the sounds.

REMEMBER
• If the vocal folds are vibrating during sound production, the consonant is referred to as a **voiced** consonant.
• If the consonants are activated by the airstream only, and there is no vibration during production, they are labeled as **voiceless** consonants.

EXERCISE 13-C: DETERMINING THE VOICING OF CONSONANT SOUNDS

Place your palm across the front of your neck and produce the following sounds. After you produce each sound, determine whether it is voiced or voiceless. Be sure to produce just the sound and not a CV syllable (i.e., produce only the "b" sound and not the syllable "buh").

ng	th(father)	zh	n	h	z	p	f	m	y	ch	g
s	th(thing)	d	w	t	sh	j	v	k	l	r	b

Voiced	*Voiceless/Unvoiced*
vocal folds vibrate	vocal folds do not vibrate during production
___ ___ ___	___ ___ ___
___ ___ ___	___ ___ ___
___ ___ ___	___ ___ ___
___ ___ ___	___ ___ ___
___ ___ ___	___ ___ ___
___ ___ ___	___ ___ ___

After you organize the consonant sounds by voicing, produce the sounds in each group. Are they all produced with the same amount of voicing? Make the necessary changes. Check your groups again. All sounds in each group should be similar in their voicing.

TRUE or FALSE   There are more consonants that are voiceless than voiced.

Support your decision with evidence: _____

_____

TRUE or FALSE   There are some consonants that are produced the same except for voicing.

Support your decision with evidence: _____

_____

Place of Articulation

The place of articulation refers to *where* along the vocal tract the sound is made. This location is the point of contact or near contact of the active (movable) and passive (immovable) articulators when a speech sound is produced (Edwards, 2003). The best way to discover a sound's place of articulation is to feel where the sound is produced in your mouth and focus on the articulators that are involved in producing it.

EXERCISE 13-D: DETERMINING PLACE OF ARTICULATION

As you produce each sound, focus on where in the mouth the sound is being produced and which articulators are necessary for producing that sound. More than enough spaces are provided for you. An "other" category is provided for you to use, if needed.

ng	th(father)	zh	n	h	z	p	f	m	y	ch	g
s	th(thing)	d	w	t	sh	j	v	k	l	r	b

Lip to lip   _____ _____ _____ _____ _____ _____ _____

Upper teeth to lower lip   _____ _____ _____ _____ _____ _____ _____

Tongue tip between teeth   _____ _____ _____ _____ _____ _____ _____

Tongue tip on or near alveolar ridge _____ _____ _____ _____ _____ _____ _____

Tongue blade/ body near hard palate _____ _____ _____ _____ _____ _____ _____

Back of tongue near soft palate   _____ _____ _____ _____ _____ _____ _____

Neck (level of vocal folds)   _____ _____ _____ _____ _____ _____ _____

Other   _____ _____ _____ _____ _____ _____ _____

After you have organized the consonant sounds by place, produce the sounds in each group. Are they all produced in the same general area? Make the necessary changes. Check your groups again. All sounds in each group should be similar in where they are produced.

Terminology for Place of Articulation

Front-to-back place of articulation is presented in Table 13.2. Articulators are given in row one; the specific place of articulation term is given in row two.

TABLE 13.2 Front-to-Back Place of Articulation

Lip to Lip	Upper Teeth to Bottom Lip	Tongue Tip Between Teeth	Tongue Tip to Alveolar Ridge	Tongue Body to Hard Palate	Back of Tongue to Soft Palate	Neck (Glottis)
Bilabial	**Labiodental**	**Interdental**	**Alveolar**	**Palatal**	**Velar**	**Glottal**
			Note: Front of tongue (most active) moves to front of mouth	Note: Middle of tongue (most active) and stays in the center of the mouth	Note: Back of tongue (most active) and connects with the back of the mouth	

Manner of Articulation

The manner of articulation describes *how the sound is formed*. It describes how the articulators control the flow of air. Because different groups of consonants range in the degree of constriction along the vocal tract, the affected flow of air ranges from one of complete stoppage to one that is relatively open and unimpeded.

The manner of consonants can be divided into two broad groups according to the amount of constriction in the vocal tract during their formation.

Obstruents describe those consonants in manner classes that are produced with greater constriction along the vocal tract (airstream encounters greater *obstru*ction). Obstruents can be produced with or without vocal cord vibration.

Sonorants describe those consonants in manner classes that are produced with less obstruction in the vocal tract. Although the vocal tract is narrowed at the place of articulation, the airstream encounters minimal obstruction. Because sonorant sounds are produced with a more open vocal tract, they are often considered to be semi-vowels because they share many of the characteristics of vowels (all voiced, more **sonority**).

> **REMINDER**
>
> The more open the vocal tract → the greater the degree of sonority.

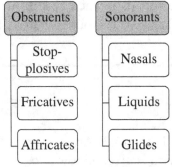

Figure 13.1

There are six manner classes: three classes are obstruents and three are sonorants. These manner classes are organized for you in Figure 13.1.

Obstruents

Stop-plosive: Stop-plosive consonants, regardless of where they are made, are formed by a complete closure of the vocal tract (stop), so that airflow ceases temporarily and air pressure builds up behind the point of closure. When the impounded air is released, it produces a small explosion of escaping air (plosive). This audible puff of air is termed **aspiration**.

Articulatory summary (Shriberg & Kent, 2003; p. 64):

- The oral cavity is completely closed at some point for a brief interval.
- The velopharynx is closed (otherwise, the air within the oral pressure chamber would escape through the nose).
- Upon release of the stop closure, a burst of noise typically is heard.
- The closing and opening movements for stops tend to be quite fast, usually the fastest movements in speech.

Fricative: Fricative sounds are produced with a narrow constriction through which air escapes with a continuous noise.

Articulatory summary (Shriberg & Kent, 2003; p. 65):

- The articulators form a narrow constriction through which airflow is channeled. Air pressure increases in the chamber behind the constriction.
- As the air flows through the narrow opening, a continuous frication noise is generated.
- Because effective noise production demands that all of the escaping air be directed through the oral constriction, fricative sounds are produced with a closed velopharynx.

Affricate: These sounds are a combination sound created by a stop closure at the place of articulation followed by a fricative release.

Articulatory summary (Shriberg & Kent, 2003; p. 67):

- Affricates are a combination of a stop closure and a fricative segment, with the frication noise closely following the stop portion.
- Affricates are made with complete closures of the velopharynx.

Sonorants

The three manner classes within the sonorant category form two groups: nasal and oral. The oral sonorants also are referred to as **approximants**. This subgroup of the sonorants are also described as *semi-vowels*. Approximants are made so that the articulators approach each other, but not to the extent that turbulence is produced. The articulators are only approximated during their production.

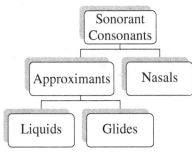

Figure 13.2

Nasals are not considered approximants because they require complete closure of the articulators, even though they are resonated through the nose (Edwards, 2003; Small, 2005). The organization of the sonorant manner classes are shown in Figure 13.2.

Nasal: Nasal consonants are produced with a complete oral closure at the place of articulation (like a stop), but with an open velopharynx, so that voicing energy travels out through the nose.

Articulatory summary (Shriberg & Kent, 2003; p. 65):

- The oral tract is completely closed, as it is for a stop.
- The velopharyngeal port is open to permit sound energy to radiate outward through the nasal cavities.
- Even if the oral closure is broken, sound may continue to travel through the nose as long as the velopharynx remains open.

Liquid: Liquids are consonants in which voicing energy passes through a vocal tract that is constricted only somewhat more than for vowels. As a result, there is only approximation of the articulators (no friction or blockage), thus producing a vowel-like quality. The shape and location of the constriction is a critical defining property, being distinctive for a given type of liquid. There are two types of liquids: lateral and rhotic. A lateral sound has midline closure and lateral opening for sound transmission. A rhotic sound has "r-coloring." There is more variation in the /r/ sounds in English when compared with any other consonant (MacKay, 1987).

Articulatory summary (Shriberg & Kent, 2003; p. 65):

- Sound energy from the vocal folds is directed through a distinctively shaped oral passage, one that can be held indefinitely for sustained production of the sound, if required.
- The velopharynx is always (or at least almost always) closed.
- The oral passageway is narrower than that for vowels but wider than that for stops, fricatives, and nasals.

Glide: Glide sounds are characterized by a rapid, gliding motion of the articulators from a partly constricted state (place of articulation) to a more open state for the following vowel. A glide is always followed by a vowel. Glides are produced with a vocal tract constriction somewhat narrower than that for vowels but less severe than that for stops and fricatives.

Articulatory summary (Shriberg & Kent, 2003; p. 67):

- The constricted state for the glide is narrower than that for a vowel but wider than that for stops and fricatives.
- The articulators make a gradual gliding motion from the constricted segment to the more open configuration for the following vowel.
- The velopharynx is generally, if not always, closed.
- The sound energy from the vocal folds passes through the mouth in a fashion similar to that for vowels.

EXERCISE 13-E: DETERMINING MANNER OF ARTICULATION

As you produce each sound, focus on how the air is controlled through the vocal tract. More than enough spaces are provided for you. An "other" category is provided for you to use if needed.

ng	th(father)	zh	n	h	z	p	f	m	y	ch	g
s	th(thing)	d	w	t	sh	j	v	k	l	r	b

Stop-plosives _____ _____ _____ _____ _____ _____ _____

Fricatives _____ _____ _____ _____ _____ _____ _____

_____ _____ _____ _____ _____ _____ _____

Affricates _____ _____ _____ _____ _____ _____ _____

Nasals _____ _____ _____ _____ _____ _____ _____

Liquids _____ _____ _____ _____ _____ _____ _____

Glides _____ _____ _____ _____ _____ _____ _____

Other _____ _____ _____ _____ _____ _____ _____

After you have organized the consonant sounds by manner, produce the sounds in each group. Are they all produced in the same way? Make the necessary changes. Check your groups again. All sounds in each group should be similar in how they are produced.

AN ADDITIONAL TERM

Cognates are those consonants that share the same place and manner, but they differ in voicing. All but one obstruent is part of a cognate pair. All sonorants are voiced (with one exception); they do not form cognate pairs. Return to the previous three exercises. Are you able to guess at which sounds form a cognate pair?

The following consonant classification sheet (page 109) will be useful to you in organizing the information that was presented in this chapter. You may wish to refer back to this sheet during the exercises that await you.

A table is also provided for you to complete (see page 110). This will be of assistance to you when you are asked to compare and contrast consonant sounds.

CONSONANT CLASSIFICATION SHEET

	Symbol	Voicing	Place	Manner
m	_____	_voiced_	_bilabial_	_nasal_
n	_____	_____	_____	_____
ng	_____	_____	_____	_____
p	_____	_____	_____	_____
b	_____	_____	_____	_____
t	_____	_____	_____	_____
d	_____	_____	_____	_____
k	_____	_____	_____	_____
g	_____	_____	_____	_____
th (thing)	_____	_____	_____	_____
th (father)	_____	_____	_____	_____
sh	_____	_____	_____	_____
zh	_____	_____	_____	_____
h	_____	_____	_____	_____
s	_____	_____	_____	_____
z	_____	_____	_____	_____
f	_____	_____	_____	_____
v	_____	_____	_____	_____
ch	_____	_____	_____	_____
j	_____	_____	_____	_____
y	_____	_____	_____	_____
w	_____	_____	_____	_____
l	_____	_____	_____	_____
r	_____	_____	_____	_____

CLASSIFICATION OF CONSONANTS

Manner of Articulation	Voicing		Bilabial	Labiodental	Interdental	Alveolar	Palatal	Velar	Glottal
Stop-plosive	Voiceless								
	Voiced								
Fricative	Voiceless								
	Voiced								
Affricate	Voiceless								
	Voiced								
Nasal	Voiceless								
	Voiced								
Liquid	Voiceless								
	Voiced								
Glide	Voiceless								
	Voiced								

Place of Articulation

OBSTRUENTS

SONORANTS

Organizational Framework of Chapters in This Unit

The consonant sounds will be presented to you in the six manner classes. Each chapter will present the sounds within a manner class and describe their characteristics. Each sound will have its own voicing, place, and manner, as well as its own phonetic symbol. Sixteen symbols will be the same as the Roman alphabet letters you already know. Other symbols will be new to you. It is important that you not only learn the sound–symbol association of each consonant, but also understand and learn its phonetic makeup (voicing, place, and manner). Once you learn the characteristics of each sound, you will be able to compare and contrast sounds with each other.

Also included in each chapter will be pronunciation information that will help you understand the sounds. This will be followed by exercises to practice the information for consonant singletons. You will be asked to "read" phonetic symbols to create a familiar word, translate or "spell" the sounds in a word in phonetic symbols, use an equation of phonetic information to create words, and write your own phonetic equation using specific phonetic information for the sounds that comprise a word. Additional exercises will be provided for you to use the phonetic characteristics (i.e., voicing, place, and manner) to compare and contrast sounds. The consonant sounds in each manner class will then be introduced to you in the context of consonant sequences. Two familiar exercises (reading phonetic symbols to make words and writing a word in phonetic symbols) will assist you in focusing on the consonant sounds in sequences.

The website http://www.uiowa.edu/~acadtech/phonetics/ serves as a useful tool for students learning how sounds are produced, as it presents animated productions of each sound in English (as well as German and Spanish).

Stop-Plosives

In a stop-plosive, the airstream is stopped or blocked completely before release.

Place of Articulation	Voicing	Stop-Plosive Symbols	
Bilabial	Voiceless	p	/p/
(lip to lip)	Voiced	b	/b/
Alveolar	Voiceless	t	/t/
(tongue tip to alveolar ridge)	Voiced	d	/d/
Velar	Voiceless	k	/k/
(back of tongue to soft palate)	Voiced	g	/g/

In the preceding chart, the six sounds that comprise the stop-plosive category create three *cognate pairs*. Remember that a cognate is a pair of sounds that share the same place and manner but differ only in voicing.

EXERCISE 14-A: COMMON BONDS

Using the phonetic characteristics of place and voicing described in the preceding chart, identify the commonality between the two sounds.

/p/   /k/   _____

/g/   /k/   _____

/b/   /p/   _____

/p/   /t/   _____

/d/   /g/   _____

/t/   /d/   _____

A Focus on Pronunciation

To form a stop-plosive sound, the breathstream is completely blocked at the place of articulation. When the air is released, it produces a small explosion of escaping air (plosive). This audible puff of air is termed **aspiration**.

Producing Stop-Plosives in Words

1. All prevocalic stop-plosive singletons are heavily aspirated when they initiate a word or begin a stressed syllable. You should be able to feel the amount of aspiration when you say the words that follow. Place your hand, palm side toward your face, in front of your mouth as you say the following words out loud. Notice the difference in aspiration in the stop-plosives in the following pairs of words when you say them out loud.

purse – upper

The /p/ in *purse* initiates the word; the /p/ in *upper* begins an unstressed syllable.

upper – appear

The /p/ in *upper* begins an unstressed syllable, whereas the /p/ in *appear* begins a stressed syllable.

purse – appear

Both /p/s are heavily aspirated: The /p/ in *purse* initiates the word; the /p/ in *appear* begins a stressed syllable.

Will this be similar for the /t/ and /k/ sounds? Find three words that contain these sounds to test the hypothesis. What about their voiced counterparts? Will these same concepts hold true when a voiced stop-plosive is in the same positions in words? Find three words that contain a /b/ or /d/ or /g/ to determine whether the aspiration changes.

2. Postvocalic stop-plosives may not be released.
3. Speakers tend to omit the voicing when sounds are in the final positions of words. Read the following words out loud. Can you detect a difference in the vowel length?

but – bud	cup – cub	cop – cob	knock – nog
bat – bad	cap – cab	back – bag	hit – hid
rate – raid	coop – cube	tote – toad	net – Ned

➜ The length of each vowel is shorter before a voiceless stop-plosive.

Allophones for Intervocalic /t/ and /d/

Read the following words out loud:

/t/	writer	attack	button	butter	little	rooster
	letter	forty	auntie	metal	planter	bottle
/d/	rider	adore	panda	medal	adapt	boulder

The intervocalic /t/ is produced similar to a prevocalic /t/ when it is part of an intervocalic sequence or when the second syllable receives the primary stress.

roo<u>st</u>er	au<u>nti</u>e	pla<u>nt</u>er	a<u>ttack</u>	a<u>tone</u>

Allophones for Intervocalic /t/

Alveolar flap: A *flap* involves a rapid movement of the tongue tip from a retracted vertical position to a (more or less) horizontal position, during which the tongue tip brushes the alveolar ridge.

OR

Alveolar tap /ɾ/:   A *tap* involves a rapid backward and forward movement of the tongue tip. This is more rapid than the typical alveolar stop production and typically occurs when the stress is on the first syllable.

> writer   butter   little   letter   forty   metal   bottle

Allophones for Intervocalic /d/

/d/ is also affected by these contexts:

> adore   adapt   panda   boulder   rider   medal

Track 17

Alveolar flap/tap: Notice the alveolar productions when you say the following words. The intervocalic /t/ is produced as an allophone /ɾ/ and not as a /d/.

beating – beading	betting – bedding	bitter – bidder
catty – caddy	coating – coding	greater – grader
hearty – hardy	heated – heeded	hurting – herding
kitty – kiddie	latter – ladder	liter – leader
matter – madder	metal – medal	neuter – nuder
otter – odder	painting – paining	rated – raided
Saturday – sadder day	seating – seeding	set it – said it
shutter – shudder	sighted – sided	title – tidal
traitor – trader	waiter – wader	whiter – wider
writing – riding	writer – rider	

Track 18

Glottal stop /ʔ/:   To produce a glottal stop, the air is stopped at the level of the vocal folds (VF) and the glottis and then is released. The VF do not vibrate, resulting in a voiceless glottal stop. More prevalent in British English, some speakers of American English produce a glottal stop in words in which /t/ or /nt/ is followed by a syllabic /n/. The tongue tip stays in place for both the /t/ and the following /n/ sounds (Small, 2005), but the sound is produced at the level of the VF.

> kitten   mountain   Dayton

Say the following words:

> sittin' – sitting

Do you detect a difference when producing intervocalic /t/?

Additional Pronunciation Points for /t/ and /d/

- Possible affrication of /t/ and /d/ in liquid /r/ sequences due to coarticulation. When *tr* or *dr* form a consonant sequence (e.g., <u>*train*</u>, <u>*drain*</u>), the manner feature (i.e., continuant) and place of the *r* consonant (i.e., palatal) may have an impact on the production of the alveolar stop-plosives /t/ and /d/.

The alveolar stop-plosive is often produced farther back in the mouth and with a longer release (more similar to an affricate production).

train → /tren/ or chrain /tʃren/

drain → /dren/ or jrain /dʒren/

- Pronunciation of past tense *–ed*. In Chapter 2, you were introduced to the term *morphophonemics* and the past tense *–ed* marker was used as an example. *Morphophonemics* refers to the changes in pronunciation that occur when bound morphemes are added to a word. The following words all have the *–ed* ending attached. Read them out loud, focusing on the sound the *–ed* ending makes in each word. Are you able to identify the pattern?

/t/	/d/
caped	clubbed
biked	jogged
decked	fined

Pronunciation Points for /k/ and /g/

- Velar stop plosives are rounded before a bilabial sound (consonant or vowel)

  Notice the difference in producing the velar stop plosives in the following words:

  quack – cat   coat – kite   go – gay   goo – guy

- Prevocalic velar placement

  Say the following words, paying attention to the velar placement of the onset:

  cot   cat   kite   cake   cup   cook   cool   kill   keep

EXERCISE 14-B: DECODING PHONETIC SYMBOLS

Pronounce the sound represented by each of the following phonetic symbols and blend them together to make a word. Write the word that is created in orthography.

/de/ _____   /bæd/ _____   /pʊt/ _____   /gɑt/ _____   /daʊt/ _____

/kɔt/ _____   /bud/ _____   /dɛɚ/ _____   /pik/ _____   /tɑp/ _____

/bɝp/ _____   /tʌb/ _____   /tub/ _____   /gʊd/ _____   /ɑd/ _____

/kæb/ _____   /daɪd/ _____   /dɝt / _____   /bɪd/ _____   /tʌk/ _____

/ɝb/ _____

EXERCISE 14-C: WRITING WORDS WITH PHONETIC SYMBOLS

Write the following words in phonetic symbols. All of these words contain stop-plosives.

guy _____   cow _____   guard _____   pack _____

court _____   up _____   dig _____   paid _____

EXERCISE 14-C: WRITING WORDS WITH PHONETIC SYMBOLS (*continued*)

boy _____   get _____   tuck _____   ache _____

could _____   pig _____   bird _____   cap _____

dope _____   dear _____   taught _____   dark _____

dared _____

EXERCISE 14-D: SOLVING WORD EQUATIONS

Provide the correct symbol for each sound description. Once all symbols are identified, blend the sounds together to form a word. Write the resulting word in orthography.

	Sound Description	*Phonetic Symbol*		*Word in Orthography*
	Voiced alveolar stop-plosive	/d/		
+	High back tense rounded vowel	/u/ =	/du/	do
	High front tense unrounded vowel	_____		
+	Voiceless alveolar stop-plosive	_____ =	_____	_____
	Voiced velar stop-plosive	_____		
+	Mid front tense unrounded vowel	_____ =	_____	_____
	Voiceless bilabial stop-plosive	_____		
+	Mid back tense rounded vowel	_____		
+	Voiceless velar stop-plosive	_____ =	_____	_____
	Voiceless velar stop-plosive	_____		
+	Mid central lax unrounded vowel	_____		
+	Voiceless bilabial stop-plosive	_____ =	_____	_____

	Sound Description	*Phonetic Symbol*	*Word in Orthography*
	Voiced bilabial stop-plosive	_____	
+	Low front lax unrounded vowel	_____	
+	Voiced velar stop-plosive	_____ = _____ _____

EXERCISE 14-E: WRITING WORD EQUATIONS

Transcribe the sounds you hear in each of the following words. For each symbol, write a word equation that accurately describes the sounds contained in each word. On each line, write the phonetic description for each consonant and vowel contained in the word.

owed   <u>mid back tense rounded vowel</u> _____

/od/   +   <u>voiced alveolar stop-plosive</u> _____

      +   _____

egg   _____

      +   _____

      +   _____

ape   _____

      +   _____

      +   _____

took   _____

      +   _____

      +   _____

      +   _____

goop   _____

      +   _____

118   *Chapter 14*

EXERCISE 14-E: WRITING WORD EQUATIONS (*continued*)

+ _____

+ _____

EXERCISE 14-F: STATE THE CHANGE

In Chapter 1, you were introduced to the concept of minimal pairs (i.e., two words that differ by one phoneme). In this exercise, two words are provided. Identify the sound change(s) and then provide an explanation on the line (using what you know about place, manner, and voicing). The change(s) may be in the onset or the coda.

pear → tear   <u>place changed from bilabial to alveolar</u>

cop → pop   _____

boat → goat   _____

tall → ball   _____

bite → kite   _____

key → T   _____

Now, create your own minimal pairs. _____

_____

EXERCISE 14-G: CREATING MINIMAL PAIRS (ONSET) WITH STOP-PLOSIVE SOUNDS

In this exercise, you will be provided with a word and then be required to change its **onset** by changing a specific phonetic characteristic (place or voicing) in order to create a new word that will form a minimal pair. For some of the words, you may be able to create more than one word.

Word	Change	New Word
beg /bɛg/	voicing	peg /pɛg/
peach	place	_____
does	place	_____
tar	place	_____
card	voicing	_____

EXERCISE 14-H: CREATING MINIMAL PAIRS (CODA) WITH STOP-PLOSIVE SOUNDS

In this exercise, you will be provided with a word and then be required to change its **coda** by changing a specific phonetic characteristic (place or voicing) in order to create a new word that will form a minimal pair.

Track 9

Practice transcribing stop-plosive in simple syllables

Word	Change	New Word
pack /pæk/	place	pat /pæt/
hug _____	place/voicing	_____
ape _____	place	_____
red _____	place/voicing	_____
hot _____	place	_____
rob _____	place/voicing	_____

Stop-Plosives in Sequences

Sound	Prevocalic Sequences (Syllable Initial)*	Postvocalic Sequences (Syllable Final)*
/p/	pr, pl, sp	ps, pt, sp, pt, lp sps
/b/	br, bl, by(u)	bz, bd
/t/	tr, tw st str	nt, pt, st, ft, lt, p, k, s, f, sh, ch, mp + t (past tense marker) ts
/d/	dr, dw	ld, nd, b, m, n, g, j, v, z, th + d (past tense marker) dz
/k/	kr, kl, kw ("q") sk skr, skw	lk, kt, ngk, ngks, sk, ks, sks
/g/	gr, gl	+d +z

*Sequences as listed are written in orthography.

Pronunciation Notes

- Voiceless stop-plosives have less of a burst of air (i.e., aspiration) in prevocalic strident clusters. This is termed an *unaspirated release*.

  Notice the difference in aspiration in the stop-plosives in the following pairs of words when you say them out loud:

  pin – spin   pot – spot   tuck – stuck   tile – style   key – ski   care – scare

EXERCISE 14-I: DECODING PHONETIC SYMBOLS: WORDS WITH SEQUENCES

Pronounce the sound represented by each of the following phonetic symbols and blend them together to make a word. Write the word that is created in orthography. The symbols for the consonant sounds that are not stop-plosives will be the same as those used in the alphabet.

/drɔ/ _____   /ekt/ _____   /klaʊd/_____   /tubz/ _____   /stups/_____

/tre/ _____   /pækt/ _____   /klind/ _____   /blu/ _____   /tʌgd/_____

/gron/_____   /bɝst/ _____   /klæpt/_____   /praɪd/ _____   /bɛlt/ _____

/kræk/_____   /glo/ _____   /dɪpt/ _____   /brok/ _____   /kɝst/ _____

/told/ _____   /plet/ _____   /tæpt/ _____   /blɛnd/ _____

EXERCISE 14-J: WRITING WORDS IN PHONETIC SYMBOLS: WORDS WITH SEQUENCES

Write the following words in phonetic symbols. The symbols for the consonants are the same as those used in the alphabet.

treat _____   spoiled _____   grabbed _____   biked _____   wasp _____

plug _____   blouse _____   brags _____   drive _____   pressed _____

typed _____   milk _____   blow _____   dabbed _____   cooked _____

poked _____   desk _____   curled _____   bugged _____   glides _____

glue _____   proud _____   twirled _____   brats _____   help _____

clap _____   bleed _____   blocks _____   cold _____   coast _____

taste _____   gross _____

15 *Fricatives*

I n a fricative, air is forced through a narrow passageway in the mouth or throat, creating continuous friction.

Place of Articulation	Voicing	Fricative Symbols	
Labiodental	Voiceless	f	/f/
(lip to teeth)	Voiced	v	/v/
Interdental	Voiceless	*thigh*	/θ/
(tongue tip between teeth)	Voiced	*thy*	/ð/
Alveolar	Voiceless	s	/s/
(tongue tip to alveolar ridge)	Voiced	z	/z/
Palatal	Voiceless	sh	/ʃ/
(tongue body to central palate)	Voiced	zh	/ʒ/
Glottal	Voiceless	h	/h/
(neck/glottis)			

In the preceding chart, eight of the nine sounds that comprise the fricative manner class form *cognate pairs*. Learning new symbols in cognates is often helpful in remembering the phonetic characteristics of each sound.

A Focus on Pronunciation

- To detect the voicing differences in interdental fricatives, a recommended strategy is to produce the word both ways (i.e., with the voiced and voiceless sounds). Which one sounds better?

Read the following pairs of words aloud, focusing on the interdental fricatives (/θ/ /ð/) in the word. Determine whether they have the same voicing (**S**ame/**D**ifferent). Write the correct symbol on the line next to each word.

Focus on Prevocalic				Voicing	
though	_____	thug	_____	S	D
thought	_____	them	_____	S	D
thunder	_____	thirsty	_____	S	D
these	_____	thumb	_____	S	D
thin	_____	third	_____	S	D

Focus on Postvocalic				*Voicing*	
north	_____	cloth	_____	S	D
smooth	_____	wreath	_____	S	D
breathe	_____	clothe	_____	S	D
soothe	_____	south	_____	S	D
myth	_____	mouth	_____	S	D

Focus on Intervocalic				*Voicing*	
either	_____	nothing	_____	S	D
leather	_____	lethal	_____	S	D
sympathy	_____	authentic	_____	S	D
gather	_____	mother	_____	S	D
worthy	_____	breathy	_____	S	D
farther	_____	father	_____	S	D

You learned in Chapter 14 that the length of the vowel is shorter before a voiceless stop-plosive. Determine whether this remains true for the fricative cognates.

bus – buzz	H – age	leaf – leave	mouth – mouthe
loss – laws	etch – edge	safe – save	teeth – teethe
rice – rise	rich – ridge	proof – prove	

The length of each vowel is shorter before a voiceless fricative. There is a common tendency for speakers to devoice final voiced fricatives; attending to the vowel length may help you determine the voicing of the final consonant.

- Pronunciation of the morpheme *–s* (plural, third-person regular, possessive): All of the following words have the bound morpheme *–s* on the end. Do you hear a difference in the final sound in each word? Is this pattern the same as for the past tense *–ed* marker?

/s/	/z/
capes	clubs
bikes	jogs
decks	fines
hits	goes

- Voicing changes in connected speech

  - Word final /v/ is devoiced in the word final position or when followed by a word that begins with a voiceless consonant (e.g., "have to" becomes /hæftə/).

  - Word final /θ/ becomes voiced (i.e., /ð/) before a word beginning with a voiced consonant (e.g., "with many" becomes /wɪðmɛnɪ/).

  - Alveolar fricatives (/s, z/) become palatal fricatives before the "y" sound (i.e., /j/) because of the palatal placement of that sound (e.g., "as you" becomes /æʒju/; "kiss you" becomes /kɪʃju/).

EXERCISE 15-A: COMMON BONDS

Using the phonetic characteristics of voicing and place described in the preceding table, identify the commonality between the two fricative sounds. Additional pairs of sounds are included that require you to use all three phonetic characteristics of voicing, place, and manner.

/s/	/θ/	V	P		/v/	/ʒ/	V	P	
/h/	/f/	V	P		/ð/	/θ/	V	P	
/θ/	/ʃ/	V	P		/ʒ/	/z/	V	P	
/ʒ/	/s/	V	P	M	/p/	/h/	V	P	M
/ʃ/	/ʒ/	V	P	M	/g/	/ð/	V	P	M
/z/	/t/	V	P	M	/f/	/v/	V	P	M

EXERCISE 15-B: DECODING PHONETIC SYMBOLS

Pronounce the sound represented by each of the following phonetic symbols and blend them together to make a word. Write the word that is created in orthography.

/vaʊ/ _____	/zu/ _____	/sɔ/ _____
/ʃɚ/ _____	/ɔf/ _____	/θaɪ/ _____
/fɛɚ/ _____	/ɝθ/ _____	/ðe/ _____
/hi/ _____	/æʃ/ _____	/ɪz/ _____
/fɪʃ/ _____	/haɪv/ _____	/sɝf/ _____
/ʃʌv/ _____	/fɔɚθ/ _____	/haʊs/ _____

EXERCISE 15-B: DECODING PHONETIC SYMBOLS (*continued*)

/ðɪs/ _____	/ʃɛf/ _____	/beʒ/ _____
/hoz/ _____	/sɔs/ _____	/θif/ _____
/bæθ/ _____	/saɪz/ _____	/fɪɚs/ _____
/vɔɪs/ _____	/fez/ _____	/hʌʃ/ _____
/suð/ _____	/sɑʊθ/ _____	/vɝs/ _____
/hɑɚt/ _____	/pʊʃ/ _____	/tɔt/ _____
/tʌf/ _____	/dæʃ/ _____	/fud/ _____
/saɪt/ _____	/bɛɚz/ _____	/huz/ _____

EXERCISE 15-C: WRITING WORDS WITH PHONETIC SYMBOLS

Write the following words in phonetic symbols. The symbols for the consonant sounds that are not fricatives or stop-plosives will be the same as those used in the alphabet.

who _____	sigh _____	their _____
shoe _____	ace _____	of _____
ease _____	that _____	his _____
those _____	safe _____	share _____
cough _____	food _____	half _____
verb _____	should _____	weave _____
gush _____	toys _____	teeth _____
third _____	hook _____	shirt _____
cash _____	puff _____	bath _____
shard _____	dive _____	thus _____
verse _____	height _____	goes _____

soaked _____   thick _____   shave _____

Zeus _____   zoos _____   shocks _____

EXERCISE 15-D: SOLVING WORD EQUATIONS

Provide the correct symbol for each sound description. Once all symbols are identified, blend the sounds together to make a word you know. Write the resulting word in orthography.

	Sound Description	Phonetic Symbol			Word in Orthography
	Voiceless alveolar fricative	/s/ _____			
+	High front tense unrounded vowel	/i/ _____	=	/si/ _____	see _____
	High front lax unrounded vowel	_____			
+	Voiceless labiodentals fricative	_____	=	_____	_____
	Voiced interdental fricative	_____			
+	Mid back tense rounded vowel	_____	=	_____	_____
	Voiceless bilabial stop-plosive	_____			
+	Low front lax unrounded vowel	_____			
+	Voiceless interdental fricative	_____	=	_____	_____
	Voiced labiodentals fricative	_____			
+	Mid front tense unrounded vowel	_____			
+	Voiceless alveolar fricative	_____	=	_____	_____
	Voiceless glottal fricative	_____			
+	High back tense rounded	_____			
+	Voiceless bilabial stop-plosive	_____	=	_____	_____

EXERCISE 15-E: WRITING WORD EQUATIONS

Transcribe the sounds you hear in each of the following words. For each symbol, write a word equation that accurately describes the sounds contained in each word. On each line, write the phonetic description for each consonant and vowel contained in the word.

he   <u>voiceless glottal fricative</u>

/hi/   +   <u>high front tense unrounded vowel</u>

     +   _____

faith   _____

     +   _____

     +   _____

zip   _____

     +   _____

     +   _____

shoes   _____

     +   _____

     +   _____

     +   _____

thus   _____

     +   _____

     +   _____

     +   _____

EXERCISE 15-F: STATE THE CHANGE

State the change in the minimal pair. In this exercise, two words are provided. Identify the sound change(s) and then provide an explanation on the line (using what you know about place, manner, and voicing). The change(s) may be in the onset or the coda.

have → has   Transcribe: /hæv/ → /hæz/   Isolate change: /v/ → /z/

THINK: voiced labiodental fricative → voiced alveolar fricative

Identify the change: <u>place changed from labiodental to alveolar</u>

shoe → zoo   _____

height → sight   _____

T → C   _____

math → mass   _____

doubt → shout   _____

fall → call   _____

Now, create your own minimal pairs. _____

_____

_____

EXERCISE 15-G: CREATING MINIMAL PAIRS (ONSET) WITH FRICATIVES

In this exercise, you will be provided with a word and then be required to change its **onset** by changing a specific phonetic characteristic (voicing, place, or manner) in order to create a new word that will form a minimal pair. For some of the words, you may be able to create more than one word.

Word	*Change*	*New Word*
fizz <u>/fɪz/</u>	place	<u>his /hɪz/</u>
share	place/voicing	_____

EXERCISE 15-G: CREATING MINIMAL PAIRS (ONSET) WITH FRICATIVES (*continued*)

Word	Change	New Word
thin	place	_____
vine	voicing/place	_____
shook	manner/place	_____
sand	place	_____
think	manner/place	_____

EXERCISE 15-H: CREATING MINIMAL PAIRS (CODA) WITH FRICATIVES

In this exercise, you will be provided with a word and then be required to change its **coda** by changing a specific phonetic characteristic (voicing, place, or manner) in order to create a new word that will form a minimal pair.

Word	Change	New Word
of /ʌv/	place	us /ʌs/
grace	place/voicing	_____
miss	place	_____
cave	voicing/place	_____
rush	place/manner	_____
loathe	place/voicing	_____

Fricatives in Sequences

	Prevocalic Sequences (Syllable Initial)	Postvocalic Sequences (Syllable Final)
/h/	hy(u)	
/f/	fl, fr	ft, fs
/v/		+v, +z

	Prevocalic Sequences (Syllable Initial)	Postvocalic Sequences (Syllable Final)
/s/	sm, sn, sw, sl, sp, st, sk, spl, spr, str, skw, skr	ps, ts, ks*, ns, ths, fs sp, st, sk sps, sks, sts, nts, ngks,
/z/		+d + z Used as a plural/third person regular marker after all voiced consonants
/θ/	thr	+t, +s, nθ
/ð/		+d +z
/ʃ/	shr	+t
/ʒ/		+d nʒ

Note: Sequences as listed are written in orthography.

*In the first unit, you were faced with making decisions about the letter "*x*". Remember that the letter "*x*" is a stop-plosive + fricative sequence /ks/.

EXERCISE 15-I: DECODING PHONETIC SYMBOLS: WORDS WITH SEQUENCES

Pronounce the sound represented by each of the following phonetic symbols and blend them together to make a word. Write the word that is created in orthography. The symbols for the consonant sounds that are not fricatives or stop-plosives will be the same as those used in the alphabet.

/ʃrʌb/ _____	/flɛʃ/ _____	/θrot/ _____
/staɚ/ _____	/splæʃ/ _____	/θraɪv/ _____
/skɝt/ _____	/stonz/ _____	/snɔɚ/ _____
/buθs/ _____	/wivz/ _____	/ʃɪft/ _____
/ʃɛlf/ _____	/faks/ _____	/hʌʃt/ _____
/pæst/ _____	/stapt/ _____	/snizd/ _____
/kɝst/ _____	/kloðd/ _____	/nɛkst/ _____
/ʃrʌgz/ _____	/θri/ _____	/flɛɚ/ _____

EXERCISE 15-J: WRITING WORDS IN PHONETIC SYMBOLS: WORDS WITH SEQUENCES

Write the following words in phonetic symbols. The symbols for the consonant sounds that are not fricatives or stop-plosives will be the same as those used in the alphabet.

throw	_____	floods	_____	slush	_____
shrimp	_____	soft	_____	zips	_____
striped	_____	smash	_____	spear	_____
swirls	_____	first	_____	froth	_____
bathed	_____	frisk	_____	flushed	_____
thrashed	_____	shelves	_____	desks	_____

16 *Affricates*

T he sound of an affricate is produced with a single impulse of air. It begins as a stop-plosive and is then released as a fricative.

Place of Articulation	*Voicing*	*Affricate Symbols*	
Palatal	Voiceless	ch	/tʃ/
(tongue body to central palate)	Voiced	j	/dʒ/

Affricates are a combination sound created by airflow blocked briefly and then released as a fricative. The stop closure occurs at the place of articulation. The audible release occurs as the air flows through the point of constriction. The two affricates are a cognate pair; they share the same place and manner but differ in voicing.

A Focus on Pronunciation

The following list of words will help you understand the manner of the affricate. Words are provided that allow you to compare a stop-plosive, fricative, and affricate production:

Stop-Plosive	*Fricative*	*Affricate Symbols*
/tu/	/ʃu/	/tʃu/
two	shoe	chew
/ti/	/ʃi/	/tʃi/
tea	she	chi
/tɛɚ/	/ʃɛɚ/	/tʃɛɚ/
tear	share	chair
/tɪn/	/ʃɪn/	/tʃɪn/
tin	shin	chin
/et/		/etʃ/
ate/8		H
/ped/	/beʒ/	/pedʒ/
paid	beige	page
/rud/	/ruʒ/	
rude	rouge	

Stop-Plosive	Fricative	Affricate Symbols
/bʌd/		/bʌdʒ/
bud		budge
/hɛd/		/hɛdʒ/
head		hedge

Confusion exists between the voiced palatal fricative /ʒ/ and the voiced palatal affricate /dʒ/ in the word's final position. Both are produced in the same place and have the same voicing; however, the fricative sound is long and the affricate is not. These two sounds can be confusing in certain words. How do you pronounce *garage*? Is the final sound a fricative or affricate?

EXERCISE 16-A: COMMON BONDS

Using the phonetic characteristics of voicing, place, and manner described in the preceding table and in the tables for stop-plosives and fricatives, identify the commonality between the two sounds given.

/ʃ/	/tʃ/	V	P	M		/θ/	/dʒ/	V	P	M
/b/	/dʒ/	V	P	M		/tʃ/	/f/	V	P	M
/ʒ/	/dʒ/	V	P	M		/s/	/ʒ/	V	P	M
/t/	/tʃ/	V	P	M		/v/	/dʒ/	V	P	M

EXERCISE 16-B: DECODING PHONETIC SYMBOLS

Pronounce the sound represented by each of the following phonetic symbols and blend them together to make a word. Write the word that is created in orthography.

/ɪtʃ/ _____	/edʒ/ _____	/tʃu/ _____
/aʊtʃ/ _____	/dʒɔɪ/ _____	/tʃɚ/ _____
/tʃip/ _____	/bædʒ/ _____	/dʒok/ _____
/dʒed/ _____	/sʌtʃ/ _____	/dʒɛt/ _____
/tʃɝtʃ/ _____	/tʃɛɚz/ _____	/tʃɑp/ _____

/dʒaɪv/ _____   /dʒip/ _____   /dʒæz/ _____

/tʃɛnd/ _____   /fʌdʒ/ _____   /tʃɛst/ _____

/tʃɪl/ _____   /dʒɝk/ _____   /pʌdʒ/ _____

/plɛdʒ/ _____   /smʌdʒ/ _____   /mætʃ/ _____

/tʃiz/ _____   /tʃʌg/ _____   /dʒaʊl/ _____

/sɝtʃ/ _____   /skɑtʃ/ _____   /rɪdʒ/ _____

EXERCISE 16-C: WRITING WORDS WITH PHONETIC SYMBOLS

Write the following words in phonetic symbols. All of these words contain affricates, fricatives, and stop-plosives. The symbols for the consonant sounds that are not obstruents will be the same as those used in the alphabet.

urge _____   each _____   G _____

chief _____   jug _____   wage _____

arch _____   couch _____   judge _____

jab _____   purge _____   roach _____

chalk _____   wedge _____   choice _____

perch _____   jock _____   patch _____

child _____   cheer _____   just _____

EXERCISE 16-D: SOLVING WORD EQUATIONS

Provide the correct symbol for each sound description. Once all symbols are identified, blend the sounds together to make a word you know. Write the resulting word in orthography.

	Sound Description	Phonetic Symbol		Word in Orthography
	Mid front lax unrounded vowel	/ɛ/		
+	Voiced palatal affricate	/dʒ/	= /ɛdʒ/	edge

EXERCISE 16-D: SOLVING WORD EQUATIONS (*continued*)

Sound Description	Phonetic Symbol		Word in Orthography
Voiceless palatal affricate	_____		
+ High back tense rounded vowel	_____ =	_____	_____
Voiceless palatal affricate	_____		
+ Mid front tense unrounded vowel	_____		
+ Voiceless alveolar fricative	_____ =	_____	_____
Voiced alveolar stop-plosive	_____		
+ Low back lax unrounded vowel	_____		
+ Voiced palatal affricate	_____ =	_____	_____
Voiceless alveolar fricative	_____		
+ Mid central tense rounded vowel	_____		
+ Voiced palatal affricate	_____ =	_____	_____
Voiceless palatal affricate	_____		
+ High front lax unrounded vowel	_____		
+ Voiceless bilabial stop-plosive	_____ =	_____	_____

EXERCISE 16-E: WRITING WORD EQUATIONS

Transcribe the sounds you hear in each of the following words. For each symbol, write a word equation that accurately describes the sounds contained in each word. On each line, write the phonetic description for each consonant and vowel contained in the word.

etch	mid front lax unrounded vowel
/ɛtʃ/ +	voiceless palatal affricate
+	_____

choke　　　　　_____

　　　+　　　_____

　　　+　　　_____

　　　+　　　_____

juice　　　　_____

　　　+　　　_____

　　　+　　　_____

nudge　　　　_____

　　　+　　　_____

　　　+　　　_____

　　　+　　　_____

cheese　　　　_____

　　　+　　　_____

　　　+　　　_____

　　　+　　　_____

EXERCISE 16-F: STATE THE CHANGE

In Chapter 1, you were introduced to the concept of minimal pairs (i.e., two words that differ by one phoneme). In this exercise, two words are provided. Identify the sound change(s) and then provide an explanation on the line (using what you know about place, manner, and voicing). The change(s) may be in the onset or the coda.

share → chair　　manner changed from fricative to affricate

jeep → cheap　　_____

job → sob　　　_____

EXERCISE 16-F: STATE THE CHANGE (*continued*)

hatch → half   _____

sail → jail   _____

vet → jet   _____

G → D   _____

Now, create your own minimal pairs. _____

_____

_____

_____

EXERCISE 16-G: CREATING MINIMAL PAIRS (ONSET) WITH OBSTRUENTS

In this exercise, you will be provided with a word and then be required to change its **onset** by changing a specific phonetic characteristic (place or voicing) in order to create a new word that will form a minimal pair. For some of the words, you may be able to create more than one word.

Word	Change	New Word
gin /dʒɪn/	voicing	chin /tʃɪn/
chore	manner	_____
junk	voicing	_____
chest	voicing/place/manner	_____
jump	voicing/place/manner	_____
chip	place/manner	_____
joke	voicing/place/manner	_____
chair	place/manner	_____
sheep	voicing/manner	_____
chat	place/manner	_____

EXERCISE 16-H: CREATING MINIMAL PAIRS (CODA) WITH OBSTRUENTS

In this exercise, you will be provided with a word and then be required to change its **coda** by changing a specific phonetic characteristic (voicing, place, or manner) in order to create a new word that will form a minimal pair.

Word	Change	New Word
age /edʒ/	voicing	H /etʃ/
hush	manner	_____
ridge	voicing	_____
search	voicing	_____
each	voicing/place/manner	_____
rose	voicing/place/manner	_____
rage	place/manner	_____

Track 10

Practice transcribing fricatives and affricates in simple syllables.

Affricates in Sequences

	Prevocalic Sequences (Syllable Initial)	Postvocalic Sequences (Syllable Final)
/tʃ/		/tʃt/
		/ntʃ/
		/ntʃt/
/dʒ/		/dʒd/
		/ndʒ/
		/ndʒd/

EXERCISE 16-I: DECODING PHONETIC SYMBOLS: WORDS WITH SEQUENCES

Pronounce the sound represented by each of the following phonetic symbols and blend them together to make a word. Write the word that is created in orthography. The symbols for the consonant sounds that are not obstruents will be the same as those used in the alphabet.

/drɛntʃ/ _____   /tʌtʃt/ _____

/rendʒ/ _____   /ræntʃ/ _____

EXERCISE 16-I: DECODING PHONETIC SYMBOLS: WORDS WITH SEQUENCES
(*continued*)

/strɛtʃt/ _____   /lʌntʃ/ _____

/mɝdʒd/_____   /pɪtʃt/ _____

/tʃendʒ/ _____   /sɪndʒd/_____

/skrætʃt/ _____   /sɝtʃt/ _____

EXERCISE 16-J: WRITING WORDS IN PHONETIC SYMBOLS: WORDS WITH SEQUENCES

Write the following words in phonetic symbols. The symbols for the consonants that are not obstruents are the same as those used in the alphabet.

lunge _____   fringe _____

charged_____   patched _____

sponge _____   lounge _____

purged _____   starched _____

dodged _____   splurged_____

17 *Nasals*

I n nasals, continuous air is released through the nasal cavity while the speech organs assume a stop-like position.

Place of Articulation	Voicing	Nasal Symbols	
Bilabial (lip to lip)	Voiced	m	/m/
Alveolar (tongue tip to alveolar ridge)	Voiced	n	/n/
Velar (back of tongue to soft palate)	Voiced	ng	/ŋ/

EXERCISE 17-A: COMMON BONDS

Using the phonetic characteristics of voicing, place, and manner, identify the commonality between the two sounds.

/m/	/b/	V	P	M	/ŋ/	/dʒ/	V	P	M
/ŋ/	/k/	V	P	M	/ʃ/	/n/	V	P	M
/m/	/v/	V	P	M	/d/	/n/	V	P	M
/z/	/n/	V	P	M	/v/	/ŋ/	V	P	M
/h/	/tʃ/	V	P	M	/ʒ/	/dʒ/	V	P	M

EXERCISE 17-B: DECODING PHONETIC SYMBOLS

Pronounce the sound represented by each of the following phonetic symbols and blend them together to make a word. Write the word that is created in orthography.

/nu/ _____   /em/ _____   /kɪŋ/ _____

/hæŋ/ _____   /tʃɝn/ _____   /mɔɚ/ _____

EXERCISE 17-B: DECODING PHONETIC SYMBOLS (*continued*)

/naʊn/ _____   /mun/ _____   /θʌm/ _____

/mætʃ/ _____   /strɔŋ/ _____   /dʒɝmz/ _____

/nɑks/ _____   /naɪs/ _____   /tʌŋ/ _____

/mɔɪst/ _____   /fæŋ/ _____   /nɪɚ/ _____

/stɪŋ/ _____   /naɪn/ _____   /mɪst/ _____

/nɝst/ _____   /dʒɔɪn/ _____   /nɔɚθ/ _____

/mɛʃ/ _____   /dʒɛm/ _____   /sʌm/ _____

EXERCISE 17-C: WRITING WORDS WITH PHONETIC SYMBOLS

Write the following words in phonetic symbols. Most of the words contain nasals and obstruents. The symbols for the consonants not yet introduced will be the same as those used in the alphabet.

on _____   shine _____   mouse _____

thing _____   none _____   mean _____

march _____   noise _____   hang _____

mouth _____   nudge _____   song _____

known _____   mix _____   gang _____

rhyme _____   mock _____   gnat _____

long _____   I'm _____   must _____

jam _____   chin _____   wing _____

gym _____   name _____   bang _____

thorn _____   them _____   gnashed _____

EXERCISE 17-D: SOLVING WORD EQUATIONS

Provide the correct symbol for each sound description. Once all symbols are identified, blend the sounds together to make a word you know. Write the resulting word in orthography.

Sound Description	*Phonetic Symbol*			*Word in Orthography*
Voiced alveolar nasal	/n/			
+ Mid front tense unrounded vowel	/e/			
+ Voiced bilabial nasal	/m/	=	/nem/	name
Voiced velar stop-plosive	_____			
+ Mid back lax rounded vowel	_____			
+ Voiced alveolar nasal	_____	=		
Voiceless bilabial stop-plosive	_____			
+ High front lax unrounded vowel	_____			
+ Voiced velar nasal	_____	=	_____	_____
Voiced interdental fricative	_____			
+ Mid front lax unrounded vowel	_____			
+ Voiced bilabial nasal	_____	=	_____	_____
Voiceless alveolar fricative	_____			
+ Voiceless alveolar stop plosive	_____			
+ Mid central lax unrounded vowel	_____			
+ Voiced alveolar nasal	_____	=	_____	_____

EXERCISE 17-E: WRITING WORD EQUATIONS

Transcribe the sounds you hear in each of the following words. For each symbol, write a word equation that accurately describes the sounds contained in each word. On each line, write the phonetic description for each consonant and vowel contained in the word.

know   <u>voiced alveolar stop-plosive</u>

/no/ + <u>mid back tense rounded vowel</u>

     + _____

gem   _____

     + _____

     + _____

thin   _____

     + _____

     + _____

     + _____

tunes   _____

     + _____

     + _____

     + _____

sting   _____

     + _____

     + _____

     + _____

EXERCISE 17-F: STATE THE CHANGE

In this exercise, two words are provided. Identify the sound change(s) and then provide an explanation on the line (using what you know about voicing, place, and manner). The change(s) may be in the onset or the coda.

rag → rang   manner change from stop-plosive to nasal

noise → toys   _____

mane → made   _____

knee → me   _____

fail → mail   _____

sick → sing   _____

north → fourth   _____

cage → cane   _____

Now, create your own minimal pairs. _____

_____

_____

_____

EXERCISE 17-G: CREATING MINIMAL PAIRS (ONSET) WITH NASALS AND OBSTRUENTS

In this exercise, you will be provided with a word and then required to change its **onset** by changing a specific phonetic characteristic (place or voicing) in order to create a new word that will form a minimal pair. For some of the words, you may be able to create more than one word.

Word	Change	New Word
more /mɔɚ/	manner	bore /bɔɚ/
near	manner	_____

EXERCISE 17-G: CREATING MINIMAL PAIRS (ONSET) WITH NASALS AND OBSTRUENTS (*continued*)

Word	Change	New Word
math	voicing/manner	_____
nose	voicing/place/manner	_____
meal	voicing/manner	_____
mug	place/manner	_____
nine	voicing/manner	_____
mop	voicing/place/manner	_____

EXERCISE 17-H: CREATING MINIMAL PAIRS (CODA) WITH NASALS AND OBSTRUENTS

In this exercise, you will be provided with a word and then required to change its **coda** by changing a specific phonetic characteristic (place or voicing) in order to create a new word that will form a minimal pair.

Word	Change	New Word
doom	place	dune
rhyme	voicing/manner	_____
pan	place	_____
beam	voicing/place/manner	_____
phone	place	_____
spin	voicing/manner	_____
train	manner	_____
bang	place/manner	_____
bang	voicing/place/manner	_____

Nasals in Sequences

	Prevocalic Sequences (Syllable Initial)	*Postvocalic Sequences (Syllable Final)*
/m/	/sm/	/md/, /mp/, /mpt/, /mz/
/n/	/sn/	/ntʃ/, /ndʒ/, /nd/, /ns/, /nt/, /nts/, /nz/
/ŋ/		/ŋz/, /ŋd/, /ŋk/, /ŋks/, /ŋkt/, /ŋθ/, /ŋθs/

Representing the velar nasal in "ng," "nk," "nks," "nx" contexts–not all of these will be a sequence.

"ng"	= /ŋ/	long, fang, singer
	= /ŋg/	finger, linger, dangle
"nk"	= /ŋk/	think, drank, dunk, blinker
"nx," "nks"	= /ŋks/	minx, links, thanks

Track 20

Listen to examples of words with /ŋ/

EXERCISE 17-I: DECODING PHONETIC SYMBOLS: WORDS WITH SEQUENCES

Pronounce the sound represented by each of the following phonetic symbols and blend them together to make a word. Write the word that is created in orthography. The symbols for the consonant sounds that are not nasals or obstruents will be the same as those used in the alphabet.

/trɛntʃ/ _____   /dʒʌmp/_____   /branz/ _____

/kaɪnd/ _____   /lɛŋθ/ _____   /tʃaɚmz/_____

/maʊnd/_____   /θæŋk/ _____   /klind/ _____

/rɪns/ _____   /tond/ _____   /smɔl/ _____

/snæk/ _____   /skrimd/_____   /ʃrʌŋk/ _____

/monz/ _____   /prɪns/ _____   /bæŋd/ _____

/pand/ _____   /paʊnd/_____   /flɪŋz/ _____

/stɪŋks/ _____   /smɛlz/ _____   /rʌnz/ _____

EXERCISE 17-J: WRITING WORDS IN PHONETIC SYMBOLS: WORDS WITH SEQUENCES

Write the following words in phonetic symbols. The symbols for the consonants that are not nasals or obstruents are the same as those used in the alphabet.

themes _____	sings _____	ground _____
honk _____	grunge _____	mink _____
smile _____	snared _____	strength _____
tanked _____	don't _____	smoke _____
counts _____	thinks _____	pants _____
trunks _____	brains _____	prince _____
snows _____	turns _____	smashed _____
worms _____	tense _____	clowns _____
joints _____	zinc _____	junk _____

CHAPTER

18 *Liquids*

To produce these sounds, the airstream moves around the tongue in a relatively unobstructed manner.

Place of Articulation	Voicing	Liquid Symbols
Alveolar (tongue tip to alveolar ridge)	Voiced	l /l/ Lateral
Palatal (tongue body to central palate)	Voiced	r /r/ Rhotic

EXERCISE 18-A: COMMON BONDS

Using the phonetic characteristics of voicing, place, and manner to identify the commonality between the two sounds.

/r/	/ʒ/	V	P	M	/l/	/d/	V	P	M
/r/	/l/	V	P	M	/dʒ/	/r/	V	P	M
/s/	/l/	V	P	M	/ð/	/l/	V	P	M
/r/	/tʃ/	V	P	M	/l/	/t/	V	P	M
/l/	/n/	V	P	M	/m/	/r/	V	P	M

EXERCISE 18-B: DECODING PHONETIC SYMBOLS

Pronounce the sound represented by each of the following phonetic symbols and blend them together to make a word. Write the word that is created in orthography.

/lɔ/ _____   /len/ _____   /lɪp/ _____

/ræŋ/ _____   /rul/ _____   /rʌʃ/ _____

/laʊd/_____   /lus/ _____   /ræntʃ/ _____

EXERCISE 18-B: DECODING PHONETIC SYMBOLS (*continued*)

/rɪst/ _____   /rɛst/ _____   /lʌŋ/ _____

/lɝn/ _____   /pɝl/ _____   /rid/ _____

/faʊl/ _____   /rɔŋ/ _____   /raɪz/ _____

/rom/ _____   /rɛɚ/ _____   /lɔŋ/ _____

/lɑks/ _____   /raɪs/ _____   /ril/ _____

/pʊl/ _____   /lɔs/ _____   /lɛft/ _____

/rɪɚ/ _____   /kɔɪl/ _____   /laɪn/ _____

/lɛgz/ _____   /rɑkt/ _____   /rʌst/ _____

/rʌts/ _____   /list/ _____   /rɪsk/ _____

/lʌv/ _____   /hɔl/ _____   /lɪft/ _____

/rɔ/ _____   /lɪnt/ _____   /lik/ _____

EXERCISE 18-C: WRITING WORDS WITH PHONETIC SYMBOLS

Write the following words in phonetic symbols. The symbols for the sounds you do not yet know are the same as the alphabet letters.

laugh _____   lime _____   rain _____

rough _____   wool _____   loan _____

limb _____   raced _____   lawn _____

rare _____   whole_____   large _____

rail _____   raft _____   room _____

rhyme_____   length_____   look _____

long _____   write _____   girl _____

gel _____   round_____   lace _____

wrap	_____	rinse	_____	lunch	_____
rose	_____	lost	_____	rude	_____
roast	_____	rise	_____	reel	_____
owl	_____	spill	_____	list	_____

EXERCISE 18-D: SOLVING WORD EQUATIONS

Provide the correct symbol for each sound description. Once all symbols are identified, blend the sounds together to make a word you know. Write the resulting word in orthography.

	Sound Description	*Phonetic Symbol*		*Word in Orthography*
	Voiced alveolar liquid	/l/		
+	Mid back tense rounded vowel	/o/	=	/lo/ low
	Voiced palatal liquid	_____		
+	High front lax unrounded vowel	_____		
+	Voiced bilabial stop-plosive	_____	=	_____ _____
	Voiced alveolar liquid	_____		
+	Mid central lax unrounded vowel	_____		
+	Voiceless velar stop-plosive	_____	=	_____ _____
	Voiced palatal liquid	_____		
+	Mid front tense unrounded vowel	_____		
+	Voiced alveolar liquid	_____	=	_____ _____
	Voiced palatal liquid	_____		
+	High front lax unrounded vowel	_____		
+	Voiced velar nasal	_____	=	_____ _____

EXERCISE 18-D: SOLVING WORD EQUATIONS (*continued*)

	Sound Description	Phonetic Symbol		Word in Orthography
	Voiced palatal liquid	_____		
+	Low back lax unrounded vowel	_____		
+	Voiced bilabial stop-plosive	_____	=	_____ _____
	Voiceless alveolar fricative	_____		
+	Voiceless bilabial stop-plosive	_____		
+	High front lax unrounded vowel	_____		
+	Voiced alveolar liquid	_____	=	_____ _____
	Voiced alveolar liquid	_____		
+	Mid back lax rounded vowel	_____		
+	Voiced velar nasal	_____	=	_____ _____
	Voiced alveolar liquid	_____		
+	Mid front lax unrounded vowel	_____		
+	Voiceless alveolar stop-plosive	_____		
+	Voiceless alveolar fricative	_____	=	_____ _____
	Voiced palatal liquid	_____		
+	High back tense rounded vowel	_____		
+	Voiced bilabial nasal	_____		
+	Voiced alveolar fricative	_____	=	_____ _____
	Voiced alveolar liquid	_____		
	Low front lax unrounded	_____		
	Voiceless palatal affricate	_____	=	_____ _____

EXERCISE 18-E: WRITING WORD EQUATIONS

Transcribe the sounds you hear in each of the following words. For each symbol, write a word equation that accurately describes the sounds contained in each word. On each line, write the phonetic description for each consonant and vowel contained in the word.

road   <u>voiced palatal liquid</u>

/rod/   +   <u>mid back tense rounded vowel</u>

            +   <u>voiced alveolar stop-plosive</u>

lodge   _____

            +   _____

            +   _____

            +   _____

fool   _____

            +   _____

            +   _____

            +   _____

rook   _____

            +   _____

            +   _____

            +   _____

load   _____

            +   _____

            +   _____

            +   _____

EXERCISE 18-E: WRITING WORD EQUATIONS (*continued*)

rage   _____

+   _____

+   _____

+   _____

live (verb)   _____

+   _____

+   _____

+   _____

wrench   _____

+   _____

+   _____

+   _____

kneel   _____

+   _____

+   _____

+   _____

rink   _____

+   _____

+   _____

+   _____

EXERCISE 18-F: STATE THE CHANGE

In this exercise, two words are provided. Identify the sound change(s) and then provide an explanation on the line (using what you know about place, manner, and voicing). The change(s) will be in the onset.

lamb → dam   <u>manner changed from liquid to stop-plosive</u>

leap → jeep   _____

rug → chug   _____

lace → race   _____

roar → door   _____

lake → cake   _____

room → zoom   _____

ring → thing   _____

rice → mice   _____

Now, create your own minimal pairs. _____

_____

_____

EXERCISE 18-G: CREATING MINIMAL PAIRS (ONSET) WITH LIQUIDS, NASALS, AND OBSTRUENTS

In this exercise, you will be provided with a word and then required to change its **onset** by changing a specific phonetic characteristic (voicing, place, and/or manner) in order to create a new word that will form a minimal pair. For some of the words, you may be able to create more than one word.

Word		Change	New Word(s)
rope	<u>/rop/</u>	voicing/place/manner	<u>soap/sop/, pope /pop/</u>
lamp	_____	place	_____

EXERCISE 18-G: CREATING MINIMAL PAIRS (ONSET) WITH LIQUIDS, NASALS, AND OBSTRUENTS (*continued*)

Word		Change	New Word(s)
ramp	_____	voicing/manner	_____
rip	_____	place/manner	_____
look	_____	place/manner	_____
line	_____	manner	_____
roast	_____	voicing/place/manner	_____
rust	_____	place/manner	_____
leap	_____	voicing/place/manner	_____

Track 19

Listen to examples of /l/ productions

Liquids in Sequences

Sound	Prevocalic Sequences (Syllable Initial)	Postvocalic Sequences (Syllable Final)
/r/	/br/, /pr/, /dr/, /tr/, /gr/, /kr/, /fr/, /θr/, /ʃr/, /skr/, /spr/, /str/	
/l/	/bl/, /pl/, /gl/, /kl/, /fl/, /sl/, /spl/	/ld/, /lk/, /lm/, /lp/, /lt/, /lθ/, /lz/, /ldz/, /lks/, /lkt/, /lmd/, /lmz/, /lps/, /lpt/, /lts/

EXERCISE 18-H: DECODING PHONETIC SYMBOLS: WORDS WITH SEQUENCES

Pronounce the sound represented by each of the following phonetic symbols and blend them together to make a word. Write the word that is created in orthography. The symbols for the consonant sounds that have not been introduced will be the same as those used in the alphabet.

/drim/ _____   /kloz/ _____   /blu/ _____

/tred/ _____   /fraɪz/ _____   /ʃrud/ _____

/plet/ _____   /praɪd/ _____   /gron/ _____

/klaʊd/ _____   /brok/ _____   /krɔld/ _____

/klind/ _____   /told/ _____   /glez/ _____

/brif/ _____   /træʃ/ _____   /spre/ _____

/ɛls/ _____   /bɛlt/ _____   /wɝld/ _____

/staɪlz/ _____   /frɛnd/ _____   /blɑkt/ _____

/traɪ/ _____   /flɪntʃ/ _____   /ʃrʌg/ _____

/pʊld/ _____   /klɪɚ/ _____   /graʊnd/_____

/graɪnd/ _____   /prɪns/ _____   /skrʌb/ _____

EXERCISE 18-I: WRITING WORDS IN PHONETIC SYMBOLS: WORDS WITH SEQUENCES

Write the following words in phonetic symbols. The symbols for the consonant sounds that have not been introduced will be the same as those used in the alphabet.

treat _____   glue _____   drive _____

plug _____   clap _____   blown _____

dreamt_____   truth _____   curls _____

wolf _____   grabbed_____   twirled _____

glides _____   health _____   blocks _____

blind _____   meals _____   vault _____

glance _____   pulled _____   glared _____

floored_____   film _____   flinch _____

false _____   prompt _____   trunk _____

bread _____   straight _____   spring _____

filled _____   valve _____   scalp _____

shrink _____   Greece _____   France _____

EXERCISE 18-I: WRITING WORDS IN PHONETIC SYMBOLS: WORDS WITH SEQUENCES (*continued*)

bruise _____	crisp _____	street _____
gulp _____	sleigh _____	shelf _____
guilt _____	willed _____	brush _____
front _____	shrimp _____	shelved _____

19 *Glides*

T hese sounds involve a gliding motion of the articulators before a vowel. There is a continued gliding movement of the articulators from one position to another that results in a change in resonance.

Place of Articulation	Voicing	Glide Symbols	
Bilabial	Voiceless	wh	/ʍ/
(lip to lip)	Voiced	w	/w/
Palatal (tongue body to central palate)	Voiced	y	/j/

Glides are only produced before a vowel: prevocalic or intervocalic positions.

Don't be fooled! There is no glide in the following words: *grow*, *now*, *joy*, *try*.

EXERCISE 19-A: COMMON BONDS

Use the phonetic characteristics of voicing, place, and manner to identify the commonality between the two sounds listed.

/r/	/j/	V	P	M		/l/	/w/	V	P	M
/j/	/b/	V	P	M		/dʒ/	/j/	V	P	M
/w/	/m/	V	P	M		/b/	/j/	V	P	M
/j/	/tʃ/	V	P	M		/w/	/ŋ/	V	P	M
/w/	/r/	V	P	M		/ʒ/	/r/	V	P	M

EXERCISE 19-B: DECODING PHONETIC SYMBOLS

Pronounce the sound represented by each of the following phonetic symbols and blend them together to make a word. Write the word that is created in orthography.

/waʊ/ _____ /jɛs/ _____ /ju/ _____

/jʌm/ _____ /wik/ _____ /wɔl/ _____

EXERCISE 19-B: DECODING PHONETIC SYMBOLS (*continued*)

/wʊd/	_____	/jus/	_____	/wæg/	_____
/wand/	_____	/juθ/	_____	/jʌŋ/	_____
/wɝd/	_____	/wʌn/	_____	/jist/	_____
/jaɚd/	_____	/wev/	_____	/wɔɚn/	_____
/waʊnd/	_____	/waɪɚd/	_____	/wɪnd/	_____

EXERCISE 19-C: WRITING WORDS WITH PHONETIC SYMBOLS

Write the following words in phonetic symbols.

way	_____	year	_____	yuck	_____
yarn	_____	wool	_____	warm	_____
want	_____	waist	_____	yawn	_____
wear	_____	yield	_____	walk	_____
Yale	_____	wealth	_____	wish	_____
witch	_____	yolk	_____	yank	_____
wing	_____	with	_____	were	_____
once	_____	weird	_____	wind (verb)	_____

EXERCISE 19-D: SOLVING WORD EQUATIONS

Provide the correct symbol for each sound description. Once all symbols are identified, blend the sounds together to make a word you know. Write the resulting word in orthography.

	Sound Description	Phonetic Symbol		Word in Orthography
	Voiced bilabial glide	/w/		
+	High front tense unrounded vowel	/i/		
+	Voiced labiodentals fricative	/v/ =	/wiv/	weave

Sound Description	Phonetic Symbol		Word in Orthography
Voiced palatal glide	_____		
+ Mid front lax unrounded vowel	_____		
+ Voiced alveolar liquid	_____ =	_____	_____
Voiced bilabial glide	_____		
+ High front lax unrounded vowel	_____		
+ Voiced alveolar nasal	_____		
+ Voiced alveolar stop-plosive	_____ =	_____	_____
Voiced palatal glide	_____		
+ High back tense rounded vowel	_____		
+ Voiced alveolar fricative	_____		
+ Voiced alveolar stop-plosive	_____ =	_____	_____
Voiced bilabial glide	_____		
+ Mid front lax unrounded	_____		
+ Voiced alveolar nasal	_____		
+ Voiceless alveolar stop plosive	_____ =	_____	_____

EXERCISE 19-E: WRITING WORD EQUATIONS

Transcribe the sounds you hear in each of the following words. For each symbol, write a word equation that accurately describes the sounds contained in each word. On each line, write the phonetic description for each consonant and vowel contained in the word.

wed   voiced bilabial glide _____

/wɛd/   +   mid front lax unrounded vowel _____

         +   voiced alveolar stop-plosive _____

EXERCISE 19-E: WRITING WORD EQUATIONS (*continued*)

yule   _____

    +   _____

    +   _____

wave   _____

    +   _____

    +   _____

yacht   _____

    +   _____

    +   _____

    +   _____

wedge   _____

    +   _____

    +   _____

    +   _____

EXERCISE 19-F: STATE THE CHANGE

In this exercise, two words are provided. Identify the sound change(s) and then provide an explanation on the line (using what you know about place, manner, and voicing). The change(s) will be in the onset.

yea → way   place changed from palatal to bilabial

will → bill   _____

yes → chess   _____

weigh → they   _____

yoke → woke   _____

wall → fall _____

yard → guard _____

wing → ring _____

wait → late _____

Now, create your own minimal pairs. _____

_____

_____

EXERCISE 19-G: CREATING MINIMAL PAIRS (ONSET) WITH SONORANTS AND OBSTRUENTS

In this exercise, you will be provided with a word and then required to change its **onset** by changing a specific phonetic characteristic (voicing, place, and/or manner) in order to create a new word that will form a minimal pair. For some of the words, you may be able to create more than one word.

Word	*Change*	*New Word(s)*
wear /wɛɚ/	manner	bear /bɛɚ/, mare /mɛɚ/
yard	voicing/place/manner	_____
wow	place/manner	_____
wool	manner	_____
world	voicing/place/manner	_____
year	voicing/manner	_____
won	voicing/place/manner	_____
yes	place/manner	_____
wick	voicing/place/manner	_____

Glides in Sequences

Sound	Prevocalic Sequences (Syllable Initial)
/w/*	/dw/, /kw/, /tw/, /sw/, /skw/, /θw/
/j/	/bj/, /fj/, /hj/,
	/kj/, /mj/

A Focus on Pronunciation

*/ʍ/ vs. /w/ in sequences: There is actually a fair degree of aspiration in prevocalic sequences that contain the bilabial glide.

- Although we seldom aspirate the onset (to produce /ʍ/ in the words *where*, *when*, *what*), note the amount of aspiration when you pronounce the following sequences containing a bilabial glide.

swear	swim	suede
square	squire	quit
quite	twig	twin
dwell	Dwight	thwart

- Focus again on the amount of aspiration you use in bilabial glide sequences by reading the following pairs of words.

wear – swear	win – swim	wade – suede
wear – square	wire – squire	wit – quit
white – quite	wig – twig	win – twin
well – dwell	white – Dwight	wart – thwart

Palatal Glide in Sequences

Read the following pairs of words. The second word in each pair has an additional sound, the palatal glide /j/. This sound is the second sound in each of these words. Do you hear the extra sound? Do you feel the difference in the onsets? The first word in each pair has an onset with a singleton, whereas the second word has a sequence as its onset.

food – feud   boot – Butte   who – hue   cool – cue

EXERCISE 19-H: DECODING PHONETIC SYMBOLS: WORDS WITH SEQUENCES

Pronounce the sound represented by each of the following phonetic symbols and blend them together to make a word. Write the word that is created in orthography. HINT: Say the word naturally. Over-pronunciation will add a vowel that does not belong.

/dwɛl/ _____   /kwɪk/ _____   /swɪm/ _____

/kwɔɚt/ _____   /skwɑʃ/ _____   /twɝld/ _____

/swɝlz/ _____   /kwin/ _____   /twɪndʒ/ _____

/skwik/ _____   /twɛlfθ/ _____   /kwaɪt/ _____

/skwɝl/ _____   /swɑmp/ _____   /kwel/ _____

/kjub/ _____   /fjud/ _____   /mjuz/ _____

/pjʊɚ/ _____   /bjut/ _____   /fjumz/ _____

/kjud/ _____   /fju/ _____   /bjutɪ/ _____

EXERCISE 19-I: WRITING WORDS IN PHONETIC SYMBOLS: WORDS WITH SEQUENCES

Write the following words in phonetic symbols.

twelve _____   swore _____   view _____

fuse _____   twine _____   mule _____

swerve _____   cure _____   dwarf _____

quack _____   feud _____   squish _____

huge _____   queer _____   swear _____

quake _____   cute _____   switch _____

quench _____   swag _____   squirt _____

rescue _____   square _____   tribute _____

20 *Term Review and Practice*

Your goals for Unit 3 included:

- Understanding the ways that consonants can be classified.
- Learning the place, manner, and voicing characteristics of each consonant sound.
- Learning the phonetic symbol for each consonant sound.
- Recognizing the similarities and differences across consonant sounds.
- Completing exercises to improve attention to consonant sounds in words.
- Becoming aware of the phonetic variations of specific sounds in the context of words.
- Becoming aware of the dialectal variations/accent influences on consonant sounds.

By completing the exercises in this chapter, you will:

- Continue your journey in becoming "ear-minded" about sounds in words.
- Solidify your understanding of the place, manner, and voicing characteristics of each consonant sound and be able to demonstrate this knowledge in a variety of ways.
- Gain additional practice with sounds that often are challenging for students.
- Continue to practice your knowledge about the key characteristics of each vowel sound.
- Increase your automaticity in reading and writing both vowel and consonant symbols.
- Review key terms.
- Establish connections between related concepts.

The following terms were introduced or used in Chapters 14 through 19.

Not only is it important for you to understand what each term means, but it is also important to understand how the terms are connected to each other. Create a concept map to assist you in understanding how the terms are related to each other. Hint: Which words are related to Place? Manner? Voicing? Which words are related to the two broad groups of consonants? Considering these questions will assist you in organizing and understanding the terms in Unit 3.

affricate	allophone/allophonic variations	alveolar
alveolar flap	alveolar tap	approximants
bilabial	cognates	fricative
glide	glottal	glottal stop
interdental	labiodental	lateral
liquid	manner of articulation	minimal pair
nasal	obstruents	palatal
place of articulation	sonorants	sonority
stop-plosive	velar	voiced
voiceless	voicing	

This review chapter will first provide you with exercises to solidify the phonetic characteristics of each consonant sound. Specific exercises will then be offered for you to focus on sounds that tend to be more problematic for students. Exercises that will ask you to read phonetic symbols to create words will assist you in increasing your automaticity in recognizing the IPA symbols. This review chapter will end with activities that focus on terminology used in the first three units.

EXERCISE 20-A: IDENTIFYING COMMON BONDS

Identify the phonetic characteristics for each sound in the pairs below. You may wish to refer to your consonant classification table used in Chapter 13 as well as your vowel quadrilateral from Unit 2. Compare the characteristics in order to determine how the two sounds are similar. You have several areas from which to choose. You may identify more than one similarity.

/p/	/f/		/ʧ/	/r/		/j/	/w/
/m/	/p/		/b/	/k/		/h/	/z/
/ð/	/θ/		/ŋ/	/k/		/j/	/ʤ/
/j/	/ŋ/		/t/	/n/		/ʃ/	/s/
/d/	/l/		/w/	/m/		/θ/	/h/
/v/	/b/		/ʒ/	/ʤ/		/ʒ/	/r/
/r/	/ŋ/		/θ/	/v/		/p/	/s/
/i/	/ɑ/		/o/	/u/		/e/	/ɔ/
/i/	/e/		/æ/	/i/		/ɪ/	/ɛ/
/ʊ/	/ɔ/		/e/	/ɛ/		/ɪ/	/ʊ/

EXERCISE 20-B: ODD ONE OUT

Identify the phonetic characteristics of each sound in the following groups. Compare the characteristics across the three sounds in order to identify the one that does not belong with the group. Explain how the two that remain are similar. Reminder: There may be more than one correct answer. See if you can find them all.

/dʒ/	/b/	/r/	/k/	/ŋ/	/h/
/ð/	/s/	/f/	/w/	/m/	/p/
/j/	/m/	/ŋ/	/t/	/n/	/s/
/ʃ/	/s/	/d/	/l/	/w/	/m/
/θ/	/h/	/s/	/dʒ/	/ʒ/	/tʃ/
/n/	/ʃ/	/s/	/g/	/v/	/ŋ/
/ð/	/θ/	/h/	/ʃ/	/tʃ/	/n/
/g/	/ŋ/	/k/	/l/	/r/	/n/
/w/	/r/	/m/	/ʒ/	/z/	/ʃ/
/l/	/t/	/n/	/ʒ/	/v/	/dʒ/
/j/	/ŋ/	/d/	/s/	/θ/	/v/
/b/	/ŋ/	/θ/	/p/	/s/	/m/
/i/	/u/	/ʊ/	/e/	/ɔ/	/ʌ/
/ɛ/	/i/	/æ/	/ɛ/	/ɑ/	/æ/
/i/	/e/	/u/	/ʊ/	/ɪ/	/ɛ/
/ɑ/	/æ/	/ɔ/	/o/	/e/	/ɛ/
/u/	/ɑ/	/o/	/e/	/ɔ/	/u/
/e/	/u/	/æ/	/e/	/ɔ/	/æ/

EXERCISE 20-C: PROVIDE THE SOUNDS THAT ARE REQUESTED

All voiced bilabials   _____   All low vowels   _____

All high vowels   _____   All voiced stridents   _____

All voiceless fricatives   _____   All velars   _____

All central vowels   _____   All labial obstruents   _____

All palatal sounds   _____   All voiceless stop-plosives   _____

All lax, front vowels   _____   All back, lax vowels   _____

All nonstrident fricatives   _____   All strident non-fricatives   _____

All rounded, tense vowels   _____   All voiced affricates   _____

All sonorants   _____   All nasals   _____

All approximants   _____   All tense, mid vowels   _____

All mid vowels   _____   All unrounded back vowels   _____

All tense, high vowels   _____   All sounds with no cognates   _____

All cognates   _____

EXERCISE 20-D: HOW ARE THE ONSETS DIFFERENT?

Minimal pairs are listed below. Transcribe the words and then decide how their onsets are different in regards to their voicing, place, and/or manner. Circle your choices.

zoo – sue	V	P	M	moo – new	V	P	M
type – pipe	V	P	M	fair – there	V	P	M
thumb – some	V	P	M	chart – part	V	P	M
get – kit	V	P	M	beg – peg	V	P	M
moan – bone	V	P	M	bough – cow	V	P	M
height – fight	V	P	M	sawed – laud	V	P	M
sought – thought	V	P	M	them – hem	V	P	M
late – wait	V	P	M	jam – sham	V	P	M
zoos – chews	V	P	M	thought – bought	V	P	M
bark – shark	V	P	M	kite – right	V	P	M
book – look	V	P	M	vine – fine	V	P	M
tent – dent	V	P	M	wrist – list	V	P	M

EXERCISE 20-D: HOW ARE THE ONSETS DIFFERENT? (*continued*)

yes – chess	V	P	M		sun – fun	V	P	M
thigh – thy	V	P	M		land – hand	V	P	M
bend – send	V	P	M		cheap – jeep	V	P	M
we're – year	V	P	M		burn – churn	V	P	M

Identify the pairs of words that have cognates in their onsets. _____

_____

_____

EXERCISE 20-E: HOW ARE THE CODAS DIFFERENT?

How are the codas of these minimal pairs different? Transcribe the words and then decide how the sounds in the codas are different in regards to their voicing, place, and/or manner. Circle your choices.

badge – batch	V	P	M		have – half	V	P	M
caught – cough	V	P	M		sing – sin	V	P	M
hard – heart	V	P	M		laugh – lass	V	P	M
force – fort	V	P	M		paid – page	V	P	M
cord – cork	V	P	M		mouth – mouse	V	P	M
peace – peas	V	P	M		leg – ledge	V	P	M
bought – ball	V	P	M		bows – bowl	V	P	M
have – hatch	V	P	M		rag – rail	V	P	M
plaid – plan	V	P	M		fourth – fort	V	P	M
dug – duck	V	P	M		fell – fetch	V	P	M
lab – laugh	V	P	M		us – of	V	P	M

Identify the pairs of words that have cognates in their codas. _____

_____

_____

EXERCISE 20-F: DECODING PHONETIC SYMBOLS

Read the following phonetic symbols. Blend them together to create a word you recognize.

/gɔn/	/bʌgd/	/fon/	/kɔɪn/
/rɪŋz/	/strɛŋθ/	/beʒ/	/ðɛɚ/
/kaʊ/	/klos/	/kloz/	/ʧik/
/ʃaʊt/	/hɔk/	/kraʊd/	/klɔθ/
/tu/	/nus/	/ʃaɪn/	/kloð/
/ðɛm/	/ɔf/	/tub/	/haɪt/
/graʊl/	/θɪŋk/	/blæk/	/buθ/
/ʃɪn/	/wʌnz/	/tuθ/	/lɪv/
/praɪs/	/ad/	/ʃep/	/mæʧ/
/ʃɛl/	/ʤʌst/	/lʊk/	/haʊs/
/kæʃ/	/beð/	/θæŋk/	/ʃɑt/
/jɛl/	/hjuʤ/	/ræp/	/hæz/
/sɔŋ/	/θrɪl/	/ʤel/	/lɔst/
/spun/	/ɝʤ/	/jɛt/	/ʃɑp/
/ʤɛt/	/daʊt/	/ʧɔk/	/kjut/
/ɔɪŋk/	/auʧ/	/mits/	/rest/

EXERCISE 20-G: FOCUS ON INTERDENTAL FRICATIVES

Read the following words out loud. Pay particular attention to the interdental fricative in each word. After saying each word, identify which interdetntal fricative is in the word. Then, determine whether the same sound is in each word. Remember the strategy of producing the word both ways (with the voiced and voiceless sounds) to determine which one sounds like the word you recognize.

thee	θ ð	the	θ ð	same	different
though	θ ð	thought	θ ð	same	different
there	θ ð	thine	θ ð	same	different

EXERCISE 20-G: FOCUS ON INTERDENTAL FRICATIVES (*continued*)

these	θ ð	thesis	θ ð	same	different
filthy	θ ð	feather	θ ð	same	different
either	θ ð	ether	θ ð	same	different
mother	θ ð	father	θ ð	same	different
soothe	θ ð	south	θ ð	same	different
both	θ ð	bother	θ ð	same	different
that	θ ð	thaw	θ ð	same	different
together	θ ð	leather	θ ð	same	different
that	θ ð	than	θ ð	same	different
north	θ ð	south	θ ð	same	different
faith	θ ð	breathe	θ ð	same	different
thaw	θ ð	author	θ ð	same	different
soothing	θ ð	loathing	θ ð	same	different
Thursday	θ ð	thousand	θ ð	same	different
lethal	θ ð	leather	θ ð	same	different
thin	θ ð	thine	θ ð	same	different
south	θ ð	soothe	θ ð	same	different
nothing	θ ð	feather	θ ð	same	different
breathy	θ ð	breathe	θ ð	same	different
think	θ ð	thick	θ ð	same	different

Continue the exercise, but now write the correct symbol next to the word.

breath	_____	cloth	_____	same	different
thin	_____	think	_____	same	different
author	_____	mother	_____	same	different
together	_____	birthday	_____	same	different
thereafter	_____	theater	_____	same	different

EXERCISE 20-H: DIFFERENTIATING BETWEEN THE INTERDENTAL FRICATIVES

Read the following groups of three words aloud, focusing on the interdental fricative (/θ/ /ð/) in the word. Circle the two that have the same voicing. Write the correct symbol on the line. You may need to rely on your strategy of producing each word two ways (with the voiced and voiceless sound).

though	(north)	(thug)	/θ/
either	leather	nothing	_____
smooth	cloth	wreathe	_____
sympathy	authentic	though	_____
them	theater	ethanol	_____
gather	thought	lethal	_____
mother	worthy	breathy	_____
together	thunder	mathematics	_____
thirsty	these	thumb	_____
thousand	weather	thin	_____
third	faithful	feather	_____
altogether	teethe	thigh	_____
ethics	clothe	therefore	_____
themselves	think	cathedral	_____
farther	author	father	_____
lather	that	enthusiast	_____
thermos	Thursday	southern	_____
the	thick	thaw	_____
bother	brother	breath	_____
neither	though	toothpaste	_____
thieves	there	theater	_____
leather	thousand	ethanol	_____
thump	thou	soothing	_____
Othello	soothing	thick	_____
apathy	worthy	bathing	_____

EXERCISE 20-H: DIFFERENTIATING BETWEEN THE INTERDENTAL FRICATIVES (*continued*)

thumb	thing	thou	_____
writhe	gothic	thermometer	_____
throw	loathe	this	_____

EXERCISE 20-I: FINDING THE PALATAL GLIDE /j/

The palatal glide /j/ is an elusive sound. Say the following words out loud and cross out the words that *do not* contain the palatal glide. Read the remaining words—you should be able to detect the palatal glide in a prevocalic or inter-vocalic singleton or sequence. Remember: Glides are *never* postvocalic.

puree	cue	fluke	use	joy
beau	beauty	volume	fusion	puny
human	cube	few	dew	view
cure	bureau	fury	furry	figure
Figaro	ambulance	million	refuse	unit
under	uvula	tortilla	yo yo	senior
curl	behavior	accuse	eye	excuse
onion	pretty	convene	convenient	yell
familiar	popular	fool	huge	ugly
value	mission	tissue	cruel	fuel

EXERCISE 20-J: FOCUS ON NASAL CONSONANTS

Pronounce each of the following words aloud and focus on the nasal singleton or sequence present in each word. Sort the words by their sounds. The first row of words is done for you.

ranger	anger	bang	pancake	hang
anchor	chunky	concur	strong	sponge
wavelength	stronger	jungle	longer	bronco
chunk	encode	danger	young	savings
spring	long	engine	dangerous	hinge

bungalow	fungus	conquer	king	tinkle
English	anguish	ginger	lounger	strange
shingle	full-strength	donkey	arrange	tank
wrinkle	Lincoln	shrink		

/ŋ/	/ŋg/	/ŋk/
bang	anger	
hang		

/nk/	/ŋθ/	/nʤ/
pancake		ranger

EXERCISE 20-J: FOCUS ON NASAL CONSONANTS (*continued*)

_____   _____   _____

_____   _____   _____

_____   _____   _____

_____   _____   _____

_____   _____   _____

_____   _____   _____

_____   _____   _____

_____   _____   _____

EXERCISE 20-K: FOLLOW THE CLUES

In the next three exercises, you will begin by identifying three sounds by their phonetic descriptions. After blending these sounds together to make a word, you will then change at least one sound by following the clue/directions. You are to do two things: write the correct phonetic symbol to reflect the change requested *and* write the resultant word in orthography. You are working with *real* words.

Clue	*Phonetic Symbol(s)*	*Resulting Word in Orthography*
Voiceless bilabial stop-plosive	_____	
Lowfront lax unrounded	_____	
Voiceless palatal affricate	_____	
What is the word?	_____	_____
Change the voicing of the onset. *Voiced bilabial stop-plosive*	_____	_____
Change the voicing of the coda. *Voiced palatal affricate*	_____	_____
Change the voicing *and* manner of the coda (keeping it an obstruent). *Voiceless palatal fricative*	_____	_____
Change the manner of the onset. *Voiced bilabial nasal*	_____	_____

EXERCISE 20-L: FOLLOW MORE CLUES

Clue	Phonetic Symbol(s)	Resulting Word in Orthography
Voiced labiodental fricative	_____	
Mid front tense unrounded	_____	
Voiceless alveolar fricative	_____	
What is the word?	_____	_____
Change the voicing of the onset.	_____	_____
Change the voicing of the coda.	_____	_____
Change the place and manner of the onset but still keeping the lips involved.	_____	_____
Change the tongue advancement and lip rounding of the vowel.	_____	_____
Change the tension of the vowel.	_____	_____

EXERCISE 20-M: EXPLAIN THE CHANGES

Now you will explain what happened to the words. The word is provided to you and the change is identified. Using your knowledge of the phonetic make-up of the consonants, describe the changes.

**Voiceless palatal fricative
+ high-back tense rounded vowel
+ voiceless alveolar stop-plosive
/ʃut/**

New Word	Word in Phonetic Symbols	State the Change __ Changed to __ →	Describe the Change
shoes	_____	t → z	What changed in the coda?
			_____
chews	_____	ʃ → tʃ	What changed in the onset?
			_____

EXERCISE 20-M: EXPLAIN THE CHANGES (*continued*)

chewed   _____   z → d   What changed?

_____

rude   _____   tʃ → r   What changed?

_____

room   _____   d → m   What changed?

_____

zoom   _____   r → z   What changed?

_____

EXERCISE 20-N: IDENTIFY MORE CHANGES

Voiceless labiodental fricative
+ high-front tense unrounded vowel
+ voiceless alveolar stop-plosive
/fit/

Word in Orthography	Word in Phonetic Symbols	State the Change _____ changed to _____ →	Describe the Change
fit	_____	_____	_____
foot	_____	_____	_____
food	_____	_____	_____
feud	_____	_____	_____
fuel	_____	_____	_____
fool	_____	_____	_____
full	_____	_____	_____
pull	_____	_____	_____
push	_____	_____	_____

EXERCISE 20-O: COUNTING AND IDENTIFYING SOUNDS IN WORDS

Complete the table.

Word	Transcription	How Many Phonemes?	What Is the First Sound?	What Is the Last Sound?
thrill				
does				
sawed				
spoke				
saws				
sauce				
ring				
showed				
thought				
shirt				
year				
straight				
mixed				
bathe				
joint				
though				
sheer				
laughed				
know				
fox				
shrink				
numb				
square				
change				
chew				

EXERCISE 20-O: COUNTING AND IDENTIFYING SOUNDS IN WORDS (*continued*)

Word	Transcription	How Many Phonemes?	What Is the First Sound?	What Is the Last Sound?
cheese				
jay				
snitch				
cash				
boy				
fresh				
gnawed				
thing				
clear				
wow				
real				
binge				

EXERCISE 20-P: IDENTIFY THE THIRD SPEECH SOUND IN WORDS

Transcribe each word. Find the third speech sound in each word. Circle all the graphemes in the word that represents that specific sound.
Example: o[n]e /wʌn/

joy[f]ul	/dʒɔɪfʊl/	tinker		talk	
known		climb		sung	
autumn		should		vision	
thought		knight		fresh	
choose		kitchen		start	
patchwork		shrink		numb	
shocks		soothe		psyche	
rough		square		napkin	
unless		gnawed		thorn	
bathe		script		shrimp	
church		chord		glow	

EXERCISE 20-Q: FIND THE WORDS THAT ARE REQUESTED

Which of the following words **begin with a voiced sound**?

| owl | think | bold | that | hat | my |

Which of the following words **do not have a coda**?

| how | far | bus | mink | joy | blow |

Which of the following words **begin with a voiceless fricative sound**?

| far | hour | joy | him | chance | shine |

Which of the following words contain **a back, tense vowel**?

| boot | juice | lock | putt | most | crowd |

Which of the following words contain **front vowels**?

| boat | beet | bit | bought | bat | bait |

Which of the following words contain a **velar nasal**?

| angel | thank | ginger | tongue | engine | sphinx |

Which of the following words are **not simple syllables**?

| green | rock | love | friend | cough | think |

Which of the following words **have four or more phonemes**?

| knock | train | rhyme | youth | join | share |

Which of the following words contain a **bilabial sound**?

| think | pop | whom | farm | me | now |

Which of the following words contain a **low vowel**?

| gnat | kite | hot | coat | cot | bet |

Which of the following words **do not have an onset**?

| who | all | honor | own | oh | what |

Which of the following words contain a **mid vowel**?

| mate | meet | mutt | might | note | nerd |

Which of the following words **begin with a fricative**?

| who | chive | cell | vast | psych | youth |

Which of the following words contain a **diphthong**?

| buy | cow | voice | caught | rhyme | house |

EXERCISE 20-Q: FIND THE WORDS THAT ARE REQUESTED (*continued*)

Which of the following words has a **sonorant for a coda**?

spin   far   wow   spell   my   comb

Which of the following words contain a **consonant sequence**?

graph   most   box   basket   park   skill

Which of the following words contain an **affricate**?

junior   treasure   chair   strange   chef   chaos

EXERCISE 20-R: MORE OR LESS

Read the statements and decide whether the quantity of the first noun is more or less than that of the second. Circle your answer.

More   Less   Graphemes than phonemes in the English language

More   Less   Allographs for the sound /h/ than for /f/

More   Less   Consonants than vowels

More   Less   Controlled-r diphthongs than nonphonemic diphthongs

More   Less   Unrounded vowels than rounded

More   Less   Tense vowels than lax

More   Less   High vowels than low

More   Less   Obstruents than sonorants

More   Less   Voiced consonants than voiceless

More   Less   Fricatives than stridents

EXERCISE 20-S: MIND YOUR MANNERS

Read each of the following statements carefully. Each statement refers to a specific manner of consonant production. Identify which manner is being described. Write the name on the line provided.

Closely blended stop and fricative occurring as
a single sound.   _____

Airstream is directed through the nasal cavity
instead of the oral cavity.   _____

Track 11, 12, 13, 14, 15

Practice transcribing all sounds in simple and complex syllables.

Less constricted than other consonants but lack audible articulatory movement

_____

Complete closure of the vocal tract at the place of articulation that stops the airstream momentarily but then is released abruptly.

_____

Produced as the articulators move from one position to another, resulting in a change of resonance.

_____

Air is forced through a narrow constriction of the vocal tract at the point of articulation, producing a turbulent, continuous sound as it passes through.

_____

Term used for oral sonorants

_____

A subgroup of sounds that are produced with high-frequency turbulence

_____

UNIT

4

Transcription: The Details

The goals for Unit 4 include the following:

- To introduce you to general rules of broad transcription
- To provide you with additional exercises on sounds that often challenge students
- To assist you in understanding the impact of stress on the sound system and to learn how to attend to stress in multisyllabic words
- To provide you with exercises to improve your attention to stress patterns in isolated words
- To increase your automaticity in using phonetic symbols in order to decode and transcribe words.

Overview of Transcription

Now that you know the sounds of the English language, how they are formed, and the IPA symbols representing each sound, you are ready for the next step: *phonetic transcription*. This is a tool used by speech–language pathologists to record the speech sounds used by others in order to diagnose a potential disorder as well as to gain information for intervention. It is also used by linguists to understand speech production, by actors and singers to learn dialects, and by broadcast professionals to improve their pronunciation. In the previous two units, you practiced reading and writing words using the sound symbols of the IPA. You are now prepared to use the IPA to transcribe the speech you hear.

Not everyone transcribes speech in the same manner. *Broad transcription* refers to the process of using the sound symbols to represent the speech that is heard without detailing the allophonic variations. When more detail about allophonic variations is warranted, *narrow transcription* is used. Narrow transcription uses additional symbols, known as *diacritic*, to provide more detail about pronunciation variations. These additional symbols are important for providing additional clinical information not communicated through the use of the IPA symbol for a particular sound. A list of diacritic symbols will be provided to you in Appendix A, but will not be emphasized during transcription practice in the next two chapters.

Transcribing Speech

General rules for transcribing speech:

MOST IMPORTANT RULE TO FOLLOW WHEN TRANSCRIBING SPEECH
Listen carefully.

- There are many phonetic symbols that are identical to the roman alphabet; however, there are no *c*, *q*, *x*, or *y* symbols in the IPA. Remember, *x* is a sequence represented by the symbols /ks/ and the spelling *qu* is most often represented by the symbols /kw/.

- Glides (/w,j/) and the fricative (/h/) are only prevocalic or intervocalic. Reminder: when you see them as letters (/w/, /y/, and /h/) at the end of words, they are part of the vowel.

- Be careful with some words that have a "hidden" sequence (not evident by looking at orthography). The palatal glide, the bilabial glide, and the velar nasal are not represented in orthography.

- When transcribing, always watch out for instances of coarticulation.

- Use the IPA symbols to represent the sounds you *hear*. Silent letters, letter doubling, and other orthographic conventions are what you see.
- The IPA does not use capital letters.

Additional reminders about specific sounds that may challenge you:

Track 20

Velar nasal in "nk," "ng," "nks," and "nx" contexts in printed words

When you see:	You may hear:	Examples:
"ng"	= /ŋ/	long, singer
	= /ŋg/	finger, linger, dangle
"nk"	= /ŋk/	think, drank, dunk, blinker
"nx," "nks"	= /ŋks/	minx, links

Vowels preceding a velar nasal

Lax vowels generally precede the velar nasal.
When it sounds like "__" transcribe it as /__/

"ing" → /ɪŋ/   "ang" → /æŋ/   "eng" → /ɛŋ/
"ong" → /ɔŋ/ or /ɑŋ/   "ung" → /ʌŋ/

Using the lax vowel before the velar nasal: An explanation—The length and quality of the lax vowel is affected by the sounds that follow it. Lax vowels are longest when they are followed by a sonorant consonant, next longest by a voiced obstruent, and the shortest when followed by a voiceless obstruent. The quality of the lax vowel also is affected when it is followed by a nasal consonant.

Read the following pairs of words. The vowel sounds stay the same, although vowel length changes.

at – an	ab – am	ag – ang
it – in	ib – im	ig – ing
et – en	eb – em	eg – eng

Read the following groups of words across. The vowel sound is the same across the words, although its length is affected by the consonant (where it is produced in the mouth and the voicing) that follows it.

Vowel	Voiceless Postvocalic Obstruent	Voiced Postvocalic Obstruent	Postvocalic Alveolar Nasal	Postvocalic Velar Nasal	Postvocalic Velar Nasal
/æ/	bat	bad	ban	bang	bank
	rat	rad	ran	rang	rank
	sat	sad	sand	sang	sank
/ɪ/	kit	kid	kin	king	kink
	pit		pin	ping	pink
			thin	thing	think
/ɔ/	sought	sawed		song	

shortest ------ longer --longest

Lax vowels are longest when they are followed by a sonorant consonant, next longest by a voiced obstruent, and shortest when followed by a voiceless obstruent. The quality of the lax vowel also is affected when it is followed by a nasal consonant.

EXERCISE 21-A: VOWEL SOUNDS WITH VELAR NASAL

Write the vowel symbol on the line next to each word.

stung _____	strong _____	thing _____	slang _____
pong _____	length _____	bank _____	hung _____
cling _____	gang _____	tongs _____	tongue _____
junk _____	sings _____	think _____	hang _____

EXERCISE 21-B: IDENTIFYING THE VELAR NASAL IN SINGLETON AND SEQUENCE CONTEXTS

Say the following words out loud. Identify the whether a velar nasal singleton or sequence is in the word. Select your choice.

bring	/ŋ/	/ŋg/	/ŋk/	/ŋks/
Jenga	/ŋ/	/ŋg/	/ŋk/	/ŋks/
blanks	/ŋ/	/ŋg/	/ŋk/	/ŋks/
morning	/ŋ/	/ŋg/	/ŋk/	/ŋks/
stronger	/ŋ/	/ŋg/	/ŋk/	/ŋks/
bongo	/ŋ/	/ŋg/	/ŋk/	/ŋks/
links	/ŋ/	/ŋg/	/ŋk/	/ŋks/
kangaroo	/ŋ/	/ŋg/	/ŋk/	/ŋks/
mink	/ŋ/	/ŋg/	/ŋk/	/ŋks/
gang	/ŋ/	/ŋg/	/ŋk/	/ŋks/
dangle	/ŋ/	/ŋg/	/ŋk/	/ŋks/
wrong	/ŋ/	/ŋg/	/ŋk/	/ŋks/

rancor	/ŋ/	/ŋg/	/ŋk/	/ŋks/
England	/ŋ/	/ŋg/	/ŋk/	/ŋks/
thinker	/ŋ/	/ŋg/	/ŋk/	/ŋks/

EXERCISE 21-C: SELECT THE CORRECT TRANSCRIPTIONS

Circle the words that are transcribed correctly (tune into the vowel before the velar nasal).

/strɛŋθ/	/pɪŋ/	/rɛŋk/	/tæŋ/
/dɪpɪŋ/	/θæŋk/	/stiŋk/	/strɔŋ/
/sɪŋ/	/drepɪŋ/	/tʌŋ/	/lɔŋgɚ/

EXERCISE 21-D: TRANSCRIPTION PRACTICE: VELAR NASAL

Transcribe the following words. Pay careful attention to whether a velar nasal is in the word. Remember the type of vowel that precedes it.

anger _____	singer _____	tango _____
hunger _____	prank _____	king _____
danger _____	English _____	clang _____
kingdom _____	angle _____	banker _____
mingle _____	ginger _____	savings _____
longer _____	finger _____	sponge _____
England _____	strengthen _____	young _____
jungle _____	spring _____	running _____

Another challenge that you will encounter during phonetic transcription concerns what happens to words when you add a prefix or a suffix.

Morphophonemics refer to the sound changes that result when morphemes are put together to make new words. Although specific morphemes are always *spelled* the same way, the way they are pronounced is determined by the sounds in the word to which they are attached.

Two common suffixes to single syllable words are the –*s* suffix that can signify plural (e.g., *cups*), third-person regular tense (e.g., *I eat, you eat, he eats*), or possessive (e.g., *mom's*) and the past tense suffix –*ed* (e.g., *jumped*). You have been working with these suffixes throughout Unit 3. As a reminder:

- Plural marker –*s*, third-person regular tense marker –*s*, possessive –*'s* is always spelled with an –*s* or –*es* but can be pronounced as an /s/, /z/, or /əz/ depending on the last sound of the word to which it is attached.

- Past tense –*ed* is always spelled with an –*ed*, but may be pronounced as a /t/, /d/, or /əd/ depending on the final sound of the word to which it is attached.

> How do you determine which sound to use?
> This is dependent on the voicing characteristics of the last sound of the root word.
>
> - If the last sound of the root word is voiceless (consonant) → use the sound that is voiceless for the morpheme marker.
> - If the last sound of the root word is voiced (consonant or vowel) → use the sound that is voiced for the morpheme marker.
> - If the last sound has similar characteristics to the morpheme marker → add the syllable.

EXERCISE 21-E: TRANSCRIBING WORDS WITH BOUND MORPHEMES /s/, /z/, /əz/ OR /t/, /d/, /əd/

Transcribing bound morphemes (i.e., plurals, third-person regular tense, and past tense markers): Pay attention to the voicing characteristic of the final sound in each word before selecting the correct sound to represent the specific morpheme marker. Say the word out loud. Can you detect the voicing difference?

Plurals

toe	/to/	→	/toz/
sack	_____	→	_____
ball	_____	→	_____
pin	_____	→	_____

cup   _____   →   _____

rub   _____   →   _____

car   _____   →   _____

boy   _____   →   _____

word   _____   →   _____

piece   _____   →   _____

branch   _____   →   _____

tax   _____   →   _____

dish   _____   →   _____

Third-Person Regular Tense (*e.g., I go, you go, he goes*)

stop   /stɑp/   →   /stɑps/

rub   _____   →   _____

put   _____   →   _____

ride   _____   →   _____

top   _____   →   _____

look   _____   →   _____

run   _____   →   _____

toss   _____   →   _____

wish   _____   →   _____

guess   _____   →   _____

Past Tense

call   /kɔl/   →   /kɔld/

stop   _____   →   _____

EXERCISE 21-E: TRANSCRIBING WORDS WITH BOUND MORPHEMES /s/, /z/, /əz/ OR /t/, /d/, /əd/ (*continued*)

rob   _____   →   _____

knock   _____   →   _____

peel   _____   →   _____

push   _____   →   _____

cough   _____   →   _____

live   _____   →   _____

munch   _____   →   _____

treat   _____   →   _____

melt   _____   →   _____

trade   _____   →   _____

EXERCISE 21-F: TRANSCRIPTION PRACTICE: VELAR NASALS AND BOUND MORPHEMES

Transcribe the following words into phonetic symbols. Remember the morphophonemic changes.

yells	_____	stayed	_____
typed	_____	hugs	_____
clapped	_____	sings	_____
lands	_____	tossed	_____
toes	_____	boys	_____
etched	_____	facts	_____
climbed	_____	grows	_____
clowns	_____	shrinks	_____

lengths _____   dimes _____

brains _____   aimed _____

counts _____   tensed _____

moaned _____   turns _____

guided _____   started _____

wishes _____   guesses _____

EXERCISE 21-G: TRANSCRIPTION PRACTICE: GLIDES

Transcribe the following words into phonetic symbols, paying attention to when a glide is present in the word.

humid _____	plow _____	bowl _____
Cuba _____	toy _____	cube _____
few _____	whose _____	cow _____
snowing _____	chewy _____	enjoy _____
once _____	destroy _____	view _____
cutest _____	future _____	cure _____
humor _____	own _____	sewer _____
employer _____	employ _____	fumes _____
thy _____	myth _____	quilt _____

EXERCISE 21-H: DETERMINING THE CORRECT TRANSCRIPTION

Read each word in orthography and the corresponding transcriptions. Find the words that are transcribed correctly. For those that are not, provide the correct transcription.

scene	/sin/	shirt	/ʃɝt/	done	/dʊn/
noise	/nɔɪs/	how	/haʊw/	use	/uz/

EXERCISE 21-H: DETERMINING THE CORRECT TRANSCRIPTION (*continued*)

what	/wʌt/	cheat	/tʃet/	yawn	/yɑn/
calm	/kælm/	teeth	/titθ/	tucked	/tʌkt/
knead	/knid/	couch	/caʊtʃ/	juice	/jus/
stormed	/stɔɚməd/	those	/ðoz/	gleam	/glim/
paint	/paɪnt/	dish	/dɪʃ/	down	/daʊn/
first	/fɪɚst/	pears	/peɚz/	fox	/faks/
grown	/gron/	who	/hʊ/	health	/hɛlθ/

EXERCISE 21-I: JUDGE THE TRANSCRIPTION

Read the following phonetic symbols. Judge the accuracy of the transcription by comparing the sounds you produced with the word next to it. If incorrect, write the correct transcription on the line provided.

/θaʊ/	though	Y	N	_____
/plʌmz/	plums	Y	N	_____
/raɪs/	rise	Y	N	_____
/cʌf/	cough	Y	N	_____
/reng/	rang	Y	N	_____
/waʊw/	wow	Y	N	_____
/jʌddʒ/	judge	Y	N	_____
/wiŋk/	wink	Y	N	_____
/ðɛm/	them	Y	N	_____
/bʊθ/	booth	Y	N	_____
/spaɪsd/	spiced	Y	N	_____
/caʊs/	cows	Y	N	_____
/θɪnk/	think	Y	N	_____

/jɔɪy/	joy	Y	N	_____
/pɪtʃ/	pitch	Y	N	_____

EXERCISE 21-J: DECODE SYMBOLS: WHAT'S THE WORD?

Read the following phonetic symbols and decide on the word they represent.

/ʃapɪŋ/	/hɛlθɪ/	/pʌblək/	/wɪðɚd/
/skwɪntəd/	/dʒæmd/	/væljud/	/ɪglu/
/dʒɛləs/	/pandɚ/	/dʒɛntəl/	/θɔtfʊl/
/plɛʒɚ/	/mɪstek/	/əmjuzd/	/sɚfəs/
/lʌkɪ/	/mɔɚnɪŋ/	/kɝnəl/	/kəkun/
/səpɔɚtəd/	/mɪljənɛɚ/	/ɪmpeʃənt/	/praɪvəsɪ/
/kaməkəl/	/əkweʒən/	/dɪskʌvɚ/	/bælərinə/
/abləgeʃən/	/sɪgnəfaɪ/	/fæntæstɪk/	/kwɔlətɪ/

22 *Stress*

In this workbook, we have been working with words in isolation. All of the words used in the second and third units have been monosyllable (i.e., single syllable) words. When words have more than one syllable, at least one of the syllables will have more prominence. If syllables in words did not have this difference, we would speak with equal stress and our intonation would sound robotic. If you recall from the first chapter of this workbook, vowels are the nucleus of each syllable and carry the intonation.

Stress affects the pronunciation of a word. We stress syllables by increasing our:

> *Definition of* **stress**: The degree of prominence associated with a particular syllable in a word.

- Breath force during vowel production
- Loudness of the vowel
- Length of the vowel
- Pitch of the vowel

The speaker can *feel* stress. The stressed syllable is produced by pushing more air out of the lungs in one syllable relative to others.

Stress is perceived by listeners as the vowel in the syllable being:

- Longer in duration
- Higher in pitch
- Greater in intensity

The listener can *hear* stress on the vowels in the word. In the stressed syllable, the vowel is often longer relative to the other vowels in the word and produced louder (but not always).

Listen as someone says the following words to you: *diplomat, diplomacy, diplomatic*. With each word, the stress moves to a different syllable. *Diplomat* has the strongest stress on the <u>first</u> syllable, *diplomacy* has the strongest stress on the <u>second</u> syllable, and *diplomatic* has the strongest stress on the <u>third</u> syllable.

Listen as someone says these words to you: *photograph, photography, photographic*. Identify the syllable that receives the most stress in those words.

Vowels in Stressed and Unstressed Syllables

 Track 21

Say the following groups of words aloud or listen as a speaker says these words. Pay attention to the vowel sounds in the syllables

Group 1: emphatic – fantastic – emphasis
Group 2: implicit – simplistic – implication
Group 4: allege – tempestuous – allegation

Ladefoged (1993) discussed three forms of vowel quality in syllables: stressed, unstressed, and reduced. Vowel sounds are produced the clearest in syllables that receive stress. The quality of the vowel sound is reduced in syllables that receive no stress.

Column 1	Column 2	Column 3
emphatic	fantastic	emphasis
implicit	simplistic	implication
allege	tempestuous	allegation

Say the words in Column 1 aloud or listen as a speaker says these words. The stress is on the second syllable in each of these words. You should clearly hear the /æ/, /ɪ/, and /ɛ/ sounds in these syllables. Now say the words in Column 2. The stress is again on the second syllable in each of these words. Again, you should clearly hear the /æ/, /ɪ/, and /ɛ/ sounds in these syllables. Say the words in Column 2 again, but this time, pay attention to the vowels in the first syllable. You can hear the /æ/, /ɪ/, and /ɛ/ sounds in these syllables, but not as clearly as in the syllable that receives the most stress. As you read the words in Column 3, listen to the vowel sounds in the second syllable in each of these words. These syllables receive no stress, and, as a result, the vowel sounds are reduced to a schwa /ə/.

 Track 22

Two-Syllable Words

Two-syllable *compound* words (also *spondee* words) have equal stress on each syllable. Notice that as you say or hear the speaker say a spondee word, you speak each syllable at the same volume (same energy used) and take the same length of time saying each syllable.

airplane	baseball	eyebrow	doorbell
popcorn	stairway	yardstick	toothpaste
cowboy	football	playground	mailman

In a word with two syllables (that are not compound words), one syllable will receive *primary* stress. The vowel in the syllable with primary stress is pronounced with greater emphasis.

A good example of the difference in stress in two-syllable words is comparing a word that can function as both a noun and verb in the English language. Say or listen to the speaker say the following words and pay attention to how the stress shifts in the word depending on which function it serves.

Track 23

Nouns	*Verbs*
produce	produce
conflict	conflict
record	record
contract	contract
protest	protest
convert	convert
permit	permit
subject	subject
rebel	rebel
conduct	conduct
address	address
object	object
insert	insert

Were you able to determine the rule?

In these words, stress serves a *phonemic* function. When the stress pattern changes in the word, the meaning also changes. The meanings of the words depend on accurate syllable stress.

Listen to the following sentences, paying attention to the stress shifts in the words that serve as nouns and verbs.

Did he *desert* you in the *desert*?
I hope my garden will *produce* a great deal of *produce* this summer.
Let's try to *record* our own *record*.
He was *content* with the *contents* of the box.
We cannot *permit* you to drive without a *permit*.
Do you *object* to including that *object* in the package?
Will you *contest* the results of the *contest*?

REMEMBER

Noun form always receives first-syllable stress.

Verb form always receives second-syllable stress.

Track 24

REMEMBER

From a speaker's point of view, stress involves using more energy during production. From a listener's point of view, stress involves hearing a longer and louder vowel.

Track 25

EXERCISE 22-A: ODD ONE OUT: STRESS PATTERNS

Listen to the stress pattern in the following groups of three words. Find the word that has a different stress pattern.

<u>in</u>stant	bet<u>ween</u>	<u>bro</u>ther
engage	hydrant	recent

diving	instead	above
boxer	fighter	enough
virus	illness	disease
succeed	table	erase
button	pretend	debrief
liquid	sizzle	away
bacon	upon	open
summer	survive	salute
balloon	trapeze	comma
focus	aware	silent
assume	problem	traffic
follow	contain	secure
declare	patrol	scarlet

Why Can Learning Stress Be So Stressful?	We know how to use stress correctly in *production of speech*. We are not accustomed to thinking about stress patterns in the *perception of speech*.

Stress Changes with the Addition of Prefixes and Suffixes

Morphophonemic changes to words will continue to challenge your phonetic transcription skills when you add a prefix and/or a suffix to a base word and the syllable length increases. The addition of syllables may affect the stress pattern in the word. As a result, the change in stress patterns may affect the vowel sound in the root/base word. The addition of the prefix and suffix may also change the consonant sounds in the word. Listen carefully.

REMEMBER
As a general rule, affixes (prefixes and suffixes) do not carry primary stress.

Suffix "–s", "–ed", "–ing"

When adding plural –s or past tense –ed to the words in Chapter 21, the addition of these suffixes did not change the word length in most of the words, so the stress patterns remained the same.

EXERCISE 22-B: TRANSCRIBING THE SUFFIX *–ING* /ɪŋ/

Transcribe the following two-syllable words. Because the suffix is unstressed, the root word will receive the most stress in the word. Reminder: Use /ɪŋ/ for the suffix *–ing*

buzzing	_____	falling	_____
lasting	_____	biking	_____
clowning	_____	curling	_____
fencing	_____	stinging	_____
meeting	_____	bowling	_____
charming	_____	running	_____
driving	_____	boxing	_____
clapping	_____	frowning	_____
typing	_____	pushing	_____
punching	_____	serving	_____
dodging	_____	touching	_____
jumping	_____	yachting	_____
styling	_____	looking	_____
owning	_____	using	_____

Suffix "–y" or "–ly"

When *–y* or *–ly* is used as a suffix and added to a word, it brings an additional syllable to the word, but the suffix does not receive primary stress. The vowel sound heard in these two suffixes is shorter in duration due to the lack of stress. Because of this, many books recommend the use of the high front lax unrounded vowel /ɪ/ rather than /i/ to represent the vowel in the suffix. Not everyone agrees, so you may see the word *happy* transcribed as /hæpɪ/ or /hæpi/.

REMEMBER
The *high front lax unrounded vowel* /ɪ/ is used to represent the sound in *–y* and *–ly* suffixes.

EXERCISE 22-C: IDENTIFYING –*Y* AND –*LY* SUFFIXES THAT WOULD USE /ɪ/

Circle those words that have a –*y* or –*ly* suffix that can be transcribed with the /ɪ/.

hungry	monkey	cry	crazy
kindly	funky	groovy	turkey
hockey	baby	truly	cowboy
rely	really	freely	handy
enjoy	sunny	play	daily
unify	simply	fully	shyly

If you thought about the sound you heard in the second syllable and then considered whether the sound was part of a suffix, you identified 15 words.

EXERCISE 22-D: TRANSCRIPTION PRACTICE: –*Y* AND –*LY* SUFFIXES

Transcribe the following words. In each word, the –*y* or the –*ly* is a suffix and is unstressed.

crazy	_____	sticky _____
softly	_____	gently _____
monthly	_____	picky _____
jumpy	_____	chilly _____
grouchy	_____	quickly _____
friendly	_____	noisy _____
curly	_____	greasy _____
bossy	_____	slowly _____
squeaky	_____	crumbly _____

REMEMBER

Identifying the number of syllables in the word

Listen for the vowel sounds.

The number of vowel sounds you *hear* equals the number of syllables in the word.

How to Decide Which Syllable Has the Primary Stress?

In words that have one syllable:

- If a word is monosyllable, then that syllable is stressed. If it has a central vowel sound, use the stressed symbol for the sound (i.e., /ʌ/, /ɝ/).

In words that have two syllables:

- Most (but not all) two-syllable words in English have the first syllable stressed.

- Listen for the syllable that has the tense vowel; it usually has the primary stress of the word. Phonemic diphthongs tend to be in syllables with either primary or secondary stress (MacKay, 1987).

- Remember that prefixes and suffixes are not stressed. Therefore, if a word has a suffix or prefix attached to it, the *base/root word generally gets the primary stress*.

  - When *–y* or *–ly* is the second syllable of a two-syllable word and functions as a suffix (bound morpheme), use /ɪ/ (not /i/):
    crazy   →   /krezɪ/
    truly   →   /trulɪ/

  - Many of our prefixes and suffixes contain the schwa or the schwar sounds.
    - Prefixes: un– sub– con– de– re– a– tele–
    - Suffixes: –er, –ure, –ward, –ern, –ment, –ion, –en, –ity, –ance, –ed, –ness, –able, –ible, –a, –ious, –less, –ble

  - When a two-syllable word has *–er* at the end of the second syllable (spelled *–er*, *–or*, *–ar*), the first syllable in these words has the primary stress and the second syllable almost always is unstressed. Use the schwar /ɚ/ to represent the unstressed *–er* sound.

    Examples: either   motor   author   brother

  - *–er* also serves as a bound morpheme, changing a verb to a noun.

    Bound morphemes   →   unstressed (use /ɚ/)
             teacher   actor

  - When *a–* begins a word, is pronounced as a mid-central vowel, and is the only sound in the first syllable of a two-syllable word → it is usually represented with a schwa. Examples include about, afraid, atone. Be careful here, however, as not all words beginning with the letter "a" are pronounced the same.

Track 26

EXERCISE 22-E: SORTING WORDS BY STRESS PATTERNS

Listen to the stress patterns in the following words. Sort the following two-syllable words according to which syllable receives primary stress.

First Syllable Stress			*Second Syllable Stress*
_____	pollute	stories	_____
_____	person	thirsty	_____
_____	amaze	sisters	_____
_____	compare	writing	_____
_____	harvest	partner	_____
_____	extreme	afford	_____
_____	fairly	feather	_____
_____	purple	yellow	_____
_____	disturb	nervous	_____
_____	foolish	fifty	_____
_____	patrol	member	_____
_____			_____
_____			_____
_____			_____
_____			_____

Track 27

EXERCISE 22-F: TRANSCRIPTION PRACTICE: /ɚ/ IN FINAL UNSTRESSED SYLLABLES

Listen to the following words that have the "er" sound in the second syllable. The first syllable in each word receives primary stress. Use /ɚ/ in the final syllable when transcribing.

under	author	lather	brother
————	————	————	————

bother	murder	summer	anchor
————	————	————	————

water	monster	thunder	shudder
————	————	————	————

shooter	anger	ringer	blusher
————	————	————	————

usher	mister	better	ladder
————	————	————	————

SAY THE FOLLOWING WORDS OUT LOUD:

USHER   ASSURE

These two words have the same sounds but do not share the same stress pattern.

How would you transcribe these two words?

Track 28

EXERCISE 22-G: TRANSCRIPTION PRACTICE: SCHWA IN SUFFIXES

Listen to the following words: The suffix in each is unstressed and contains a schwa.

vision	acceptance	likable	mutant
————	————	————	————

mission	wondrous	action	gorgeous
———————	———————	———————	———————
motion	servant	strident	judgment
———————	———————	———————	———————
version	confusion	nation	commotion
———————	———————	———————	———————

Track 29

EXERCISE 22-H: TRANSCRIPTION PRACTICE: UNSTRESSED FIRST SYLLABLES

The following words contain the schwa /ə/ sound in the first syllable (it is unstressed). The second syllable in these words receives the primary stress. Transcribe accordingly.

abide	abound	abrupt	afraid
———————	———————	———————	———————
abuse	account	accuse	alone
———————	———————	———————	———————
acquire	adjourn	afford	away
———————	———————	———————	———————
avoid	about	above	allow
———————	———————	———————	———————
annoy	assure	across	amid
———————	———————	———————	———————

Special kind of unstressed syllable: *syllabic consonants*

Definition: consonant that acts like a vowel in an *unstressed* syllable. Only specific consonants can do this: /m,n,l/. Syllabics can be transcribed with a diacritic marking under the symbol or they can be transcribed with a schwa + symbol.

Syllabic syllables may be present in words ending in *–le*, *–al*, *–ol*, and so forth, pronounced as /əl/; words ending in *–en*, *–on*, pronounced as /ən/; and words ending in *–om*, pronounced as /əm/. Some phonetics books hesitate to turn all instances of these syllables into syllabic syllables. Others place certain conditions before a syllabic can be marked (i.e., preceding consonant is the same place as /m/ or /n/). We will use the /əl/, /ən/, /əm/ during our transcription of these sounds in unstressed syllables.

Track 30

EXERCISE 22-I: TRANSCRIPTION PRACTICE: SYLLABIC /l/

Listen to these words. The final syllable is unstressed. Use /əl/ in the final syllable.

circle	journal	colonel	table
_____	_____	_____	_____
thermal	buckle	knuckle	candle
_____	_____	_____	_____
stumble	nickel	jungle	pistol
_____	_____	_____	_____
angle	shingle	kernel	trouble
_____	_____	_____	_____

REMEMBER

Although the above exercises show general tendencies in the English language, there are always exceptions. The best way to improve your ability to identify stress is to *listen* to others.

Track 31

EXERCISE 22-J: TWO-SYLLABLE CENTRAL VOWEL SORT

In Chapter 9, the central vowels were presented. There were two symbols for each of the sounds (i.e., "uh" = /ʌ/ and /ə/ and "er" = /ɝ/ and /ɚ/. Because we have been using single-syllable words, you have been using the stressed symbols. The following exercise provides you with practice with stress and in using all central vowel symbols.

Listen to the following two-syllable words. Each word contains two mid-central vowel sounds. Sort the words by their vowel symbols. These will be determined by the stress pattern in each word.

shovel	butter	circus	assure	murder	above	convulse
dozen	culture	hunger	colonel	mural	avert	allure
fungus	muscle	bummer	surface	merger	murmur	stumbled
combust	annul	worker	succumb	courage	person	sculpture
muffler	turnip	nervous	usher	bubble	among	nurture
urgent	serpent	secure	journal	thunder	troubled	budget
junction	further					

/ɝ/ /ə/

circus _____

_____

_____

_____

_____

_____

_____

_____

_____

_____

_____

/ʌ/ /ə/

shovel _____

_____

_____

_____

_____

_____

_____

_____

_____

_____

_____

/ə/ /ɝ/

assure _____

_____

_____

_____

_____

_____

_____

_____

_____

_____

_____

/ə/ /ʌ/

above _____

_____

_____

_____

/ɝ/ /ɚ/

murder _____

_____

_____

_____

/ʌ/ /ɚ/

butter _____

_____

_____

_____

EXERCISE 22-J: TWO-SYLLABLE CENTRAL VOWEL SORT (*continued*)

_____   _____   _____

_____   _____   _____

_____   _____   _____

_____   _____   _____

Track 32

EXERCISE 22-K: SORTING WORDS BY STRESS PATTERN

In this activity, take turns with a partner saying each word *naturally. Listen* for the stress pattern. Decide which syllable has the stress and write the word in the appropriate column. Check your answers by listening to the CD.

First Syllable Stress   *Second Syllable Stress*

	Group A		
_____	easy	elite	_____
_____	either	elect	_____
_____	eagle	enough	_____
_____	eclipse	erupt	_____
_____	even	Egypt	_____
	emote	equate	

	Group B		
_____	omen	oboe	_____
_____	okra	obey	_____
_____	ogre	oblige	_____
_____	oblique	obese	

First Syllable Stress			*Second Syllable Stress*
_____	odor	open	_____
_____	overt	oppress	_____

First Syllable Stress			*Second Syllable Stress*
_____	*Group C*		_____
_____	inner	indeed	_____
_____	intrude	infant	_____
_____	instant	inflict	_____
_____	infer	inches	_____
_____	instead	involve	_____
_____	insect	index	_____

First Syllable Stress			*Second Syllable Stress*
_____	*Group D*		_____
_____	around	alike	_____
_____	avoid	avenge	_____
_____	achieve	anoint	_____
_____	afraid	aloof	_____
_____	atone	adore	_____
_____	abuse	arise	_____
_____	amass	adapt	_____
_____	astound		_____

EXERCISE 22-L: WHERE'S THE STRESS?

After listening to the speaker, circle the number that corresponds to which syllable receives primary stress in the following two-syllable words.

success	1	2	pleasant	1	2	relief	1	2
debate	1	2	couple	1	2	urgent	1	2
create	1	2	embrace	1	2	decay	1	2
enough	1	2	gallop	1	2	thunder	1	2
mother	1	2	culture	1	2	journal	1	2
believe	1	2	purpose	1	2	perturb	1	2
easel	1	2	ideal	1	2	intend	1	2
leather	1	2	heavy	1	2	agree	1	2

EXERCISE 22-M: JUDGE THE ACCURACY OF THE TRANSCRIPTION

Judge whether the transcription provided is correct. Remember to not only focus on the stress patterns, but also the correct vowel and consonant symbols. If incorrect, write the correct transcription.

alone	/ʌlon/	Y	N	_____
region	/ridʒən/	Y	N	_____
couple	/kəpəl/	Y	N	_____
neutral	/nutrəl/	Y	N	_____
judgment	/dʒʌdʒmɛnt/	Y	N	_____
mother	/mʌðɚ/	Y	N	_____
nickels	/nikʌls/	Y	N	_____
thunder	/θʌndɚ/	Y	N	_____
quarters	/kaɚtɚz/	Y	N	_____

fingers	/fɪŋɚz/	Y	N	_____
motion	/moʃən/	Y	N	_____
papers	/papɚz/	Y	N	_____
running	/rənɪŋ/	Y	N	_____
thinker	/θɪŋkɚ/	Y	N	_____

Track 34

EXERCISE 22-N: IDENTIFYING STRESS PATTERNS IN TWO-SYLLABLE WORDS

Listen to the following groups of words and find the word that has a different stress pattern from the others. After you identify the word that has the different stress pattern, transcribe all of the words.

absent	manage	sincere
seldom	improve	deny
emblem	demand	honest
mammal	return	select
balloon	cement	cartoon
tragic	redeem	jargon
dainty	complain	party
mistake	attach	guitar
agent	instead	garlic
safety	treasure	harvest
assure	alert	onion
govern	reverse	button
occur	career	ultra
affirm	herbal	convulse
secure	emerge	luggage

EXERCISE 22-0: IDENTIFY THE CORRECT TRANSCRIPTION

Read each word aloud. Focus on which syllable the stress is located. Determine the correct transcription that matches the stress pattern.

control	/kəntrol/	/kʌntrol/	/kəntrəl/
assist	/æsɪst/	/əsəst/	/əsɪst/
pertain	/pɚten/	/pɝrten/	/pɝten/
lucky	/lʊkɪ/	/ləki/	/lʌkɪ/
happen	/hæpɛn/	/hæpən/	/hæpʌn/
siphon	/saɪfon/	/saɪfən/	/saɪfʌn/
provoke	/provoke/	/prəvok/	/prʌvok/
western	/wɛstɚn/	/wɛstɝn/	/wɛstən/
language	/leŋgwʌdʒ/	/læŋgwədʒ/	/leŋgwədʒ/
stagnant	/stægnənt/	/stegnænt/	/stægnʌnt/
loser	/lusɚ/	/luzɝ/	/luzɚ/
unsure	/ənʃɝ/	/ʌnʃɝ/	/ənʃɚ/
twenty	/twɛnti/	/twɛntɪ/	/twɛntɪ/

In words with more than two syllables, one syllable will receive *primary* stress, another syllable may receive *secondary* stress (receives some emphasis but not as much as the syllable with primary stress), and another syllable (or more than one) receives no stress. Stress influences vowel quality. Vowel quality will be most distinct in syllables that receive primary stress. Vowel quality is less distinct in unstressed syllables; in fact, there is a tendency to reduce lax vowels to a schwa when in a syllable that receives no stress.

You were introduced to these words earlier in the chapter. Say the words out loud and identify which syllable receives primary stress. Underline it. Notice the vowel sounds in the other syllables.

emphatic	/ɛmfætək/	emphasis	/ɛmfəsɪs/
implicit	/ɪmplɪsət/	implication	/ɪmpləkeʃən/
allege	/əlɛdʒ/	allegation	/æləgeʃən/

Find the Word That Does Not Have the Same Stress Pattern as the Others.	Try Again......	Now Try Identifying Stress in 4-Syllable Words. Which Word Has a Different Stress Pattern?
amnesia	remember	chronology
electric	vacation	academy
impression	audience	celebration
clinician	outstanding	geometry
criminal	addition	combustible

Regional dialects can have an impact on the way we stress our words. Say the words *umbrella* and *insurance*. Speakers in the southeastern part of the country place the primary stress on the first syllable. Midwesterners place the primary stress on the second syllable.

Track 35

EXERCISE 22-P: IDENTIFYING THE SYLLABLE THAT IS *NOT* STRESSED

Below is a list of compound words with more than two syllables. This means that there is a weaker syllable included with the two syllables that have equal stress. Find that syllable (circle it) and transcribe the word. Note: The unstressed syllable will most likely need the schwa /ə/ or the schwar /ɚ/.

afternoon   _____

basketball   _____

bookkeeper   _____

businessman   _____

candlestick   _____

hamburger   _____

commonplace   _____

fingerprint   _____

furthermore   _____

gingerbread   _____

otherwise   _____

EXERCISE 22-P: IDENTIFYING THE SYLLABLE THAT IS *NOT* STRESSED (*continued*)

summertime   _____

nevertheless (has 2)   _____

EXERCISE 22-Q: SORTING U.S. STATES BY STRESS PATTERNS

/sɔɚtðəfɑlowɪŋjuɛstetsbaɪstrɛspætɚnz/

/rodaɪlənd/	/tɛksəs/	/ɛɚəzonə/	/tɛnəsi/
/jutɔ/	/nudʒɝzi/	/kənɛtəkət/	/əlæskə/
/mɑntænə/	/vɚdʒɪnjə/	/numɛksəko/	/waʃɪŋtən/
/wɪskɑnsən/	/okləhomə/	/waɪjomɪŋ/	/mɛɚələnd/
/mæsətʃusɪts/	/dʒɔɚdʒə/	/pɛnsəlvenjə/	/ɪlənɔɪ/
/vɚmɑnt/	/nuhæmpʃɚ/	/ɔɚəgən/	/nəvædə/
/kæləfɔɚnjə/	/kænzəs/	/flɔɚədə/	/aɪdəho/
/dɛləwɛɚ/	/aɚkənsɔ/	/həwaɪi/	/aɪəwə/
/kəntʌki/	/mɪʃəgən/	/məzɝi/	/mɪnəsotə/
/saʊθdəkotə/	/ohaɪjo/	/ɪndiænə/	/nəbræskə/
/nudʒɝzi/	/kalərado/	/mɪsəsɪpi/	

❶ ○○○	○ ❷ ○○	○○ ❸ ○	○○○ ❹

❶○○○	○❷○○	○○❸○	○○○❹

Track 36

EXERCISE 22-R: DETERMINING WHICH SYLLABLE RECEIVES PRIMARY STRESS

Listen to the stress pattern in the following words. Decide which syllable receives *primary* stress. Write 1, 2, or 3 to indicate which syllable carries the primary stress. Then transcribe each word accordingly.

surrounded _____	daffodil _____	India _____
example _____	pharyngeal _____	ebony _____
outrageous _____	misery _____	caribou _____
clavicle _____	stupendous _____	discover _____
bananas _____	clarinet _____	violin _____
creative _____	plantation _____	asterisk _____
persona _____	spectacle _____	terrified _____
distinctive _____	calendar _____	subscription _____
expertise _____	magical _____	majestic _____
magenta _____	arabesque _____	foundation _____
assessment _____	phonetics _____	anatomy _____

Reduction of Vowels to Schwa in Unstressed Syllables

In words with more than one syllable, only one syllable gets primary stress and the others are either unstressed or given secondary stress. Often, lax vowels will be pronounced as a neutral schwa when they are in syllables that are unstressed. The schwa is the most commonly spoken vowel in English, accounting for 20% of all vowels uttered.
Read the following words:

One Syllable With Stress	Two Syllables; First Syllable Has Primary Stress	
pest /pɛst/	tempest	/tɛmpəst/
	deepest	/dipəst/

Because the first syllable in *tempest* and *deepest* receives primary stress, the vowel sounds in the monosyllable *pest* and the first syllable *tem* are identical (i.e., /ɛ/). This cannot be said, however, for the vowel sounds in the monosyllable *pest* and the second syllable *pest* in *tempest* and *deepest*. Because the second syllable is unstressed, the lax vowel /ɛ/ is reduced to a schwa.

Pronounce these words, paying particular attention to the vowel in the second syllable:

/tɛmpɛst/   /tɛmpəst/   /dipɛst/   /dipəst/

Try another pair of words:

One Syllable With Stress		Two Syllables; First Syllable Has Primary Stress	
shin	chin	mission	/mɪʃən/
/ʃɪn/	/tʃɪn/	caution	/kɔʃən/
		kitchen	/kɪtʃən/

Because the first syllable in *mission*, *caution*, and *kitchen* receives primary stress, the lax vowel sound in the second syllable is not pronounced as distinct as it is in the monosyllable word *shin* or *chin*, and therefore, the sound in the second syllable is reduced to a schwa. Because of the stress pattern, the vowel sounds in the syllables in the words *mission* and *kitchen* are different.

Pronounce these words, paying particular attention to the vowel in the second syllable:

/mɪʃɪn/   /mɪʃən/   /kɪtʃɪn/   /kɪtʃən/

Additional examples are provided for the *–ence/–ance* suffix:

One Syllable With Stress		Two–Three Syllables; First Syllable Has Primary Stress	
tense	dense	sentence	/sɛntəns/
/tɛns/	/dɛns/	evidence	/ɛvədəns/

Track 37

HERE ARE SOME ADDITIONAL WORD PAIRINGS

Listen to the speaker read each pair of words. The vowel sound in the mono syllable word should sound different from the vowel sound in the second syllable of the two-syllable word. This is due to which syllable receives the primary stress.

pest	tempest	shin	mission	chin	kitchen		
tense	sentence	dense	evidence	sip	gossip	sent	absent
kit	biscuit	wren	children	brick	fabric	den	garden
Tom	bottom	ate	immediate	lad	salad		
lance	vigilance	fast	breakfast	lop	gallop		

Do you hear the reduction of the vowel sound in the second word of each pair?

The previous examples emphasized words with two syllables. Words with more than two syllables present the same type of vowel reduction.

In the word *ambition*, /æmbɪʃən/, the second syllable receives primary stress, resulting in a similar situation. The vowel sounds in the second and third syllables are not pronounced in the same manner. This word provides an example of what Ladefoged (1993) describes as *vowel reduction*. The neutral vowel, the schwa (the mid-central lax unrounded vowel), is pronounced in the final syllable, which receives the least amount of stress among the three syllables.

Here are other examples:

One Syllable; Vowel in Stressed Syllable		*Two Syllables; Vowel in Unstressed Syllable*		*Three Syllables; Second Syllable Has Primary Stress*	
meant	tent	ailment		department	/dəpaɚtmənt/
/mɛnt/	/tɛnt/	payment	/mənt/	competent	/kɑmpətənt/
		fragment			

The suffixes *–ment* and *–ent* do not receive primary stress. Although the lax vowel /ɛ/ is clearly perceived in the monosyllable words on the left, the vowel sound in the syllable is neutralized to a schwa when it is unstressed. This may be more noticeable in a three-syllable word than in a two-syllable word.

Let's focus on only two-syllable words.

–ment is Stressed Syllable	*–ment is Unstressed Syllable*
cement	ailment
lament	payment
	fragment

Noticing Vowel Alternations with Changes in Stress Patterns

The purpose of this activity is for you to pay attention to the stress and sound changes that occur in words as a result of adding morphemes.

    LISTEN to yourself pronounce each word, or better yet, listen to another person say the words.

    IDENTIFY the syllable that receives primary stress and circle the vowel sound in that syllable.

    TRANSCRIBE the words, paying attention to the stress patterns.

    DESCRIBE the morphophonemic changes.

    THINK OF other related words and transcribe them.

c(a)ve   /kev/   c(a)vity   /kævɪtɪ/ or /kævətɪ/

Describe the change: vowel change: mid front tense to low front lax

Additional words: cavern /kævɚn/   cavernous /kævɚnəs/

p o s e   _____ p o s i t i o n   _____

Describe the change: _____

Additional words: _____

a t h l e t e   _____ a t h l e t i c   _____

Describe the change: _____

Additional words: _____

f a m o u s   _____ i n f a m o u s   _____

Describe the change: _____

Additional words: _____

i n t r o d u c e   _____ i n t r o d u c t i o n _____

Describe the change: _____

Additional words: _____

p r o v i d e   _____ p r o v i s i o n   _____

Describe the change: _____

Additional words: _____

m i c r o s c o p e _____ m i c r o s c o p i c_____

Describe the change: _____

Additional words: _____

e x c e l _____ e x c e l l e n t _____

Describe the change: _____

Additional words: _____

c h r o n i c _____ c h r o n o l o g y _____

Describe the change: _____

Additional words: _____

v o l c a n o _____ v o l c a n i c _____

Describe the change: _____

Additional words: _____

p o l i t i c s _____ political _____

Describe the change: _____

Additional words: _____

p r e s i d e _____ p r e s i d e n t _____

Describe the change: _____

Additional words: _____

d i s t r i b u t e _____ d i s t r i b u t i o n_____

Describe the change: _____

Additional words: _____

a c a d e m i c _____ a c a d e m y _____

Describe the change: _____

Additional words: _____

n a t i o n   _____ n a t i o n a l   _____

Describe the change: _____

Additional words: _____

c o n v e n e   _____ c o n v e n t i o n   _____

Describe the change: _____

Additional words: _____

a s s u m e   _____ a s s u m p t i o n   _____

Describe the change: _____

Additional words: _____

The Impact of Morphophonemic Changes on Stress and Vowel/Consonant Changes

(Stress Syllable is Marked in Underlined Type)

Suffix

–ity **Major stress is always on the syllable before the suffix.**

active	<u>æk</u>tɪv	activity	æk<u>tɪ</u>vətɪ
able	<u>e</u>bəl	ability	ə<u>bɪ</u>lətɪ
ethnic	_____	ethnicity	_____
public	_____	_____	_____
solemn	_____	_____	_____
divine	_____	_____	_____
similar	_____	<u>similarity</u>	_____
abnormal	_____	_____	_____
sensitive	_____	_____	_____

–ic   **Major stress is always on the syllable before the suffix.**

athlete	<u>æθlit</u>	athletic	<u>æθlɛtɪk</u>
magnet	_____	<u>magnetic</u>	_____
chaos	_____	<u>chaotic</u>	_____
melody	_____	<u>melodic</u>	_____
nomad	_____	<u>nomadic</u>	_____

–ical   **Major stress is on the syllable before the suffix.**

history	_____	_____	_____
hysterics	_____	_____	_____
politics	_____	_____	_____

–tion
–sion   **Major stress is always on the syllable before the – *tion/-sion*.**

locate	_____	<u>location</u>	_____
invite	_____	<u>invitation</u>	_____
create	_____	_____	_____
devote	_____	_____	_____
celebrate	_____	_____	_____
separate	_____	_____	_____

What consonant changes did you notice in this group of words when the suffix *–tion* was added?

decide	_____	<u>decision</u>	_____
invade	_____	<u>invasion</u>	_____
divide	_____	_____	_____

collide   _____   _____   _____

conclude   _____   _____   _____

What consonant changes did you notice in this group of words when the suffix *–sion* was added?

fuse   _____   <u>fusion</u>   _____

revise   _____   <u>revision</u>   _____

televise   _____   _____   _____

immerse   _____   _____   _____

confuse   _____   _____   _____

What consonant changes did you notice in this group of words when the suffix *–sion* was added?

Track 38

EXERCISE 22-S: TRANSCRIBING STRESS CHANGES

Listen to the following words. Note the change in stress pattern and sound alternations when prefixes and suffixes are added.

detain   _____   detention   _____

gene   _____   genetic   _____

ignite   _____   ignition   _____

exclaim   _____   exclamation   _____

partial   _____   partition   _____

substance   _____   substantial   _____

stable   _____   stability   _____   stabilizer   _____

apply   _____   applicable   _____   application   _____

local   _____   location   _____   locality   _____

confide   _____   confident   _____   confidential   _____

receive   _____   receptor   _____   reception   _____

vocal   _____   vocalic   _____   vocalize   _____

brief	_____	brevity	_____	abbreviate	_____
vision	_____	revise	_____	visionary	_____
sign	_____	signal	_____	signify	_____
diction	_____	indicate	_____	contradict	_____
social	_____	associate	_____	association	_____
legal	_____	illegal	_____	legality	_____
recite	_____	citation	_____	recitation	_____
impose	_____	imposter	_____	imposition	_____
fate	_____	fatal	_____	fatality	_____
elastic	_____	elasticity	_____	elasticize	_____

EXERCISE 22-T: SELECT THE MOST REASONABLE TRANSCRIPTION FROM THE CHOICES PROVIDED

First, read the sounds in the three choices of phonetic transcription. Second, select the most reasonable transcription for the word given in the first column by circling it.

forced	forɛst	fɔrsd	fɔ˞st
newspaper	nuzpepɚ	nuspepɚ	nʊzpepɚ
thirsty	θɚsti	ðɝsty	θɝstɪ
yawning	yɔnɪŋ	jɔnɪŋ	jɑnɪŋ
angel	endʒəl	ændʒəl	æŋdʒəl
bounced	bounsd	baɪnst	baʊnst
thank you	θæŋkju	θænkju	θeŋkju
Asian	eʒən	edʒən	eʒʌn
stings	stiŋs	stɪŋs	stɪŋz
hungry	hʌŋgrɪ	həngrɪ	hʌŋgri
adorn	ədan	ʌdo˞n	ədɔrn
butcher	bʊtʃɚ	butʃɝ	bʊdʒɚ

EXERCISE 22-T: SELECT THE MOST REASONABLE TRANSCRIPTION FROM THE CHOICES PROVIDED (*continued*)

drinks	drɪŋks	drɪŋks	drinks
onion	ənjʌn	ʌniən	ʌnjən
delicacy	dɛlɛkəsi	dɛləkəsɪ	dɜlʌkɛsɪ
disruption	dɪsrəpʃʌn	dɪsrʌptʃən	dɪsrʌpʃən
domestic	dəmɛstək	dɪmestɪk	dʌmɛstək
sequence	səkwɛns	sikwəns	sekwəns
awkward	ɔkwɔˑd	ɔkwɚd	ʌkwɝd
musicbox	musɪkbaks	mjuzɪkbaks	mjusɪkbaks
commander	kʌmændɚ	kəmendɝ	kəmændɚ
thereafter	ðɛɚæftɚ	ðiɚæftɝ	θɜɚæftɚ
dangerous	dendʒərəs	deŋdʒɚəs	denjərəs
icecubes	aɪskjubz	aɪskjubs	aɪskubz
gangster	gæŋgstɚ	gæŋstɚ	geŋgstɚ
cucumber	cucʌmbɚ	kjukʌmbɚ	kjukəmbɚ
betrayed	betrɑd	bʌtræd	bətred
unworthy	ənwɝθɪ	ʌnwɝðɪ	ənwɝˑðɪ
reached	ritʃəd	ritʃt	ritʃət
phonology	fʌnɑlodʒɪ	fənalədʒɪ	fənologɪ
articulation	ɔɚtɪcjəletʃən	aɚtɪkələʃən	aɚtɪkjələʃən
underneath	ʌndɚniθ	əndɝniθ	əndɚnið
excellent	ɛksələnt	ɛgzələnt	ɛkzələnt
computer	kəmputɚ	kəmpjutɚ	kʌmputɝ
thinking	ðɪŋkɪŋ	θɪŋkɪŋ	θɪŋkɪŋ
sixteenth	sɪktinθ	sɪkstinθ	sɪkstinð
classify	klæsəfɪ	klæsəfaɪ	klæssəfaɪ
sympathy	sɪmpʌθi	sɪmpæθɪ	sɪmpəθɪ
examine	ɛgzæmɪn	ɛksamɪn	ɛgsæmɪn
indication	ɪndəkeʃən	ɪndiceʃən	əndəkəʃən

positive	pɑzɪtɪv	posɪtəv	pɑsitɪv
accidentally	æskɪdentəli	æksɪdɛntəlɪ	æksɪdɛntəli
exchange	ɛkstendʒ	ɛkstʃendʒ	ɛktʃændʒ
handful	hænful	hændfʊl	hɑndfʊl
luscious	lʌʃʌs	ləʃʌs	lʌʃəs
phonemes	fonims	fonemz	fonimz

Track 39

EXERCISE 22-U: SORTING WORDS BY STRESS PATTERN

Listen to the following words and categorize them by which syllable receives the primary stress. Once you have organized them by stress pattern, transcribe the words.

comedy	agility	imitation	constitution	essence	uncommon
unusual	generator	useful	iodine	camera	banana
romantic	definition	election	vacation	average	unstable
attendant	dominance	population	reluctant	expecting	ignore
diagnosis	debate	Mississippi	awful	October	never

❶ ○ ○	○ ❷ ○	○ ○ ❸

EXERCISE 22-T: SORTING WORDS BY STRESS PATTERN (*continued*)

❶ ○ ○	○ ❷ ○	○ ○ ❸

Track 40

EXERCISE 22-V: DETERMINING WHICH SYLLABLE RECEIVES PRIMARY STRESS

Listen to the following words and determine which syllable receives the primary stress. Circle 1, 2, or 3 depending on which syllable the primary stress falls in the word. Then, write an acceptable transcription on the line.

Syllable Stress

1	2	3	instrument	_____
1	2		famous	_____
1	2		after	_____
1	2	3	opponent	_____
1	2		learning	_____
1	2		study	_____
1	2	3	calendar	_____
1	2		server	_____
1	2	3	industry	_____
1	2		certain	_____
1	2		partner	_____
1	2	3	cultural	_____
1	2		country	_____

1	2	3		division	_____
1	2	3		telephone	_____
1	2	3		Canada	_____
1	2	3		occurrence	_____
1	2	3		personal	_____
1	2	3		condition	_____
1	2	3		commercial	_____
1	2	3		commencement	_____
1	2	3		processional	_____
1	2	3	4	humanity	_____
1	2	3		magnify	_____
1	2			assure	_____
1	2	3		prediction	_____
1	2	3		construction	_____

Track 41

EXERCISE 22-W: TRANSCRIPTION PRACTICE: SCHWA IN UNSTRESSED SYLLABLES

Transcribe the following words. Be sure to include the schwa and/or the schwar in the unstressed syllables.

service	_____	graceful	_____
naughty	_____	achiever	_____
bubble	_____	leveled	_____
again	_____	dominoes	_____
giggled	_____	prisoner	_____

EXERCISE 22-W: TRANSCRIPTION PRACTICE: SCHWA IN UNSTRESSED SYLLABLES (*continued*)

pleasantries	_____	absence	_____
consolable	_____	gorgeous	_____
sufficient	_____	sufficiency	_____
entrance	_____	reliable	_____
prevention	_____	revolution	_____
persistence	_____	convene	_____
partial	_____	convention	_____
brilliant	_____	moment	_____
brilliance	_____	momentous	_____
resident	_____	courageous	_____
debatable	_____	courage	_____
vibration	_____	convenient	_____
traveler	_____	difference	_____
violent	_____	vengeance	_____
improvise	_____	architect	_____
December	_____	April	_____
frequently	_____	thoughtful	_____
tasting	_____	athletic	_____
nationality	_____	national	_____
electricity	_____	electric	_____
confusion	_____	unable	_____
brother	_____	circus	_____

incompletion _____   imbalance _____

contender _____   committee _____

impossible _____   abundant _____

affair _____   suspicion _____

companion _____   bicycle _____

amusement _____   assertion _____

syllable _____   critical _____

empathy _____   musician _____

EXERCISE 22-X: WHAT'S THE WORD?

Identify the following words.

/fɑnɪks/	/ɛndʒɔɪ/	/stæljən/	/əhɛd/
/glænsɪŋ/	/maɪsɛlf/	/strɛŋθən/	/tæŋgo/
/mɛdʒɚ/	/kampaʊnd/	/klaɪmət/	/jɛlo/
/mɛʒɚ/	/æmniʒə/	/valjum/	/feməs/
/junjən/	/pɔɪzən/	/sɚvaɪvɚ/	/lɔfʊl/
/jɛstɚde/	/kənɛkʃən/	/trɛʒɚ/	/əwe/
/dʒunjɚ/	/tʃɔklət/	/pəluʃən/	/lʌvlɪ/
/bijand/	/lɛŋθən/	/onɚʃɪp/	/madəl/
/fɪŋgɚz/	/æθlit/	/əkrɔs/	/aʊtɚ/
/titʃɚ/	/flaʊwɚ/	/tɛləfon/	/ɔfən/
/ənfæsən/	/rɪtən/	/kwotə/	/ʃælo/
/sɛntɚ/	/pæsəfaɪ/	/dɪskwɔləfaɪd/	/klazət/
/ʃustrɪŋ/	/daɪnəsɔɚ/	/kəmpæʃən/	/læftɚ/
/junəvɚsətɪ/	/lɪkwəd/	/æŋgwɪʃ/	/bænded/

Appendix

The International Phonetic Alphabet, Diacritics, and Extended IPA Symbols for Disordered Speech

THE INTERNATIONAL PHONETIC ALPHABET (revised to 2005)

CONSONANTS (PULMONIC) © 2005 IPA

	Bilabial	Labiodental	Dental	Alveolar	Postalveolar	Retroflex	Palatal	Velar	Uvular	Pharyngeal	Glottal
Plosive	p b			t d		ʈ ɖ	c ɟ	k g	q ɢ		ʔ
Nasal	m	ɱ		n		ɳ	ɲ	ŋ	N		
Trill	B			r					R		
Tap or Flap		ⱱ		ɾ		ɽ					
Fricative	ɸ β	f v	θ ð	s z	ʃ ʒ	ʂ ʐ	ç ʝ	x ɣ	χ ʁ	ħ ʕ	h ɦ
Lateral fricative				ɬ ɮ							
Approximant		ʋ		ɹ		ɻ	j	ɰ			
Lateral approximant				l		ɭ	ʎ	L			

Where symbols appear in pairs, the one to the right represents a voiced consonant. Shaded areas denote articulations judged impossible.

CONSONANTS (NON-PULMONIC)

Clicks		Voiced implosives		Ejectives	
ʘ	Bilabial	ɓ	Bilabial	ʼ	Examples:
ǀ	Dental	ɗ	Dental/alveolar	pʼ	Bilabial
ǃ	(Post)alveolar	ʄ	Palatal	tʼ	Dental/alveolar
ǂ	Palatoalveolar	ɠ	Velar	kʼ	Velar
ǁ	Alveolar lateral	ʛ	Uvular	sʼ	Alveolar fricative

OTHER SYMBOLS

ʍ	Voiceless labial-velar fricative
w	Voiced labial-velar approximant
ɥ	Voiced labial-palatal approximant
ʜ	Voiceless epiglottal fricative
ʢ	Voiced epiglottal fricative
ʡ	Epiglottal plosive

ɕ ʑ	Alveolo-palatal fricatives
ɺ	Voiced alveolar lateral flap
ɧ	Simultaneous ʃ and x

Affricates and double articulations can be represented by two symbols joined by a tie bar if necessary.   k͡p t͡s

VOWELS

Front   Central   Back

Close i • y —————— ɨ • ʉ —————— ɯ • u
ɪ ʏ   ʊ
Close-mid e • ø ——— ɘ • ɵ ——— ɤ • o
ə
Open-mid ɛ • œ — ɜ • ɞ — ʌ • ɔ
æ
ɐ
Open a • ɶ ————— ɑ • ɒ

Where symbols appear in pairs, the one to the right represents a rounded vowel.

SUPRASEGMENTALS

ˈ	Primary stress
ˌ	Secondary stress ˌfoʊnəˈtɪʃən
ː	Long eː
ˑ	Half-long eˑ
˘	Extra-short ĕ
ǀ	Minor (foot) group
‖	Major (intonation) group
.	Syllable break ɹi.ækt
‿	Linking (absence of a break)

TONES AND WORD ACCENTS

LEVEL			CONTOUR		
e̋ or	˥	Extra high	ě or	˩˥	Rising
é	˦	High	ê	˥˩	Falling
ē	˧	Mid	e᷄	˧˥	High rising
è	˨	Low	e᷆	˩˧	Low rising
ȅ	˩	Extra low	e᷅	˧˩˧	Rising-falling
↓		Downstep	↗		Global rise
↑		Upstep	↘		Global fall

DIACRITICS   Diacritics may be placed above a symbol with a descender, e.g. ŋ̊

̥	Voiceless	n̥ d̥	̤	Breathy voiced	b̤ a̤	̪	Dental	t̪ d̪
̬	Voiced	s̬ t̬	̰	Creaky voiced	b̰ a̰	̺	Apical	t̺ d̺
ʰ	Aspirated	tʰ dʰ	̼	Linguolabial	t̼ d̼	̻	Laminal	t̻ d̻
̹	More rounded	ɔ̹	ʷ	Labialized	tʷ dʷ	̃	Nasalized	ẽ
̜	Less rounded	ɔ̜	ʲ	Palatalized	tʲ dʲ	ⁿ	Nasal release	dⁿ
̟	Advanced	u̟	ˠ	Velarized	tˠ dˠ	ˡ	Lateral release	dˡ
̠	Retracted	e̠	ˤ	Pharyngealized	tˤ dˤ	̚	No audible release	d̚
̈	Centralized	ë	̴	Velarized or pharyngealized	ɫ			
̽	Mid-centralized	e̽	̝	Raised	e̝	(ɹ̝ = voiced alveolar fricative)		
̩	Syllabic	n̩	̞	Lowered	e̞	(β̞ = voiced bilabial approximant)		
̯	Non-syllabic	e̯	̘	Advanced Tongue Root	e̘			
˞	Rhoticity	ɚ a˞	̙	Retracted Tongue Root	e̙			

Source: From International Phonetic Association, Department of Theoretical and Applied Linguistics, School of English, Aristotle University of Thessaloniki, Thessaloniki 54124, Greece.

NOTE: The International Phonetic Alphabet may be freely copied on condition that acknowledgment is made to the International Phonetic Association.

229

DIACRITICS   Diacritics may be placed above a symbol with a descender, e.g. ŋ̊

̥	Voiceless	n̥ d̥	̤	Breathy voiced	b̤ a̤	̪	Dental	t̪ d̪
̬	Voiced	s̬ t̬	̰	Creaky voiced	b̰ a̰	̺	Apical	t̺ d̺
ʰ	Aspirated	tʰ dʰ	̼	Linguolabial	t̼ d̼	̻	Laminal	t̻ d̻
̹	More rounded	ɔ̹	ʷ	Labialized	tʷ dʷ	̃	Nasalized	ẽ
̜	Less rounded	ɔ̜	ʲ	Palatalized	tʲ dʲ	ⁿ	Nasal release	dⁿ
̟	Advanced	u̟	ˠ	Velarized	tˠ dˠ	ˡ	Lateral release	dˡ
̠	Retracted	e̠	ˤ	Pharyngealized	tˤ dˤ	̚	No audible release	d̚
̈	Centralized	ë	̴	Velarized or pharyngealized	ɫ			
̽	Mid-centralized	e̽	̝	Raised	e̝	(ɹ̝ = voiced alveolar fricative)		
̩	Syllabic	n̩	̞	Lowered	e̞	(β̞ = voiced bilabial approximant)		
̯	Non-syllabic	e̯	̘	Advanced Tongue Root	e̘			
˞	Rhoticity	ɚ a˞	̙	Retracted Tongue Root	e̙			

Source: From International Phonetic Association, Department of Theoretical and Applied Linguistics, School of English, Aristotle University of Thessaloniki, Thessaloniki 54124, Greece.

Note: The International Phonetic Alphabet may be freely copied on condition that acknowledgment is made to the International Phonetic Association.

extIPA SYMBOLS FOR DISORDERED SPEECH
(Revised to 2002)

CONSONANTS (other than on the IPA Chart)

	bilabial	labiodental	dentolabial	labioalv.	linguolabial	interdental	bidental	alveolar	velar	velophar.
Plosive		p̪ b̪	p̄ b̄	p̺ b̺	t̼ d̼	t̪ d̪				
Nasal			m̄	m̠	n̼	n̪				
Trill					r̼	r̪				
Fricative median			f̄ v̄	f̠ v̠	θ̼ ð̼	θ̪ ð̪	h̪ ɦ̪			f̝ŋ
Fricative lateral+median								ʪ ʫ		
Fricative nareal	m̃								ñ	ŋ̃
Percussive	w̩ w̩						ᴴ			
Approximant lateral					l̼	l̪				

Where symbols appear in pairs, the one to the right represents a voiced consonant. Shaded areas denote articulations judged impossible.

DIACRITICS

↔	labial spreading	s̲↔	"	strong articulation	f̬	˚	denasal	m̃
͢	dentolabial	v̄	˺	weak articulation	v̬	˷	nasal escape	ṽ
͞	interdental/bidental	n̪	\	reiterated articulation	p\p\p	≋	velopharyngeal friction	š
͟	alveolar	t̲	ˏ	whistled articulation	s̟	↓	ingressive airflow	p↓
͜	linguolabial	d̼	→	sliding articulation	θs̲	↑	egressive airflow	!↑

CONNECTED SPEECH

(.)	short pause
(..)	medium pause
(...)	long pause
f	loud speech [{f laʊd f}]
ff	louder speech [{ff laʊdɚ ff}]
p	quiet speech [{p kwaɪət p}]
pp	quieter speech [{pp kwaɪətɚ pp}]
allegro	fast speech [{allegro fɑst allegro}]
lento	slow speech [{lento sloʊ lento}]
crescendo, ralentando, etc. may also be used	

VOICING

ˬ	pre-voicing	ˬz
ˬ	post-voicing	zˬ
(̬)	partial devoicing	z̦
(̬	initial partial devoicing	z̦
̬)	final partial devoicing	z̦
(̭	partial voicing	s̬
̭	initial partial voicing	s̬
̭)	final partial voicing	s̬
꞊	unaspirated	p꞊
h	pre-aspiration	ʰp

OTHERS

(◌̄), (C̄)	indeterminate sound, consonant	(( ))	extraneous noise	((2 sylls))
(V̄), (P̄l̄.v̄l̄s̄)	indeterminate vowel, voiceless plosive, etc.	¡	sublaminal lower alveolar percussive click	
(N̄), (v̄)	indeterminate nasal, probably [v], etc.	‼	alveolar and sublaminal clicks (cluck-click)	
( )	silent articulation (ʃ), (m)	*	sound with no available symbol	

© ICPLA 2002

Source: From International Phonetic Association, Department of Theoretical and Applied Linguistics, School of English, Aristotle University of Thessaloniki, Thessaloniki 54124, Greece.

Note: The International Phonetic Alphabet may be freely copied on condition that acknowledgment is made to the International Phonetic Association.

References

Ash, S., Boberg, C., & Labov, W. (1997). A national map of the regional dialects of American English. Linguistic geography of the mainland United States. Retrieved from http://www.evolpub.com/Americandialects/AmDialMap.html

Ash, S., Boberg, C., & Labov, W. (1997). North American English dialects, based on pronunciation patterns. Retrieved from http://aschmann.net/AmEng/

Avery, P., & Ehrlich, S. (1992). *Teaching American English pronunciation.* Oxford, United Kingdom: Oxford University Press.

Baer, D., Invernizzi, M., Templeton, S., & Johnston, F. (2000). *Words their way* (2nd ed.). Upper Saddle River, NJ: Pearson Education.

Barwick, J., & Barwick, J. (1999). *The spelling skills handbook for the word wise.* York, ME: Stenhouse Publishers.

Bauman-Waengler, J. (2008). *Articulatory and phonological impairments: A clinical focus* (3rd ed.). Boston, MA: Pearson Education.

Bernthal, J. E., & Bankson, N. W. (2004). *Articulation and phonological disorders* (5th ed.). Boston, MA: Pearson Education.

Blockcolsky, V. (1990). *Book of words.* Austin, TX: Pro-Ed.

Blockcolsky, V., Frazer, J., & Frazer, J. (1987). *40,000 selected words.* Tucson, AZ: Communication Skill Builders.

Celce-Murcia, M., Brinton, D., & Goodwin, J. (1996). *Teaching pronunciation.* New York, NY: Cambridge University Press.

Edwards, H. T. (1992). *Applied phonetics: The sounds of American English* (3rd ed.). Clifton Park, NY: Thomson Delmar Learning.

Eisenson, J. (1979). *Voice and diction* (4th ed.). New York, NY: Macmillan Publishing.

Fry, E., & Kress, J. (2006). *The reading teacher's book of lists* (5th ed.). San Francisco, CA: Jossey-Bass.

Ganske, K. (2000). *Word journeys.* New York, NY: Guilford Press.

Ganske, K. (2008). *Mindful of words.* New York, NY: Guilford Press.

Garr-Nunn, P., & Lynn, J. (2004). *Calvert's descriptive phonetics* (3rd ed.). New York, NY: Thieme Publishers.

Goldstein, B. (2000). *Cultural and linguistic diversity resource guide for speech-language pathologists.* San Diego, CA: Delmar Learning.

Henry, M. (2003). *Unlocking literacy.* Baltimore, MD: Paul H. Brookes Publishing.

Labov, W. (1996). The organization of dialect diversity in North America. University of Pennsylvania. Retrieved from http://www.ling.upenn.edu/phono_atlas/ICSLP4.html#Heading2

Labov, W., Ash, S. & Boberg, C. (1997). A national map of the regional dialects of American English. Retrieved from http://www.ling.upenn.edu/phono_atlas/NationalMap/NationalMap.html#Heading3

Labov, W., Ash, S., & Boberg, C. (2006). *The atlas of North American English: Phonetics, phonology, and sound change.* Berlin, Germany: Walter de Gruyter GmbH & Co. Retrieved from http://www.atlas.mouton-content.com.proxy.lib.ilstu.edu/

Ladefoged, P. (1993). *A course in phonetics* (3rd ed.). Fort Worth, TX: Harcourt Brace Jovanovich College Publishers.

Western Washington University. (n.d.). *Linguistics 201: The dialects of American English.* Retrieved from http://pandora.cii.wwu.edu/vajda/ling201/test3materials/AmericanDialects.htm

Mackay, I. (1987). *Phonetics: The science of speech production* (2nd ed.). Boston, MA: Allyn & Bacon.

Mayer, L. (2004). *Fundamentals of voice and articulation* (13th ed.). Boston, MA: McGraw-Hill.

Mendoza-Denton, N., Hendricks, S., & Kennedy, R. (2001). *Varieties of English.* Retrieved from http://www.ic.arizona.edu/~lsp/main.html

Moats, L. (1995). *Spelling: Development, disability, and instruction.* Baltimore, MD: York Press.

Moats, L. (2000). *Speech to print: Language essentials for teachers.* Baltimore, MD: Paul H. Brookes Publishing.

Modisett, N., & Luter, J. (1988). *Speaking clearly: The basics of voice and articulation* (3rd ed.). Edina, MN: Burgess Publishing.

Owens, R. E. (2008). *Language development: An introduction* (7th ed.). Boston, MA: Pearson Education.

Nye, C. (1999). *Target word resource for speech-language pathologists.* Austin, TX: Pro-Ed.

Phenix, J. (2003). *The spelling teacher's book of lists* (2nd ed.). Portland, ME: Stenhouse.

Roseberry-McKibbin, C. (2002). *Multicultural students with special language needs: Practical strategies for assessment and intervention.* Oceanside, CA: Academic Communication Associates.

Shriberg, L., & Kent, R. (2003). *Clinical phonetics* (3rd ed.). Boston, MA: Allyn & Bacon

Secord, W., Boyce, S., Fox, R., Donohue, J., & Shine, R. (2007). *Eliciting sounds: Techniques and strategies for clinicians* (2nd ed). Clifton Park, NY: Delmar Cengage Learning.

Singh, S., & Singh, K. (2006). *Phonetics: Principles and practice* (3rd ed.). San Diego, CA: Plural Publishing.

Small, L. (2012). *Fundamentals of phonetics* (3rd ed.). Boston, MA: Pearson.

VanRiper, C., & Smith, D. (1979). *An introduction to general American phonetics* (3rd ed.). Prospect Heights, IL: Waveland Press.

Wolfram, W. (1991). *Dialects and American English.* Englewood Cliffs, NJ: Prentice Hall.

Glossary

accent   the specific way individuals pronounce words based on a national or regional tendency; the influence of sounds from one's first language when producing a second language.

affricate   a manner of articulation; sounds that are created by a stop closure at the place of articulation followed by a fricative release.

allograph   the different spellings for each sound in our language. For example, the /f/ sound can be spelled with an *f*, *ph*, *ff*, *gh*, *lf*; the /o/ sound (i.e., *boat*) can be spelled with a silent *e*, an *o*, or with the vowel digraphs *oe*, *oa*, *ow*, *ou*, and *eau*.

allophone/allophonic variations   the different pronunciations of a particular phoneme that do not change the meaning of the word, often caused by the position of the sound in a word.

alveolar   a place of articulation; sounds that are produced by bringing the tongue tip close to the alveolar ridge.

approximants   sounds that are made by the articulators approaching each other, but not to the extent that turbulence is produced; oral sonorants (liquids and glides).

articulation   the actions of the speech organs (i.e., lips, teeth, tongue, jaw, etc.) in the production of speech sounds.

articulators   anatomical features (i.e., lips, front teeth, lower jaw, tongue, or the velum) that close the vocal tract in some way by interfering with, obstructing, or modifying the outgoing breath stream to produce different sounds.

articulatory phonetics   a branch of phonetics that examines the production features of speech sounds and categorizes/classifies them according to specific parameters in the effort to describe how sounds are formed.

aspiration   articulation accompanied by an audible puff of air; produced during the production of obstruents (i.e., in the release of a stop-plosive or affricate and during fricative production).

assimilation   The changes that a sound undergoes when influenced by its sound environment; often the result of coarticulation.

bilabial   a place of articulation; sounds that are produced with both lips.

closed syllable   any syllable ending with a consonant sound(s); these syllables have a coda.

coarticulation   the process of individual phonemes overlapping each other during the production of syllables, words, phrases, and sentences.

coda   the consonant(s) that follow the vowel in a syllable.

cognates   those consonants that share the same place and manner, but differ in voicing.

complex syllable   A syllable that contains at least one sequence.

consonants   speech sounds produced as a result of air encountering some constriction or obstruction when moving through the vocal tract; referred to as *closed* sounds.

dialect   any variety of a language that is shared by a group of speakers.

digraph   two letters that stand for one sound (either a consonant or vowel), for example, *sh*, *th*, *ch*, are common digraphs in the English language.

diphthong   type of vowel sound that is created by a rapid blending of two separate vowels sounds that create one sound; the quality of a diphthong changes from beginning to end.

fricative   a manner of articulation; sounds that are produced with a narrow constriction through which air escapes with continuous noise.

glide   a manner of articulation; sounds that are characterized by a gliding motion of the articulators from a partly constricted state to a more open state

glottal   a place of articulation; sounds that are made at the level of the glottis.

grapheme   a letter or group of letters used to represent one sound.

idiolect   the uniqueness of our speech caused by our vocal tract anatomy as well as our personal experiences (e.g., travel, education); comprised of distinct language characteristics, including rate of speech, stress and intonation patterns, vocal quality, as well as use of vocabulary, and pronunciations.

interdental   a place of articulation; sounds that are made by bringing the tongue tip between the teeth.

intervocalic consonants   a position of consonants in words; those consonants that are between vowels in a word with two or more syllables (e.g., *rubber*: the /b/ is in the intervocalic position).

labiodental   a place of articulation; sounds that are produced by bringing the upper teeth to the bottom lip.

liquid   a manner of articulation; vowel-like consonants in which voicing energy passes through a vocal tract that is constricted only somewhat more than for vowels.

manner of articulation   describes how the articulators control the flow of air to form a sound.

minimal pair   a pair of words that differ by one phoneme (e.g., bat–cat).

monophthong   considered "pure" vowels; their production is qualitatively the same from beginning to end.

morphophonemic   changes in pronunciation that occur when bound morphemes are added to a word.

nasal   a manner of articulation; consonants that are produced with a complete oral closure at the place of articulation (like a stop), but with an open velopharynx, so that voicing energy travels out through the nose; there are only three nasal consonants in the English phonology system.

nucleus   the vowel sound within a syllable; also known as the peak of the syllable.

obstruents   those consonants in manner classes that are produced with greater constriction along the vocal tract; the obstruent consonants include stop-plosives, fricatives, and affricates.

off-glide   the second vowel in a diphthong that is weaker and shorter in duration than the first vowel.

on-glide   the first vowel in a diphthong that is acoustically more prominent and longer in duration than the second vowel.

onset   the consonant(s) that precede the vowel in a syllable.

open syllable   any syllable that ends with a vowel sound; no coda is present.

orthographic awareness   what an individual knows about a language's writing system.

orthography   a language's writing (spelling) system, which includes symbol-sound associations and rules for combining those symbols.

palatal   a place of articulation; sounds that are made by bringing the tongue body near the hard palate.

peak   the part of the syllable that has the strongest acoustic energy (i.e. vowel); also known as the vowel nucleus.

perception   the manner in which sounds are heard.

phone   a speech sound.

phoneme   when a speech sound is used to differentiate meaning in words.

phonemic awareness   an individual's awareness and understanding of individual sounds in a word.

phonetics   an area that focuses on how speech sounds are produced.

phonogram   the written representation of the rime; a word family (e.g., -at).

phonological awareness   an individual's ability to attend to the sound structure of the language apart from meaning.

phonology   the sound system of a language consisting of the sounds of a given language, all their variations, and the rules for combining those sounds.

phonotactic constraints   the allowable combinations of sounds in a particular language.

place of articulation   refers to where, along the vocal tract, the sound is made.

postvocalic consonants   those consonants (singleton or sequence) that come after the vowel in a syllable or word.

prevocalic consonants   those consonants (singleton or sequence) that come before the vowel in a syllable or word.

rhotic diphthong   created when *r* follows a vowel in the same syllable (a.k.a. controlled-r diphthong, "r-colored" vowel).

rime   the part of the syllable that includes the vowel (nucleus/peak) and the consonants that follow it (coda); used to create rhymes.

schwar   the symbol /ɚ/ used to represent the "er" sound in an unstressed syllable.

schwa   the symbol /ə/ used to represent the "uh" sound in an unstressed syllable.

sequence, consonant   adjacent consonants within a word that retain their identity during production (e.g., in the word *stops*, "st" and "ps" are sequences).

simple syllable   a syllable that contains only a vowel or a vowel with singleton consonants.

singleton, consonant   consonants that are by themselves in a word (e.g., in the word *bat*, "b" and "t" are consonant singletons).

sonorants   those consonants in manner classes that are produced with less obstruction in the vocal tract; the sonorant consonants include liquids, glides, and nasals.

sonority   characteristic of a sound that refers to its loudness relative to other sounds similar in length, stress, and pitch.

stop-plosive   a manner of articulation; consonant sounds formed by a complete closure of the vocal tract (stop) at the place of articulation, so that airflow ceases temporarily and air pressure builds up behind the point of closure. When the impounded air is released, it produces a small explosion of escaping air (plosive).

syllable   a unit of pronunciation consisting of a vowel sound alone or a vowel sound with the consonants that precede or follow it.

transcription   sound-by-sound interpretation of speech using the symbols in the IPA.

triphthong   a diphthong combined with the postvocalic /r/; /aɪɚ/ and /aʊɚ/ are triphthongs.

velar   place of articulation; sounds that are produced by bringing the back of the tongue close to the soft palate.

voiced   refers to a sound that is produced with vocal fold vibration.

voiceless   refers to a sound that is produced without vocal fold vibration.

voicing   determined by whether or not the vocal folds are vibrating during sound production.

vowel quadrilateral   a visual used to aid in the understanding of how vowels are classified; depicts two features: tongue advancement and tongue height.

vowels   speech sounds that are produced as a result of air moving through a relatively *open* vocal tract and contain the most acoustic energy.

Answer Key

CHAPTER 1

Exercise 1-A: happy 2; catastrophe 4; sequential 3; alphabet 3; alligator 4; boys 1; retroactive 4; appropriate 4; introduce 3; imagination 5; ditches 2; oncoming 3; psychological 5; include 2; overwhelming 4; grounded 2; computer 3; spindle 2; unspeakable 4; spilled 1; unilateral 5

Exercise 1-B

Word	Prevocalic	Intervocalic	Postvocalic
me	m		
up			p
not	n		t
vase	v		s
skip	sk		p
bend	b		nd
helps	h		lps
wagon	w	g	n
basket	b	sk	t
consonants	c	ns, n	nts

Exercise 1-C

Word	Onset	Coda
goat	g	t
path	p	th
snake	sn	k
try	tr	–
word	w	d
bulb	b	lb
eight	–	t
rips	r	ps
frost	fr	st
book	b	k
own	–	n
thread	thr	d
left	l	ft
if	–	f
be	b	–

Exercise 1-D: picks, fox; noise, nose; mouth, bath; comb, some; eyes, cheese; cape, deep; feud, mud; vague, dog; sponge, arrange; slept, hoped; laugh, leaf; licorice, mustache; hunks, sphinx; talked, strict; whisk, flask

Exercise 1-E: thaw, thumb; chorus, kite; horse, who; sure, shot; cube, cure; there, this; suede, sweat; one, world; cheese, chief; join, gel; quick, choir; king, court; skirt, scoop; you, use; Xerox, zoo

Exercise 1-F

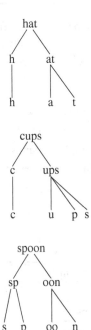

Exercise 1-G

rug, bug, mug, hug	ug	bell, well, yell	ell
back, sack, track	ack	cry, fly, by, my	y
made, paid, grade	ade/aid	care, hair, pear	air
does, buzz, was	uzz	done, won, bun	un
fur, blur, stir	ur	dog, hog, frog, log	og

Exercise 1-H

Word	Vowel Nucleus/Peak	Onset	Coda	Rime
knot	o	kn	t	ot
look	oo	l	k	ook
moist	oi	m	st	oist
sound	ou	s	nd	ound
laugh	au	l	gh	augh
frown	ow	fr	n	own
joy	oy	j	–	oy
gift	i	g	ft	ift
odd	o	–	dd	odd

Word	Vowel Nucleus/Peak	Onset	Coda	Rime
one	o	(w)	n	uhn
twice	i	tw	c(e)	ice
sky	y	sk	–	y
nest	e	n	st	est

Exercise 1-I: sit C; hope C; can C; off C; pick C; eye O; buzz C; twig C; am C; call C; row O; wash C; tray O; grass C; knew O; sing C; cough C; though O

Exercise 1-J

comb	CVC	Simple	truck	CC VC	Complex
town	CVC	Simple	most	CV CC	Complex
slip	CC VC	Complex	lamps	CV CCC	Complex
this	CVC	Simple	sign	CVC	Simple

CHAPTER 2
Exercise 2-A

Word	Sequence	Digraph
the	–	th
chains	ns	ch
swing	sw	ng
throat	thr	th
chilled	lled (ld)	ch
scold	sc, ld	–
through	thr	th
shrink	shr, nk	sh
rough	–	gh
scratch	scr	ch
mix	x (ks)	–
walked	ked (kt)	–
thumb	–	th
phone	–	ph
slither	sl	th
quick	qu	ck

CHAPTER 3
Exercise 3-A

Group #1: wild 4; put 3; fist 4; has 3; elf 3; cabin 5; stem 4; trip 4; log 3; busy 4; wag 3; grand 5; wasp 4; jump 4; gift 4

Group #2: could 3; hymn 3; scene 3; listen 5; who 2; debt 3; knock 3; answer 4; thyme 3; walk 3; gnaw 2; known 3; castle 5 (4); lamb 3; calf 3; might 3; wrote 3; align 4

Group #3: laugh 3; month 4; whole 3; with 3; phone 3; wish 3; chord 3; thigh 2; tough 3; swing 4; though 2; thing 3; showed 3; chime 3; choose 3

Group #4: thumb 3; six 4; branch 5; shrink 5; chalk 3; thought 3; threw 3; fright 4; should 3; ghost 4; soften 5; nation 5; autumn 4; pseudo 4; bridge 4; honest 5; breathe 4; catcher 4

Group #5: meant 4; obey 3; aim 2; said 3; plaid 4; blood 4; guide 3; mauve 3; cruised 5; niece 3; weigh 2; you've 3; snow 3; young 3; crowd 4; coins 4; joy 2; mouse 3

Challenge Group: mix 4; quote 4; cute 4; music 6; exit 5; view 3; quipped 5; amusing 7; anguish 6

Exercise 3-B

Word 1			Word 2	
stop	CCVC	>	ship	CVC
jog	CVC	=	badge	CVC
back	CVC	<	milk	CVCC
ouch	VC	=	itch	VC
toad	CVC	>	toe	CV
bees	CVC	>	eyes	VC
all	CV	<	ox	VCC
hear	CV	=	here	CV
adult	VCVCC	>	away	VCV
bouquet	CVCV	=	mother	CVCV
night	CVC	=	weight	CVC
who	CV	=	how	CV
came	CVC	<	crane	CCVC
missed	CVCC	=	mist	CVCC

Exercise 3-C

Word	My Answer	Box	C & V	Your Answer
pill	4	p i ll	CVC	3
speech	5	s p ee ch	CCVC	4
ships	5	sh i p s	CVCC	4
pocket	6	p o ck e t	CVCVC	5
foolish	5	f oo l i sh	CVCVC	—
blurred	4	b l urr e d	CCVC	—
itch	3	i t ch	VC	2

Word	My Answer	Box	C & V	Your Answer
squirt	4	s qu i r t	CCCVC	5
highlights	6	h igh l igh t s	CVCVCC	—
eight	3	e i gh t	VC	2
honest	5	h o n e s t	VCVCC	—
thought	4	t h ou gh t	CVC	3
trophy	5	t r o ph y	CCVCV	—
stayed	5	s t ay ed	CCVC	4

CHAPTER 4

Exercise 4-A

2	3	4	5
belong	marvelous	kilometer	denominator
rhythm	commotion	community	abbreviated
athlete	atmosphere	accompany	anthropology
excused	accident	retrospective	procrastination
crisis	quintuplet	legislature	organization
preview	companion	presidential	asymmetrical
	maneuver	recreation	contamination
	addition	conversation	
	another	spectacular	
	intrusion	communism	
	settlement	mathematician	
	principle	reliable	
	collection		

Exercise 4-B

Word	Onset	Coda	New Word	Permissible?
dock	d	ck	cod	**Yes** / No
sing	s	ng	ngis	Yes / **No**
beige	b	ge (zh)	zhabe	Yes / **No**
step	st	p	pest	**Yes** / No
tubs	t	bs	bsut	Yes / **No**
jumped	j	mpt	mptuj	Yes / **No**
grass	gr	ss	sagr	Yes / **No**
mask	m	sk	skam	**Yes** / No
toads	t	ds	dsoat	Yes / **No**
wagged	w	gged	gdaw	Yes / **No**
twice	tw	ce	sitw	Yes / **No**
land	l	nd	ndal	Yes / **No**

Exercise 4-C

f oo d 3; ough t 2 ; c (y) u te 4; s t ore 3;
q u ee n 4; w a t er 4; ch ew 2; c a lf 3; t e n se 4;
wh i ch 3; ch ur ch 3; s u g ar 4; s ure 2; f a ng 3;
th a n k 4; b o x s 4; s o ck s 4; m igh t 3;
l oo se 3; kn ow n 3; t r a ck 4; l o se 3; m o th er 4;
b ir th d ay 5; r ow b oa t 5; c ou gh 3; th i ck 3

Exercise 4-D

Word 1			Word 2	
comb	CVC	>	itch	VC
align	VCVC	<	aghast	VCVCC
guys	CVC	=	guide	CVC
fright	CCVC	<	friend	CCVCC
quote	CCVC	=	quit	CCVC
rhymes	CVCC	<	shrimp	CCVCC
there	CV	<	once	CVCC
coughed	CVCC	<	glasses	CCVCVC
chrome	CCVC	>	charge	CVC
brown	CCVC	=	brain	CCVC
glisten	CCVCVC	>	ocean	VCVC
tighter	CVCV	<	brother	CCVCV

Exercise 4-E: sick, kiss; nose, zone; enough, funny; foe, oaf; chip, pitch; nuts, stun; ice, sigh; scope, pokes; light, tile; Knicks, skin; peace, seep; gave, vague; might, time; knack, can; teach, cheat

Exercise 4-F

2	3	4	5	6
s aw	c l ay	f l oo d	s i l v er	s t in k s
r ow	ch ee se	m i l x /mɪks/	s p o k es	s w i mm ing
th ough	h a l f	v oi c ed	c r e p t	b a n a n a
th y	th r ew	g r a ph	s c r a m	f r o z en
ch ew	h ou se	t w i g	m a ch i ne	n u m b er ed
kn ee	s l ow	w or k s	f umes /fjumz/	d i c t a te
j oy	ch ar ge	c l ute /kjut/	qu e s t	
		l o s t	qu o t a	
		ch a n ge	shr i m p	
		s u n k	s i l x th /sɪksə/	

2	3	4	5	6
			m‸i‸x‸ed /mikst/	
			c‸l‸a‸s‸p	

Exercise 4-G

No coda: how, far, joy, blow
No onset: all, honor, own, oh
Sequence: cups, quick, tossed
Consonant digraph: dishes, chief, moth, known
Simple syllables: comb, pitch, ice, shoes
Complex syllables: cups, quick, tossed
Three or fewer phonemes: know, play, who, hour, eye, where

Exercise 4-H: rime; vowel nucleus/peak; onset; coda

Exercise 4-I: open; complex; postvocalic; simple; intervocalic; closed; prevocalic

Exercise 4-J

False	There are more sounds than phonetic symbols.
True	The phonological system of a language consists not only of the specific sounds used in that language, but also the rules for combining those sounds.
True	There can be only one vowel sound in a syllable.
True	There are fewer graphemes than phonemes in the English language.
False	A syllable onset refers to a postvocalic consonant.
False	A consonant sequence refers to two graphemes that represent one sound.
True	There are more allographs for the sound /f/ than for /h/.
True	A syllable coda can be a consonant singleton or sequence.
True	When consonants are in a sequence, each consonant sound retains its identity during pronunciation.
True	All syllables contain a vowel.
False	Phonetics refers to the overlapping process of sounds when produced in words, phrases, or sentences.
False	Consonants are produced as a result of air moving through a relatively *open* vocal tract.
False	All syllables contain a coda.

True	Coarticulation may occur because of time; because connected speech occurs so rapidly, there is not enough time to hit the "targets" of each sound.
True	An accent refers to the influence of one's first language on the pronunciation of sounds of one's second language.
True	When sounds are modified during coarticulation, assimilation may result.

Exercise 4-K: sequence; grapheme; phonology; vowel; idiolect; allograph; phonotactic constraints; syllable; phonetics; phoneme; allophone; consonants; dialect; digraph; rime

CHAPTER 5

Exercise 5-A: eight, shade, change; tough, but, rough; patch, zap, calf; schwa, odd, tock; jeans, quiche, chief; sign, buy, wild; limb, quilt, gym; down, cow, howl; squad, swat, cot; full, hood, push; cheer, here, weird; talk, moss, ought; whose, cool, juice; mouth, shout, ground; cork shore, forge; loose, few, do; joy, boys, voice; though, growth, known; yes, etch, dense; most, comb, sold; stare, fair, bear; wolf, would, wool; said, guess, friend; laugh, quack, plaid; glow, moan, own; length, bread, bend; wound (vb), brown, chow; worst, swirl, hers; flood, rub, does; pick, big, ding; if, quiz, hymn; quartz, storm, corpse; sharp, chart, yarn; wound (n), moon, womb

CHAPTER 6

Exercise 6-A

Vowel #1	Vowel #2	Vowel #3	Vowel #4	Vowel #5
key	prince	they	let	stand
ease	fill	beige	guess	that
he's	big	change	said	have
chief	will	gaze	head	black
each	his	claim	help	hand
green	bridge	lay	bend	laugh

Exercise 6-B: /it/ eat; /bif/ beef; /wik/ week; /stil/ steal/ steel; /mi/ me; /pis/ peace; /kiz/ keys; /pliz/ please; /iz/ ease; /bin/ bean; /ski/ ski; /sniz/ sneeze; /hi/ he; /pli/ plea; /bist/ beast; /spik/ speak; /ni/ knee; /fri/ free; /grin/ green; /blid/ bleed

Exercise 6-C: east /ist/; geese /gis/; he's /hiz/; steam /stim/; beep /bip/; leaf /lif/; niece /nis/; street /strit/; zeal /zil/; tease

/tiz/; brief /brif/; freak /frik/; heave /hiv/; keep /kip/; need /nid/; grease /gris/

Exercise 6-D: /ɪn/ in; /wɪt/ wit; /rɪb/ rib; /kwɪk/ quick; /ɪz/ is; /stɪk/ stick; /mɪlk/ milk; /spɪl/ spill; /dɪg/ dig; /sɪks/ six; /grɪn/ grin; /lɪft/ lift; /fɪl/ fill; /trɪp/ trip; /klɪf/ cliff; /swɪm/ swim; /hɪz/ his; /gɪv/ give; /tɪpt/ tipped; /rɪns/ rinse

Exercise 6-E: dim /dɪm/; build /bɪld/; film /fɪlm/; skipped /skɪpt/; fizz /fɪz/; rip /rɪp/; slim /slɪm/; splint /splɪnt/; kiss /kɪs/; sick /sɪk/; strip /strɪp/; gift /gɪft/; pig /pɪg/; wilt /wɪlt/; limb /lɪm/; trimmed /trɪmd/

Exercise 6-F: /he/ hay; /med/ made; /kes/ case; /stret/ straight; /em/ aim; /nel/ nail; /fent/ faint; /ples/ place; /bek/ bake; /rest/ raced; /kle/ clay; /swed/ suede; /det/ date; /test/ taste; /sem/ same; /kwek/ quake; /kep/ cape; /rez/ raise; /gren/ grain; /bled/ blade

Exercise 6-G: ate /et/; lay /le/; wave /wev/; traced /trest/; fake /fek/; paid /ped/; praise /prez/; grapes /greps/; face /fes/; paste /pest/; flame /flem/; snake /snek/; game /gem/; paint /pent/; trade /tred/; sleigh /sle/

Exercise 6-H: /ɛnd/ end; /nɛk/ neck; /sɛnd/ send; /sɛns/ sense; /ɛg/ egg; /dɛnt/ dent; /fɛl/ fell; /gɛst/ guest/ guessed; /bɛl/ bell; /bɛst/ best; /stɛm/ stem; /wɛpt/ wept; /hɛn/ hen; /lɛs/ less; /fɛns/ fence; /spɛk/ speck; /gɛs/ guess; /hɛd/ head; /nɛlt/ knelt; /blɛd/ bled

Exercise 6-I: elf /ɛlf/; get /gɛt/; tense /tɛns/; beg /bɛg/; debt /dɛt/; lend /lɛnd/; spread /sprɛd/; spent /spɛnt/; desk /dɛsk/; kept /kɛpt/; friend /frɛnd/; stepped/stɛpt/; belt /bɛlt/; tell /tɛl/; meant /mɛnt/; cent /sɛnt/

Exercise 6-J: /æt/ at; /bæk/ back; /hænd/ hand; /træns/ trance; /mæp/ map; /pæs/ pass; /kræb/ crab; /læm/ lamb; /hæt/ hat; /kænt/ can't; /dæns/ dance; /snæp/ snap; /fæn/ fan; /plæd/ plaid; /læst/ last; /hæf/ half; /næg/ nag; /fækt/ fact; /krækt/ cracked; /wæks/ wax

Exercise 6-K: bag /bæg/; act /ækt/; has /hæz/; glad /glæd/; add /æd/; gas /gæs/; calf /kæf/; staff /stæf/; band /bænd/; have /hæv/; laugh /læf/; plan /plæn/; damp /dæmp/; fast /fæst/; van /væn/; flag /flæg/

CHAPTER 7

Exercise 7-A

Vowel #1	Vowel #2	Vowel #3	Vowel #4*	Vowel #5*
flew	could	no	ought	mom
room	pull	toe	dog	spa
group	wood	show	all	lock
shoot	foot	mold	caught	drop
fruit	put	road	claw	hot

Vowel #1	Vowel #2	Vowel #3	Vowel #4*	Vowel #5*
true	shook	oak	long	cot

* dependent upon your pronounciation

Exercise 7-B: /tun/ tune; /sup/ soup; /tub/ tube; /klu/ clue; /plum/ plume; /muv/ move; /bum/ boom; /gus/ goose; /kluz/ clues; /snuz/ snooze; /zu/ zoo; /lup/ loop; /ful/ fool; /grups/ groups; /spun/ spoon; /hu/ who; /blu/ blue; /gru/ grew; /skul/ school; /pruv/ prove

Exercise 7-C: boot /but/; room /rum/; goose /gus/; stoop /stup/; ooze /uz/; suit /sut/; two /tu/; spool /spul/; moose /mus/; soup /sup/; true /tru/; flute /flut/; food /fud/; soon /sun/; new /nu/; broom /brum/

Exercise 7-D: /fʊt/ foot; /wʊlf/ wolf; /wʊdz/ woods; /pʊt/ put; /lʊk/ look; /gʊd/ good; /fʊl/ full; /kʊks/ cooks; /hʊd/ hood; /stʊd/ stood; /kʊd/ could; /wʊd/ wood; /bʊk/ book; /kʊkt/ cooked; /brʊks/ brooks /rʊk/ rook;

Exercise 7-E: hook /hʊk/; bull /bʊl/; crook /krʊk/; pull /pʊl/; brook /brʊk/; books /bʊks/; took /tʊk/; would /wʊd/; cook /kʊk/; hoods /hʊdz/; wool /wʊl/; looked /lʊkt/

Exercise 7-F: /on/ own; /kom/ comb; /wok/ woke; /tost/ toast; /fom/ foam; /poz/ pose; /kloz/ clothes/close (vb); /rod/ road/rode; /bolz/ bowls; /bon/ bone; /hol/ hole/ whole; /spok/ spoke; /hop/ hope; /kold/ cold; /bost/ boast; /kwot/ quote; /zon/ zone; /roz/ rose; /krom/ chrome; /glob/ globe

Exercise 7-G: boat /bot/; goes /goz/; robe /rob/; grown /gron/; fold /fold/; loaf /lof/; nose /noz/; stove /stov/; home /hom/; froze /froz/; roll /rol/; phone /fon/; hose /hoz/; goal /gol/; glow /glo/; crow /kro/

Exercise 7-H: /rɔt/ wrought; /gɔz/ gauze; /kɔzd/ caused; /stɔk/ stalk; /ɔf/ off; /sɔft/ soft; /kɔf/ cough; /flɔz/ flaws; /bɔld/ bald; /dɔg/ dog; /tɔl/ tall; /sɔlt/ salt; /fɔl/ fall; /pɔ/ paw; /bɔs/ boss; /fɔls/ false; /lɔn/ lawn; /drɔ/ draw; /kɔt/ caught; /brɔt/ brought

Exercise 7-I: all /ɔl/; lost /lɔst/; pawn /pɔn/; straw /strɔ/; dawn /dɔn/; hawk /hɔk/; call /kɔl/; broad /brɔd/; fought /fɔt/; gone /gɔn/; called /kɔld/; fault /fɔlt/; haunt /hɔnt/; pause /pɔz/; fraud /frɔd/; scald /skɔld/

Exercise 7-J: /dat/ dot; /gab/ gob; /rak/ rock; /baks/ box; /mab/ mob; /spa/ spa; /spat/ spot; /pram/ prom; /ad/ odd; /gat/ got; /drap/ drop; /stamp/ stomp; /hap/ hop; /plap/ plop; /drapt/ dropped; /klak/ clock; /nad/ nod; /mam/ mom; /skwad/ squad; /bland/ blond

Exercise 7-K: bond /band/; tops /taps/; knocks /naks/; stopped /stapt/; hot /hat/; wasp /wasp/; swamp /swamp/; swap /swap/; pop /pap/; slob /slab/; clocks

/klaks/; plot /plat/; knot /nat/; stock /stak/; hopped /hapt/; fox /faks/

CHAPTER 8

Exercise 8-A

/ɛ/	/ʊ/	/ɑ/	all are lax vowels
/e/	/o/	/ɔ/	all are mid vowels
/u/	/o/	/ɔ/	all are back vowels and rounded vowels
/æ/	/ɑ/	/ɔ/	all are lax vowels
/ɛ/	/ɔ/	/ʊ/	all are lax vowels
/ʊ/	/o/	/u/	all are back vowels and rounded vowels
/i/	/e/	/u/	all are tense vowels
/æ/	/ɪ/	/ɛ/	all are lax vowels, unrounded vowels, and front vowels
/ɪ/	/ʊ/	/i/	all are high vowels
/ʊ/	/ɔ/	/ɑ/	all are lax vowels and back vowels

Exercise 8-B

Mid front tense unrounded	/e/	Mid back tense rounded	/o/
High front tense unrounded	/i/	Low back lax unrounded	/ɑ/
Mid front lax unrounded	/ɛ/	High back lax rounded	/ʊ/
Mid back lax rounded	/ɔ/	High back tense rounded	/u/
Low front lax unrounded	/æ/	High front lax unrounded	/ɪ/

Exercise 8-C

	Symbol	Word
"b" + high back tense rounded vowel + "t"	/u/	boot
high **front** tense **unrounded** vowel	/i/	beat
high **front lax unrounded** vowel	/ɪ/	bit
Mid front lax unrounded vowel	/ɛ/	bet
Mid **back** lax **rounded** vowel	/ɔ/	bought
Mid back **tense** rounded vowel	/o/	boat
Mid **front** tense **unrounded** vowel	/e/	bait
Low front **lax** unrounded vowel	/æ/	bat

Exercise 8-D

Word	Vowel Symbol	Tongue Height	Tongue Advancement	Tongue Tension	Lip Rounding
→ took	/ʊ/	high	back	lax	rounded
talk	/ɔ/	✓ (mid)			
tock	/ɑ/	✓ (low)			✓ (un-rounded)
tack	/æ/		✓ (front)		
take	/e/	✓ (mid)		✓ (tense)	
tick	/ɪ/	✓ (high)		✓ (lax)	

Word	Vowel Symbol	Tongue Height	Tongue Advancement	Tongue Tension	Lip Rounding
→ lad	/æ/	low	front	lax	unrounded
lead (verb)	/i/	✓ (high)		✓ (tense)	
lead (noun)	/ɛ/	✓ (mid)		✓ (lax)	
load	/o/		✓ (back)	✓ (tense)	✓ (rounded)
lid	/ɪ/	✓ (high)	✓ (front)	✓ (lax)	✓ (un-rounded)
laid	/e/	✓ (mid)		✓ (tense)	

Word	Vowel Symbol	Tongue Height	Tongue Advancement	Tongue Tension	Lip Rounding
→ hope	/o/	mid	back	tense	rounded
hip	/ɪ/	✓ (high)	✓ (front)	✓ (lax)	✓ (un-rounded)
hop	/ɑ/	✓ (low)	✓ (back)		
hoop	/u/	✓ (high)		✓ (tense)	✓ (rounded)
heap	/i/		✓ (front)		✓ (un-rounded)

Word	Vowel Symbol	Tongue Height	Tongue Advancement	Tongue Tension	Lip Rounding
→ bought	/ɔ/	mid	back	lax	rounded
boat	/o/			✓ (tense)	
bat	/æ/	✓ (low)	✓ (front)	✓ (lax)	✓ (unrounded)

Word	Vowel Symbol	Tongue Height	Tongue Advancement	Tongue Tension	Lip Rounding
bait	/e/	✓ (mid)		✓ (tense)	
bit	/ɪ/	✓ (high)		✓ (lax)	
boot	/u/		✓ (back)	✓ (tense)	✓ (rounded)
bet	/ɛ/	✓ (mid)	✓ (front)	✓ (lax)	✓ (unrounded)
beet	/i/	✓ (high)		✓ (tense)	

Exercise 8-E

"s" + mid front tense unrounded	/e/	say
"h" + high back tense rounded	/u/	who
High front lax unrounded + "t"	/ɪ/	it
Mid back lax rounded + "f"	/ɔ/	off
High front tense unrounded + "z"	/i/	ease
Mid back tense rounded + "n"	/o/	own
Low back lax unrounded + "k" + "s"	/ɑ/	ox
"l" + high back tense rounded + "p"	/u/	loop
"b" + mid back lax rounded + "s"	/ɔ/	boss
"p" + high front tense unrounded + "s"	/i/	peace
"ch" + mid back lax rounded + "k"	/ɔ/	chalk
"j" + low front lax unrounded + "m"	/æ/	jam
"w" + high front lax unrounded + "g"	/ɪ/	wig
"h" + high back lax rounded + "d"	/ʊ/	hood
"r" + high front tense unrounded + "ch"	/i/	reach
"b" + mid front tense unrounded + "zh"	/e/	beige
"t" + high back tense rounded + "th"	/u/	tooth
"sh" + high back lax rounded + "d"	/ʊ/	should
"k" + mid back lax rounded + "z"	/ɔ/	cause
"w" + low back lax unrounded + " ch"	/ɑ/	watch
"th" + "r" + mid back tense rounded	/o/	throw
"p" + mid front tense unrounded + "s" + "t"	/e/	paste
"p" + mid back tense rounded + "s" + "t"	/o/	post
"r" + high front lax unrounded + "s" + "k"	/ɪ/	risk
"s" + mid front lax unrounded + "n" + "s"	/ɛ/	sense

Exercise 8-F: rook /ʊ/; rack /æ/; wreck /ɛ/; wreak /i/; rake /e/; plaid /æ/; plod /ɑ/; played /e/; pled /ɛ/; plead /i/; soup /u/; sop /ɑ/; sip /ɪ/; seep /i/; soap /o/; John /ɑ/; gin /ɪ/; June /u/; jean /i/; Jane /e/; teal /i/; tall /ɔ/; tail /e/; till /ɪ/; tool /u/; cap /æ/; cape /e/; cope /o/; coop /u/;

keep /i/; sit /ɪ/; soot /ʊ/; seat /i/; sat /æ/; suit /u/; flew /u/; flowed /o/; flee /i/; flawed /ɔ/; fled /ɛ/

Exercise 8-G: /zu/ zoo; /pik/ peek; /læm/ lamb; /tɔs/ toss; /læf/ laugh; /gʊd/ good; /fud/ food; /nɑk/ knock; /hɪz/ his; /wæg/ wag; /wet/ wait; /lon/ loan; /mun/ moon; /dɛf/ deaf; /tep/ tape; /pɛg/ peg; /gɪv/ give; /pʊt/ put; /hom/ home; /lɔg/ log; /kon/ cone; /bɛts/ bets; /bruz/ bruise; /fɛns/ fence; /plænt/ plant; /rost/ roast; /ples/ place; /brum/ broom; /stræp/ strap; /fist/ feast

CHAPTER 9

Exercise 9-A: /dʌn/ done; /lʌk/ luck; /bʌg/ bug; /mʌd/ mud; /stʌd/ stud; /kʌps/ cups; /pʌk/ puck; /tʌn/ ton; /ʌs/ us; /stʌf/ stuff; /plʌm/ plum; /drʌm/ drum; /klʌk/ cluck; /sʌm/ some/sum; /lʌvd/ loved; /hʌnt/ hunt; /mʌg/ mug; /pʌls/ pulse

Exercise 9-B: bus /bʌs/; of /ʌv/; none /nʌn/; pup /pʌp/; won /wʌn/; dump /dʌmp/; plus /plʌs/; stuck /stʌk/; come /kʌm/; fuzz /fʌz/; dust /dʌst/; gulf /gʌlf/; lump /lʌmp/; punt /pʌnt/; rough /rʌf/

Exercise 9-C: /dɝt/ dirt; /gɝl/ girl; /lɝn/ learn; /wɝm/ worm; /stɝ/ stir; /kɝb/ curb; /pɝk/ perk; /tɝn/ turn; /sɝv/ serve; /skɝt/ skirt; /ɝn/ earn/urn; /bɝd/ bird; /vɝb/ verb; /hɝt/ hurt; /sɝ/ sir; /fɝst/ first; /kɝs/ curse; /nɝd/ nerd

Exercise 9-D: burn /bɝn/; her /hɝ/; work /wɝk/; slurp /slɝp/; clerk /klɝk/; purse /pɝs/; nurse /nɝs/; herb /ɝb/ or /hɝb/; burp /bɝp/; heard /hɝd/; burst /bɝst/; turf /tɝf/; swirl /swɝl/; term /tɝm/; world /wɝld/

Challenge Exercise 9-E: /mɝdɚ/ murder; /sɝkəs/ circus; /hʌndrəd/ hundred; /pʌzəl/ puzzle; /bɝglɚ/ burglar; /əlɝt/ alert; /bʌtən/ button; /mɝmɚ/ murmur; /əbʌv/ above; /dʌzən/ dozen; /fɝnəs/ furnace; /ʌndɚ/ under

CHAPTER 10

Exercise 10-A

Group A: rhyme, wind, mine, quite, eye, time, cycle, buys, tile, height
Group B: ouch, round, lounge, doubt, cow, cloud
Group C: join, enjoy, toys, choice, oil, voice, noise, soy
Extra words: *group, clue, laugh, caught, bridge, key.*
   (They are monophthongs).

Exercise 10-B

Word	Choice of Vowel Symbols
life	/aɪ/
house	/aʊ/
claim	vowel sound not given

Word	Choice of Vowel Symbols
loud	/aʊ/
soy	/ɔɪ/
plaid	vowel sound not given
beach	vowel sound not given
clown	/aʊ/
void	/ɔɪ/
head	vowel sound not given

Exercise 10-C: frown 4; shine 3; taupe 3; wife 3; moose 3; sound 4; poise 3; high 2; lounge 4; how 2; joy 2; chai 2; doubt 3; heard 3; voice 3
The 12 words that contained diphthongs: frown, shine, wife, sound, poise, high, lounge, how, joy, chai, doubt, voice.

Exercise 10-D: /bɔɪ/ boy; /waʊ/ wow; /aɪs/ ice; /taɪ/ tie /vɔɪs/; voice; /naʊ/ now; /daʊt/ doubt; /laɪf/ life; /laʊd/ loud; /spɔɪl/ spoil; /haʊs/ house; /kɔɪ/ coy; /kaɪt/ kite; /taʊn/ town; /twaɪs/ twice; /braʊn/ brown; /spaɪn/ spine; /faɪv/ five; /praɪz/ prize; /aʊl/ owl; /raʊnd/ round

Exercise 10-E: how /haʊ/; fry /fraɪ/; toy /tɔɪ/; sound /saʊnd/; time /taɪm/; noun /naʊn/; slide /slaɪd/; foil /fɔɪl/; coin /kɔɪn/; pounce /paʊns/; kind /kaɪnd/; down /daʊn/; line /laɪn/; trout /traʊt/; point /pɔɪnt/; spice /spaɪs/; cries /kraɪz/; proud /praʊd/; swipe /swaɪp/; moist /mɔɪst/; clown /klaʊn/

CHAPTER 11

Exercise 11-A
Group 1: barn, guard, heart, carve, charge
Group 2: here, deer, weary pierced, smeared
Group 3: sword, chore, hoarse, four, warm, poor*
Group 4: larynx, merit, where, share, dairy, bury, marry, bare
Group 5: sure*, tour, poor*, pure*
Group 6: tired, choir, wire
Group 7: (central vowel monophthong) flirt, burnt, pearl, sure*, herb, burn, pure

*dependent on your pronunciation.

Exercise 11-B: where /ɛɚ/; heart /ɑɚ/; fierce /ɪɚ/; pear /ɛɚ/; nurse vowel sound not given; here /ɪɚ/; they're /ɛɚ/; fourth /ɔɚ/; word vowel sound not given; arch /ɑɚ/

Exercise 11-C: /kɔɚk/ cork; /kɑɚt/ cart; /klɪɚ/ clear; /skwɛɚ/ square; /fɔɚs/ force; /fɑɚs/ farce; /tʊɚz/ tours; /skɛɚd/ scared; /gɑɚd/ guard; /dɪɚ/ deer/dear; /sɔɚ/ sore; /glɛɚ/ glare

Exercise 11-D: steer /stɪɚ/; store /stɔɚ/; stare /stɛɚ/; star /stɑɚ/; warm /wɔɚm/; beard /bɪɚd/; barn /bɑɚn/; heir /ɛɚ/; rare /rɛɚ/; fork /fɔɚk/; mare /mɛɚ/; park /pɑɚk/; tier /tɪɚ/; arm /ɑɚm/; more /mɔɚ/; hard /hɑɚd/

Chapter 12

Exercise 12-A
Low vowel: laugh, shot, rob, match
Central vowel: blunt, blur, from, girl
Back vowel: bloom, book, boat
Monophthong: piece, cat, shoe
Open syllables: car, may, how, eye, shoe, boy
Rounded vowel: blue, sew, bird, cook
Phonemic diphthong: tribe, joy, now, noise
Lax vowel: men, bomb, fig
Mid vowel: men, mope, muck, make
Closed syllables: tribe, trip, own, noise
No onset: hour, own, eye
Coda: comb
Front vowel: mint, back, piece
Tense vowel: late, seen, boat
Voiced sound: honor, all, eye, eat, law, own

Exercise 12-B: feet 3; steak 4; spell 4; shawl 3; plant 4; row 2; ounce 3; chew 2; thought 3; half 3; flood 4; cough 3; noise 3; beige 3; hogs 4; jazz 3; whole 3; gnaw 2; want 4; thank 4

Exercise 12-C

		Similarity	Difference
/ʌ/	/o/	TH (mid)	TA, TT, LR
/ʊ/	/u/	TH (high), TA (back), LR (rounded)	TT
/ə/	/ʌ/	TH, TA, TT, LR	depends on syllable stress
/ɛ/	/ɪ/	TA (front), TT (lax), LR	TH
/i/	/ʊ/	TH (high)	TA, TT, LR
/ɪ/	/æ/	TA (front), TT (lax), LR	TH
/ɝ/	/ʌ/	TA (mid), TH (central)	TT, LR
/o/	/e/	TH (mid), TT (tense)	TA, LR

Exercise 12-D

brook	pull	/ʊ/
down	ground	/aʊ/
tooth	blue	/u/
toy	point	/ɔɪ/
bird	word	/ɝ/
spies	spice	/aɪ/
where	stare	/ɛɚ/
left	etch	/ɛ/

myth	inch	/ɪ/
laugh	quack	/æ/
large	sharp	/ɑɚ/
earth	nerd	/ɝ/
rough	mud	/ʌ/
boat	throw	/o/
these	she	/i/
horn	storm	/ɔɚ/
must	putt	/ʌ/
sell	men	/ɛ/
twice	find	/aɪ/

Exercise 12-E: rough /ʌ/; heard /ɝ/; warn /ɔr/; gauze /ɔ/; coin /ɔɪ/; square /ɛɚ/; kind /aɪ/; good /ʊ/; text /ɛ/; ground /aʊ/; each /i/; weird /ɪɚ/; shoot correct vowel sound not provided; fin /ɪ/; growth /o/; shirt /ɝ/

Exercise 12-F

Word	Characteristics	Change to	New Word
ought	mid, back, lax, rounded	TT	oat
pack	low, front, lax, unrounded	TH to mid	peck
cupped	mid, central, lax, unrounded	TA to front	kept
cheek	high, front, tense, unrounded	TT	chick
blond	low, back, lax, unrounded	TA front	bland
boat	mid, back, tense, rounded	TT	bought
fill	high, front, lax, unrounded	TA back/LR	full
bowl	mid, back, tense, rounded	TH high/TT	bull
cake	mid, front, tense, unrounded	TA back/LR	coke
shut	mid, central, lax, unrounded	LR/TT	shirt
back	low, front, lax, unrounded	TH high/TA back/LR	book

Exercise 12-G: stake /e/; stuck /ʌ/; stock /ɑ/; stack /æ/; grinned /ɪ/; grand /æ/; ground /aʊ/; grind /aɪ/; pest /ɛ/; post /o/; past /æ/; pieced /i/; key /i/; cow /aʊ/; car /ɑɚ/; core /ɔɚ/; June /u/; gin /ɪ/; jean /i/; join /ɔɪ/; took /ʊ/; tuck /ʌ/; tike /aɪ/; tack /æ/; note /o/; not /ɑ/; neat /i/; night /aɪ/; wind (n) /ɪ/;

wand /ɑ/; warned /ɔɚ/; wound (n) /u/; pout /aʊ/; put /ʊ/; putt /ʌ/; pot /ɑ/; clean /i/; clone /o/; clan /æ/; clown /aʊ/; drop /ɑ/; droop /u/; drape /e/; drip /ɪ/; first /ɝ/; feast /i/; fast /æ/; fist /ɪ/; least /i/; lust /ʌ/; list /ɪ/; last /æ/; grown /o/; green /i/; grain /e/; grin /ɪ/; spike /aɪ/; speck /ɛ/; spark /ɑɚ/; spook /u/

Exercise 12-H

Words transcribed accurately		
claim	/klem/	
peak	/pik/	
flight	/flaɪt/	
dark	/dɑɚk/	
home	/hom/	

Words transcribed inaccurately		
knit	/nit/	/nɪt/
beard	/bɛɚd/	/bɪɚd/
verb	/vɛɚb/	/vɝb/
gum	/gum/	/gʌm/
house	/hoʊs/	/haʊs/
high	/hi/	/haɪ/
test	/test/	/tɛst/
who	/ho/	/hu/

Exercise 12-I

"h" + high, back, tense, rounded + "z"	whose
"n" + high, front, tense, unrounded	knee
"sh" + high, back, lax, unrounded + "d"	should
"g" + mid, front, lax, unrounded + "s"	guess
"n" + mid, back, tense, rounded + "z"	nose
"sh" + low, back, lax, unrounded + "p"	shop
"p" + high, front, tense, unrounded + "z"	peas
"r" + mid, back, lax, unrounded	raw
"p" + high, back, lax, rounded + "l"	pull
"d" + mid, front, lax, unrounded + "t"	debt
"l" + low, front, lax, unrounded + "f"	laugh
"f" + high, front, lax, unrounded + "sh"	fish
"h" + high, back, tense, rounded + "m"	whom
"j" + high, front, lax, unrounded + "m"	gym
"f" + low, front, lax, unrounded + "n"	fan
"h" + high, back, lax, rounded + "f"	hoof
"r" + mid, front, tense, unrounded + "z"	raise
"b" + mid, back, tense, rounded + "l"	bowl
"l" + high, back, tense, rounded + "z"	lose
"w" + mid, front, tense, unrounded	way

"r" + mid, front, lax, unrounded + "d"	red
"k" + high, back, lax, rounded + "d"	could
"h" + mid, back, lax, rounded + "l"	hall
"h" + high, front, tense, unrounded + "t"	heat
"p"+ low, back, lax, unrounded + "p"	pop
"l" + high, back, tense, rounded + "s"	loose

Exercise 12-J: /lof/ loaf; /naɪt/ night; /wæks/ wax; /blʌd/ blood; /sef/ safe; /gost/ ghost; /fæst/ fast; /klɪɚ/ clear; /bland/ blond; /gɪlt/ guilt; /nɛlt/ knelt; /fɜ˞nz/ ferns; /haʊnd/ hound; /prun/ prune; /kɔɪn/ coin; /spɛnd/ spend; /temd/ tamed; /slæpt/ slapped; /kɔf/ cough; /dɛɚd/ dared; /raɪm/ rhymed; /wʊl/ wool; /told/ told; /bruz/ bruise

CHAPTER 13

Exercise 13-A

Same Onset	Different Onset
phone – far	cake – cell
sugar – chef	chair – train
judge – gem	cope – ghost
theme – them	tape – cape
look – lick	who – hue
thing – think	girl – gem
use – yours	drop – dot
there – they	food – feud
one – wind	sip – ship
me – knee	

Exercise 13-B

Same Coda		Different Coda	
match	such	peas	peace
calf	buff	cup	mob
knocks	fox	vague	beige
cage	edge	walk	milk
league	log	breath	breathe
rink	thank	lodge	luge
		backed	bagged
		bang	bank
		nest	nets
		should	yield
		dumb	dub
		most	coats

Exercise 13-C

Voiced: ng th(father) zh n z m y g d w j v l r b
Voiceless/unvoiced: h p f ch s th (thing) t sh k

Exercise 13-D

LIP to LIP: p, b, m, w
UPPER TEETH TO LOWER LIP: f, v
TONGUE TIP between TEETH: th(father) th (thing)
TONGUE TIP on or near ALVEOLAR RIDGE: n, z, s, d, t, l
TONGUE BLADE/ BODY near HARD PALATE: zh, y, ch, sh, j, r
BACK OF TONGUE near SOFT PALATE: ng, g, k
NECK (LEVEL OF VOCAL FOLDS): h

Exercise 13-E

STOP-PLOSIVES: p, g, d, t, k, b
FRICATIVES: th (father), zh, z, h, f, s, th (thing), sh, v
AFFRICATES: ch, j
NASALS: ng, n, m
LIQUIDS: l, r
GLIDES: y, w

CHAPTER 14

Exercise 14-A: /p/ /k/ both voiceless (V); /g/ /k/ both velar (P); /b/ /p/ both bilabial (P); /p/ /t/ both voiceless (V); /d/ /g/ both voiced (V); /t/ /d/ both alveolar (P)

Exercise 14-B: /de/ day; /bæd/ bad; /pʊt/ put; /got/ goat; /daʊt/ doubt; /kɔt/ caught; /bud/ booed; /dɛɚ/ dare; /pik/ peak; /tap/ top; /bɝp/ burp; /tʌb/ tub; /tub/ tube; /gʊd/ good; /ad/ odd; /kæb/ cab; /daɪd/ dyed/died; /dɝt/ dirt; /bɪd/ bid; /tʌk/ tuck; /ɝb/ herb

Exercise 14-C: guy /gaɪ/; cow /kaʊ/; guard /gaɚd/; pack /pæk/; court /kɔɚt/; up /ʌp/; dig /dɪg/; paid /ped/; boy /bɔɪ/; get /gɛt/; tuck /tʌk/; ache /ek/; could /kʊd/; pig /pɪg/; bird /bɝd/; cap /kæp/; dope /dop/; dear /dɪɚ/; taught /tɔt/; dark /daɚk/; dared /dɛɚd/

Exercise 14-D: /it/ eat; /ge/ gay; /pok/ poke; /kʌp/ cup; /bæg/ bag

Exercise 14-E

egg	/ɛg/	mid front lax unrounded vowel
+		voiced velar stop plosive
ape	/ep/	mid front tense unrounded vowel
+		voiceless bilabial stop plosive

took	/tʊk/	voiceless alveolar stop plosive
+		high back lax rounded vowel
+		voiceless velar stop plosive
goop	/gup/	voiced velar stop plosive
+		high back tense rounded vowel
+		voiceless bilabial stop plosive

Exercise 14-F

cop → pop	place changed from velar to bilabial
boat → goat	place changed from bilabial to velar
tall → ball	place changed from alveolar to bilabial; voicing changed from voiceless to voiced
bite → kite	place changed from bilabial to velar; voicing changed from voiced to voiceless
key → T	place changed from velar to alveolar

Exercise 14-G: teach; bow, doe; took, cook; buzz; par, car; guard

Exercise 14-H: hut; ate, ache; wreck, rep; hop; rot, rock

Exercise 14-I: /drɔ/ draw; /ekt/ ached; /klaʊd/ cloud; /tubz/ tubes; /stups/ stoops; /tre/ tray; /pækt/ packed; /klind/ cleaned; /blu/ blue; /tʌgd/ tugged; /gron/ grown; /bɝst/ burst; /klæpt/ clapped; /praɪd/ pride; /bɛlt/ belt; /kræk/ crack; /glo/ glow; /dɪpt/ dipped; /brok/ broke; /kɝst/ cursed; /told/ told; /plet/ plate; /tæpt/ tapped; /blɛnd/ blend

Exercise 14-J: treat /trit/; spoiled /spɔɪld/; grabbed /græbd/; biked /baɪkt/; wasp /wɑsp/; plug /plʌg/; blouse /blaʊs/; brags /brægz/; drive /draɪv/; pressed /prɛst/; typed /taɪpt/; milk /mɪlk/; blow /blo/; dabbed /dæbd/; cooked /kʊkt/; poked /pokt/; desk /dɛsk/; curled /kɝld/; bugged /bʌgd/; glides /glaɪdz/; glue /glu/; proud /praʊd/; twirled /twɝld/; brats /bræts//brɑts/; help /hɛlp/; clap /klæp/; bleed /blid/; blocks /blɑks/; cold /kold/; coast /kost/; taste /test/; gross /gros/

CHAPTER 15

Exercise 15-A

/s/	/θ/	V			/v/	/ʒ/	V		
/h/	/f/	V			/ð/	/θ/		P	
/θ/	/ʃ/	V			/ʒ/	/z/	V		
/ʒ/	/s/			M	/p/	/h/	V		M
/ʃ/	/ʒ/		P	M	/g/	/ð/	V		
/z/	/t/		P		/f/	/v/			P	M

Exercise 15-B: /vaʊ/ vow; /zu/ zoo; /sɔ/ saw; /ʃɔɚ/ shore; /ɔf/ off; /θaɪ/ thigh; /fɛɚ/ fair; /ɝθ/ earth; /ðe/ they; /hi/ he; /æʃ/ ash; /ɪz/ is; /fɪʃ/ fish; /haɪv/ hive; /sɝf/ surf; /ʃʌv/ shove; /fɔɚθ/ forth; /haʊs/ house; /ðɪs/ this; /ʃɛf/ chef; /beʒ/ beige; /hoz/ hose; /sɔs/ sauce; /θif/ thief; /bæθ/ bath; /saɪz/ size; /fɪɚs/ fierce; /vɔɪs/ voice; /fez/ phase; /hʌʃ/ hush; /suð/ soothe; /saʊθ/ south; /vɝs/ verse; /hɑɚt/ heart; /pʊʃ/ push; /θɔt/ thought; /tʌf/ tough; /dæʃ/ dash; /fud/ food; /saɪt/ sight; /bɛɚz/ bears; /huz/ whose

Exercise 15-C: who /hu/; sigh /saɪ/; their /ðɛɚ/; shoe /ʃu/; ace /es/; of /ʌv/; ease /iz/; that /ðæt/; his /hɪz/; those /ðoz/; safe /sef/; share /ʃɛɚ/; cough /kɔf/; food /fud/; half /hæf/; verb /vɝb/; should /ʃʊd/; weave /wiv/; gush /gʌʃ/; toys /tɔɪz/; teeth /tiθ/; third /θɝd/; hook /hʊk/; shirt /ʃɝt/; cash /kæʃ/; puff /pʌf/; bath /bæθ/; shard /ʃɑɚd/; dive /daɪv/; thus /ðʌs/; verse /vɝs/; height /haɪt/; goes /goz/; soaked /sokt/; thick /θɪk/; shave /ʃev/; Zeus /zus/; zoos /zuz/; shocks /ʃɑks/

Exercise 15-D: /ɪf/ if; /ðo/ though; /pæθ/ path; /ves/ vase; /hup/ hoop

Exercise 15-E

faith	/feθ/	voiceless labiodentals fricative
+		mid front tense unrounded vowel
+		voiceless interdental fricative
zip	/zɪp/	voiced alveolar fricative
+		high front lax unrounded vowel
+		voiceless bilabial stop plosive
shoes	/ʃuz/	voiceless palatal fricative
+		high back tense rounded vowel
+		voiced alveolar fricative
thus	/ðʌs/	voiced interdental fricative
+		mid central lax unrounded vowel
+		voiceless alveolar fricative

Exercise 15-F

shoe → zoo	voicing changed from voiceless to voiced; place changed from palatal to Alveolar
height → sight	place changed from glottal to alveolar
T → C	manner changed from stop-plosive to fricative
math → mass	place changed from interdental to alveolar
doubt → shout	voicing changed from voiced to voiceless; place changed from alveolar

to palatal; manner changed from stop-plosive to fricative

fall → call   placed changed from labiodental to velar; manner changed from fricative to stop-plosive

Exercise 15-G: their; sin, fin, shin; sign, shine; took, cook; hand, fanned; pink, kink

Exercise 15-H: grave; myth; case; rut; loaf

Exercise 15-I: /ʃrʌb/ shrub; /flɛʃ/ flesh; /θrot/ throat; /stɑɚ/ star; /splæʃ/ splash; /θraɪv/ thrive; /skɝt/ skirt; /stonz/ stones; /snɔɚ/ snore; /buθs/ booths; /wivz/ weaves; /ʃɪft/ shift; /ʃɛlf/ shelf; /faks/ fox; /hʌʃt/ hushed; /pæst/ past/passed; /stapt/ stopped; /snizd/ sneezed; /kɝst/ cursed; /kloðd/ clothed; /nɛkst/ next; /ʃrʌgz/ shrugs; /θri/ three; /flɛɚ/ flare

Exercise 15-J: throw /θro/; floods /flʌdz/; slush /slʌʃ/; shrimp /ʃrɪmp/; soft /sɔft/; zips /zips/; striped /straɪpt/; smash /smæʃ/; spear /spɪɚ/; swirls /swɝlz/; first /fɝst/; froth /frɔθ/; bathed /beðd/; frisk /frɪsk/; flushed /flʌʃt/; thrashed /θræʃt/; shelves /ʃɛlvz/; desks /dɛsks/

CHAPTER 16
Exercise 16-A

/ʃ/	/tʃ/	V	P		/θ/	/dʒ/			
/b/	/dʒ/	V			/tʃ/	/f/	V		
/ʒ/	/dʒ/	V	P		/s/	/ʒ/			M
/t/	/tʃ/	V			/v/	/dʒ/	V		

Exercise 16-B: /ɪtʃ/ itch; /edʒ/ age; /tʃu/ chew; /aʊtʃ/ ouch; /dʒɔɪ/ joy; /tʃɔɚ/ chore; /tʃip/ cheap; /bædʒ/ badge; /dʒok/ joke; /dʒed/ jade; /sʌtʃ/ such; /dʒɛt/ jet; /tʃɝtʃ/ church; /tʃɛɚz/ chairs; /tʃap/ chop; /dʒaɪv/ jive; /dʒip/ jeep; /dʒæz/ jazz; /tʃend/ chained; /fʌdʒ/ fudge; /tʃɛst/ chest; /tʃɪl/ chill; /dʒɝk/ jerk; /pʌdʒ/ pudge; /plɛdʒ/ pledge; /smʌdʒ/ smudge; /mætʃ/ match; /tʃiz/ cheese; /tʃʌg/ chug; /dʒaʊl/ jowl; /sɝtʃ/ search; /skatʃ/ scotch; /rɪdʒ/ ridge

Exercise 16-C: urge /ɝdʒ/; each /itʃ/; "G" /dʒi/; chief /tʃif/; jug /dʒʌg/; wage /wedʒ/; arch /ɑɚtʃ/; couch /kaʊtʃ/; judge /dʒʌdʒ/; jab /dʒæb/; purge /pɝdʒ/; roach /rotʃ/; chalk /tʃɔk/; wedge /wɛdʒ/; choice /tʃɔɪs/; perch /pɝtʃ/; jock /dʒak/; patch /pætʃ/; child /tʃaɪld/; cheer /tʃɪɚ/; just /dʒʌst/

Exercise 16-D: /tʃu/ chew; /tʃes/ chase; /dadʒ/ dodge; /sɝdʒ/ surge; /tʃɪp/ chip

Exercise 16-E
choke	/tʃok/	voiceless palatal affricate
+		mid back tense rounded vowel
+		voiceless velar stop plosive
juice	/dʒus/	voiced palatal affricate
+		high back tense rounded vowel
+		voiceless alveolar fricative
nudge	/nʌdʒ/	voiceless alveolar nasal
+		mid central lax unrounded vowel
+		voiced palatal affricate
cheese	/tʃiz/	voiceless palatal affricate
+		high front tense unrounded vowel
+		voiced alveolar fricative

Exercise 16-F

jeep → cheap   voicing changed from voiced to voiceless

job → sob   voicing changed from voiced to voiceless; place changed from palatal toalveolar; manner changed from affricate to fricative

hatch → half   place changed from palatal to labiodental; manner changed from affricate to fricative

sail → jail   voicing changed from voiceless to voiced; place changed from alveolar to palatal; manner changed from fricative to affricate

vet → jet   place changed from labiodental to palatal; manner changed from fricative to affricate

G → D   place changed from palatal to alveolar; manner changed from affricate to stop-plosive

Exercise 16-G: shore; chunk; vest, best, zest, guest; hump, pump, thump; tip, sip, hip; poke, coke, soak, folk; pair, tear, care, hair, share; jeep, deep, beep; pat, cat, fat, hat, sat

Exercise 16-H: hutch; rich; surge; eve, ease; rope, wrote, roach; raid, raise, rave

Exercise 16-I: /drɛntʃ/ drench; /tʌtʃt/ touched; /rendʒ/ range; /ræntʃ/ ranch; /strɛtʃ/ stretch; /lʌntʃ/ lunch; /mɝdʒd/ merged; /pɪtʃt/ pitched /tʃendʒ/ change; /sɪndʒd/ singed; /skrætʃt/ scratched; /sɝtʃt/ searched

Exercise 16-J: lunge /lʌndʒ/; fringe /frɪndʒ/; charged /tʃɑɚdʒd/; patched /pætʃt/; sponge /spʌndʒ/ lounge /laʊndʒ/; purged /pɝdʒd/; starched /stɑɚtʃt/; dodged /dadʒd/; splurged /splɝdʒd/

CHAPTER 17

Exercise 17-A

/m/	/b/	V	P	/ŋ/	/dʒ/	V	
/ŋ/	/k/		P	/ʃ/	/n/		nothing in common
/m/	/v/	V		/d/	/n/	V	
/z/	/n/	V	P	/v/	/ŋ/	V	
/h/	/tʃ/	V		/ʒ/	/dʒ/	V	P

Exercise 17-B: /nu/ new/knew; /em/ aim; /kɪŋ/ king; /hæŋ/ hang; /tʃɝn/ churn; /mɔɚ/ more; /naʊn/ noun; /mun/ moon; /θʌm/ thumb; /mætʃ/ match; /strɔŋ/ strong; /dʒɝmz/ germs; /naks/ knocks; /naɪs/ nice; /tʌŋ/ tongue; /mɔɪst/ moist; /fæŋ/ fang; /nɪɚ/ near; /stɪŋ/ sting; /naɪn/ nine; /mɪst/ missed/mist; /nɝst/ nursed; /dʒɔɪn/ join; /nɔɚθ/ north; /mɛʃ/ mesh; /dʒɛm/ gem; /sʌm/ some/sum

Exercise 17-C: on /ɔn//ɑn/; shine /ʃaɪn/; mouse /maʊs/; thing /θɪŋ/; none /nʌn/; mean /min/; march /mɑɚtʃ/; noise /nɔɪz/; hang /hæŋ/; mouth /maʊθ/; nudge /nʌdʒ/; song /sɔŋ/; known /non/; mix /mɪks/; gang /gæŋ/; rhyme /raɪm/; mock /mak/; gnat /næt/; long /lɔŋ/; I'm /aɪm/; must /mʌst/; jam /dʒæm/; chin /tʃɪn;/ wing /wɪŋ/; gym /dʒɪm/; name /nem/; bang /bæŋ/; thorn /θɔɚn/; them /ðɛm/; gnashed /næʃt/

Exercise 17-D: /gɔn/ gone; /pɪŋ/ ping; /ðɛm/ them; /stʌn/ stun

Exercise 17-E

gem	/dʒɛm/	voiced palatal affricate
+		mid front lax unrounded vowel
+		voiced bilabial nasal
thin	/θɪn/	voiceless interdental fricative
+		high front lax unrounded vowel
+		voiced alveolar nasal
tunes	/tunz/	voiceless alveolar stop-plosive
+		high back tense rounded vowel
+		voiced alveolar nasal
+		voiced alveolar fricative
sting	/stɪŋ/	voiceless alveolar fricative
+		voiceless alveolar stop-plosive
+		high front lax unrounded vowel
+		voiced velar nasal

Exercise 17-F

noise →toys	manner change from nasal to stop-plosive; voicing change from voiced to voiceless
mane → made	manner change from nasal to stop-plosive
knee → me	place change from alveolar to bilabial
fail → mail	voicing change from voiceless to voiced; place change from labiodental to bilabial; manner change from fricative to nasal
sick → sing	voicing change from voiceless to voiced; manner change from stop-plosive to nasal
north → fourth	voicing change from voiced to voiceless; place change from alveolar to labiodental; manner change from nasal to fricative
cage → cane	place change from palatal to alveolar; manner change from affricate to nasal

Exercise 17-G: dear; path, hath; pose, hose, chose, foes, shows; peal; bug, dug, jug; sign; top, cop, sop, shop, hop, chop

Exercise 17-H: ripe; pam, pang; beat, beak, beach, beef; foam; spit; trays, trade; bad, badge; bat, batch, bath, bash

Exercise 17-I: /trɛntʃ/ trench; /dʒʌmp/ jump; /branz/ bronze; /kaɪnd/ kind; /lɛŋθ/ length; /tʃɑɚmz/ charms; /maʊnd/ mound; /θæŋk/ thank; /klind/ cleaned; /rɪns/ rinse; /tond/ toned; /smɔl/ small; /snæk/ snack; /skrimd/ screamed; /ʃrʌŋk/ shrunk; /monz/ moans; /prɪns/ prince; /bæŋd/ banged; /pand/ pond; /paʊnd/ pound; /flɪŋz/ flings; /stɪŋks/ stinks; /smɛlz/ smells; /rʌŋz/ rungs

Exercise 17-J: themes /θimz/; sings /sɪŋz/; ground /graʊnd/; honk /hɔŋk/; grunge /grʌndʒ/; mink /mɪŋk/; smile /smaɪl/; snared /snɛɚd/; strength /strɛŋθ/; tanked /tæŋkt/; don't /dont/; smoke /smok/; counts /kaʊnts/; thinks /θɪŋks/; pants /pænts/; trunks /trʌŋks/; brains /brenz/; prince /prɪns/; snows /snoz/; turns /tɝnz/; smashed /smæʃt/; worms /wɝmz/; tense /tɛns/; clowns /klaʊnz/; joints /dʒɔɪnts/; zinc /zɪŋk/; junk /dʒʌŋk/

CHAPTER 18

Exercise 18-A

/r/	/ʒ/	V	P		/l/	/d/	V	P
/r/	/l/	V		M	/dʒ/	/r/	V	P
/s/	/l/		P		/ð/	/l/	V	
/r/	/tʃ/		P		/l/	/t/		P
/l/	/n/	V	P		/m/	/r/	V	

Page 250 — Answer Key

Exercise 18-B: /lɔ/ law; /len/ lane; /lɪp/ lip; /ræŋ/ rang; /rul/ rule; /rʌʃ/ rush; /laʊd/ loud; /lus/ loose; /ræntʃ/ ranch; /rɪst/ wrist; /rɛst/ rest; /lʌŋ/ lung; /lɜ˞n/ learn; /pɝl/ pearl; /rid/ read; /faʊl/ fowl/foul; /rɔŋ/ wrong; /raɪz/ rise; /rom/ roam; /rɛɚ/ rare; /lɔŋ/ long; /laks/ locks; /raɪs/ rice; /ril/ real; /pʊl/ pull; /lɔs/ loss; /lɛft/ left; /rɪɚ/ rear; /kɔɪl/ coil; /laɪn/ line; /lɛgz/ legs; /rakt/ rocked; /rʌst/ rust; /rʌts/ ruts; /list/ least; /rɪsk/ risk; /lʌv/ love; /hɔl/ haul; /lɪft/ lift; /rɔ/ raw; /lɪnt/ lint; /lik/ leak

Exercise 18-C: laugh /læf/; lime /laɪm/; rain /ren/; rough /rʌf/; wool /wʊl/; loan /lon/; limb /lɪm/; raced /rest/; lawn /lɔn/; rare /rɛɚ/; whole /hol/; large /laɚdʒ/; rail /rel/; raft /ræft/; room /rum/; rhyme /raɪm/; length /lɛnθ/; look /lʊk/; long /lɔŋ/; write /raɪt/; girl /gɝl/; gel /dʒɛl/; round /raʊnd/; lace /les/; wrap /ræp/; rinse /rɪns/; lunch /lʌntʃ/; rose /roz/; lost /lɔst/; rude /rude/; roast /rost/; rise /raɪz/; reel /ril/; owl /aʊl/; spill /spɪl/; list /lɪst/

Exercise 18-D: /rɪb/ rib; /lʌk/ luck; /rel/ rail; /rɪŋ/ ring; /rab/ rob; /spɪl/spill; /lɔŋ/ long; /lɛts/ let's; /rumz/ rooms; /lætʃ/ latch;

Exercise 18-E

lodge	/ladʒ/	voiced alveolar liquid
+		low back lax unrounded vowel
+		voiced palatal affricate
fool	/ful/	voiceless labiodentals fricative
+		high back tense rounded vowel
+		voiced alveolar liquid
rook	/rʊk/	voiced palatal liquid
+		high back lax rounded vowel
+		voiceless velar stop-plosive
load	/lod/	voiced alveolar liquid
+		mid back tense rounded vowel
+		voiced alveolar stop -plosive
rage	/redʒ/	voiced palatal liquid
+		mid front tense unrounded vowel
+		voiced palatal affricate
live (verb)	/lɪv/	voiced alveolar liquid
+		high front lax unrounded vowel
+		voiced labiodental fricative
wrench	/rɛntʃ/	voiced palatal liquid
+		mid front lax unrounded vowel
+		voiced alveolar nasal
+		voiceless palatal affricate

kneel	/nil/	voiced alveolar nasal
+		high front tense unrounded vowel
+		voiced alveolar liquid
rink	/rɪŋk/	voiced palatal liquid
+		high front lax unrounded vowel
+		voiced velar nasal
+		voiceless velar stop-plosive

Exercise 18-F

leap → jeep	place changed from alveolar to palatal; manner changed from liquid to affricate
rug → chug	voicing changed from voiced to voiceless, manner changed from liquid to affricate
lace → race	place changed from alveolar to palatal
roar → door	place changed from palatal to alveolar; manner changed from liquid to stop-plosive
lake →cake	voicing changed from voiced to voiceless; place changed from alveolar to velar; manner changed from liquid to stop-plosive
room → zoom	place changed from palatal to alveolar; manner changed from liquid to fricative
ring → thing	voicing changed from voiced to voiceless; place changed from palatal to interdental; manner changed from liquid to fricative
rice →mice	place changed from palatal to bilabial; manner changed from liquid to nasal

Exercise 18-G: ramp; champ; dip, zip; book; dine, nine; toast, coast; dust, bust, must, gust; peep, keep, heap, sheep, cheap

Exercise 18-H: /drim/ dream; /kloz/ close /clothes/; /blu/ blue; /tred/ trade; /fraɪz/ fries; /ʃrud/ shrewd; /plet/ plate; /praɪd/ pride; /gron/ grown; /klaʊd/ cloud; /brok/ broke; /krɔld/ crawled; /klind/ cleaned; /told/ told; /glez/ glaze; /brif/ brief; /træʃ/ trash; /spre/ spray; /ɛls/ else; /bɛlt/ belt; /wɝld/ world; /staɪlz/ styles; /frɛnd/ friend; /blakt/ blocked; /traɪ/ try; /flɪntʃ/ flinch; /ʃrʌg/ shrug; /pʊld/ pulled; /klɪɚ/ clear; /graʊnd/ ground; /graɪnd/ grind; /prɪns/ prince; /skrʌb/ scrub

Exercise 18-I: treat /trit/; glue /glu/; drive /draɪv/; plug /plʌg/; clap /klæp/; blown /blon/; dreamt /drɛmt/; truth /truθ/; curls /kɝlz/; wolf /wʊlf/; grabbed /græbd/; twirled /twɝld/; glides /glaɪdz/; health /hɛlθ/; blocks /blaks/; blind /blaɪnd/; meals /milz/; vault /vɔlt/; glance /glæns/; pulled /pʊld/; glared /glɛɚd/; floored /flɔɚd/; film /fɪlm/; flinch /flɪntʃ/; false /fɔls/; prompt /pramt/; trunk /trʌŋk/;

bread /brɛd/; straight /stret/; spring /sprɪŋ/; filled /fɪld/; valve /vælv/; scalp /skælp/; shrink /ʃrɪŋk/; Greece /gris/; France /fræns/; bruise /bruz/; crisp /krɪsp/; street /strit/; gulp /gʌlp/; sleigh /sle/; shelf /ʃɛlf/; guilt /gɪlt/; willed /wɪld/; brush /brʌʃ/; front /frʌnt/; shrimp /ʃrɪmp/; shelved /ʃɛlvd/

CHAPTER 19

Exercise 19-A

/r/	/j/	V	P	/l/	/w/	V	
/j/	/b/	V		/dʒ/	/j/	V	P
/w/	/m/	V	P	/b/	/j/	V	
/j/	/tʃ/		P	/w/	/ŋ/	V	
/w/	/r/	V		/ʒ/	/r/	V	P

Exercise 19-B: /waʊ/ wow; /jɛs/ yes; /ju/ you; /jʌm/ yum; /wik/ week; /wɔl/ wall; /wʊd/ wood/would; /jus/ use; /wæg/ wag; /wɑnd/ wand; /juθ/ youth; /jʌŋ/ young; /wɝd/ word; /wʌn/ won; /jist/ yeast; /jɑɚd/ yard; /wev/ wave; /wɔɚn/ worn; /waʊnd/ wound; /waɪɚd/ wired; /wɪnd/ wind

Exercise 19-C: way /we/; year /jɪɚ/; yuck /jʌk/; yarn /jɑɚn/; wool /wʊl/; warm /wɔɚm/; want /wʌnt/wɑnt/; waist /west/; yawn /jɔn/; wear /wɛɚ/; yield /jild/; walk /wɔk/; Yale /jel/; wealth /wɛlθ/; wish /wɪʃ/; witch /wɪtʃ/; yolk /jok/; yank /jæŋk/; wing /wɪŋ/; with /wɪθ/; were /wɝ/; once /wʌns/; weird /wɪɚd/; wind (vb) /waɪnd/

Exercise 19-D: /jɛl/ yell; /wɪnd/ wind; /juzd/ used; /wɛnt/ went

Exercise 19-E

yule	/jul/	voiced palatal glide
+		high back tense rounded vowel
+		voiced alveolar liquid
wave	/wev/	voiced bilabial glide
+		mid front tense unrounded vowel
+		voiced labiodentals fricative
yacht	/jɑt/	voiced palatal glide
+		low back lax unrounded vowel
+		voiceless alveolar stop-plosive
wedge	/wɛdʒ/	voiced bilabial glide
+		mid front lax unrounded vowel
+		voiced palatal affricate

Exercise 19-F

will → bill	manner changed from glide to stop-plosive
yes → chess	voicing changed from voiced to voiceless; manner changed from glide to affricate
weigh → they	place changed from bilabial to interdental; manner changed from glide to fricative
yoke → woke	place changed from palatal to bilabial
wall → fall	voicing changed from voiced to voiceless; place changed from bilabial to labiodental; manner changed from glide to fricative
yard → guard	place changed from palatal to velar; manner changed from glide to stop-plosive
wing → ring	place changed from bilabial to palatal; manner changed from glide to liquid
wait → late	place changed from bilabial to alveolar; manner changed from glide to liquid

Exercise 19-G: hard, card; vow, thou, now; bull; curled, hurled; cheer, sheer; pun, ton, sun, fun, shun; guess, mess, less; pick, tick, kick, thick, sick, chick, hick

Exercise 19-H: /dwɛl/ dwell; /kwɪk/ quick; /swɪm/ swim; /kwɔɚt/ quart; /skwɑʃ/ squash; /twɝld/ twirled; /swɝlz/ swirls; /kwin/ queen; /twɪndʒ/ twinge; /skwik/ squeak; /twɛlfθ/ twelfth; /kwaɪt/ quite; /skwɝl/ squirrel; /swɑmp/ swamp; /kwel/ quail; /kjub/ cube /fjud/ feud /mjuz/ muse; /pjʊɚ/ pure; /bjut/ Butte; /fjumz/ fumes; /kjud/ cued; /fju/ few; /bjutɪ/ beauty

Exercise 19-I: twelve /twɛlv/; swore /swɔɚ/; view /vju/; fuse /fjuz/; twine /twaɪn/; mule /mjul/; swerve /swɝv/; cure /kjʊɚ/ /kjɝ/; dwarf /dwɔɚf/; quack /kwæk/; feud /fjud/; squish /skwɪʃ/; huge /hjudʒ/; queer /kwɪɚ/; swear /swɛɚ/; quake /kwek/; cute /kjut/; switch /swɪtʃ/; quench /kwɛntʃ/; swag /swæg/; squirt /skwɝt/; rescue /rɛskju/; square /skwɛɚ/; tribute /trɪbjut/

CHAPTER 20

Exercise 20-A

V = voicing; P = place; M = manner

p f	**VPM** obstruents	tʃ r	**VPM** sonorants	j w	**VPM** sonorants
m p	**VPM** obstruents	b k	**VPM** obstruents	h z	**PMV** obstruents
ð θ	**VPM** obstruents	ŋ k	**VPM**	j dʒ	**VPM**
j ŋ	**VPM** sonorants	t n	**VPM**	ʃ s	**VPM** obstruents
d l	**VPM**	w m	**VPM** sonorants	θ h	**VPM** obstruents

v b **VPM**   ʒ dʒ **VPM**   ʒ r **VPM**
  obstruents   obstruents

r ŋ **VPM**   θ v **VPM**   p s **VPM**
  sonorants   obstruents   obstruents

H = tongue height; A = tongue advancement; T = tongue
tension; R = lip rounding

i ɑ HAT**R**   o u HAT**R**   e ɔ HAT**R**
i e HA**T**R   æ i HA**T**R   ɪ ɜ HAT**R**
ʊ ɔ HAT**R**   e ɛ HA**TR**   ɪ ʊ HATR

Exercise 20-B

dʒ ƀ r **VPM**   k ŋ ħ **VPM**
dʒ b f obstruents   k ꞃ h **VPM**
                                     obstruents
ð s f **VPM**   w m ꝑ **VPM**
  stridents   sonorants
j m ŋ **VPM**   t ꞃ s **VPM**
                                     obstruents
ʃ s đ **VPM**   ɫ w m **VPM**
  stridents
ʃ s d **VPM**V

θ h ꞩ nonstridents   dʒ ʒ ʧ **VPM**
                                   dʒ ʒ tʃ **VPM**
ꞃ ʃ s **VPM**   g ⱱ ŋ **VPM**
  obstruents   g v ŋ obstruents
  stridents

n f s **VPM**
ð θ ħ **VPM**   ʃ tʃ ꞃ **VPM**
ð θ h **VPM**   obstruents
                                     stridents
g ŋ ꝁ **VPM**   l ꞃ n **PMV**
g ꞃ k **VPM**   l r ꞃ **VPM**
  obstruents

w f m **VPM**   ʒ z ʃ **VPM**
                                   ʒ ᵶ ʃ **VPM**
l ꞇ n **PMV**   ʒ ⱱ dʒ **VPM**
                                   ʒ v đʒ **VPM**
j ŋ d **VPM**   s θ ⱱ **VPM**
j ŋ đ sonorants   s θ v **stridents**
                                     obstruents
b ŋ θ **VPM**   p s ꝳ **VPM**
b ꞃ θ obstruents   obstruents
                                   p ꞩ m **VPM**

H = tongue height; A = tongue advancement; T = tongue
tension; R = lip rounding

i u ꝷ **HATR**   e ə ʌ **HATR**
ꞟ u ʊ **HATR**   ɛ ꞽ æ **HATR**
ɛ ɑ æ **HATR**   ɛ ɑ æ **HATR**
i e ꝷ **HATR**   ʊ ɪ ɛ **HATR**
i e u **HATR**   ʊ ɪ ɛ **HATR**
ɑ æ ə **HATR**   θ e ɛ **HATR**

ɑ æ ɔ HATR   ɔ e ɛ HATR
u ɑ o HATR   e ʊ c HATR
e ə u HATR   e ɔ ꞇ HATR
e u æ HATR   e ɔ æ HATR
e ꞇ æ HATR   æ e ə HATR
e ɔ æ HATR

Exercise 20-C:

Voiced bilabials: /b/, /w/, /m/
High vowels: /ɪ/, /i/, /u/, /ʊ/
Voiceless fricatives: /f/, /s/, /θ/, /ʃ/ h/
Low vowels: /æ/, /ɑ/
Voiced stridents: /v/, /z/, /ʒ/, /dʒ/
Velars: /k/, /g/, /ŋ/
Central vowels: /ʌ/, /ə/, /ɚ/, /ɝ/
Palatal sounds: /ʃ/, /ʒ/, /tʃ/, /dʒ/ /j/, /r/
Lax, front vowels: /ɪ/, /ɛ/, /æ/
Nonstrident fricatives: /θ/, /ð/, /h/
Rounded, tense vowels: /u/, /o/, /ɝ/
Sonorants: /m/, /n/, /ŋ/, /w/, /j/, /r/, /l/
Approximants: /l/, /r/, /w/, /j/
Mid vowels: /e/, /ɛ/, /o/, /ɔ/, /ʌ/, /ə/, /ɚ/, /ɝ/
Tense, high vowels: /i/, /u/
Cognates: /p/- /b/, /t/-/d/, /k/- /g/, /s/- /z/, /f/- /v/, /θ/-/ð/,
    /ʃ/-/ʒ/, /tʃ/-/dʒ/
Labial obstruents: /p/, /b/, /f/, /v/
Voiceless stop-plosives: /p/, /t/, /k/
Back, lax vowels: /ʊ/, /ɔ/, /ɑ/
Strident non-fricatives: /tʃ/, /dʒ/
Voiced affricates: /dʒ/
Nasals: /m/, /n/, /ŋ/
Tense, mid vowels: /e/, /o/, /ɝ/
Unrounded, back vowels: /ɑ/
No cognates: /m/, /n/, /ŋ/, /h/, /j/, /l/, /r/

Exercise 20-D:

zoo – sue V; moo – new P; type – pipe P ; fair – there V P;
thumb – some P; chart – part P M; get – kit V;
beg – peg V; moan – bone M; bough – cow V P;
height – fight P; sawed – laud V M; sought – thought P;
them – hem V P; late – wait P M; jam – sham V M;
zoos – chews V P M; thought – bought V P M;
bark – shark V P M; kite – right V P M; book – look P M;
vine – fine V; tent – dent V; wrist – list P; yes – chess V M;
sun – fun P; thigh – thy V; land – hand V P M;
bend – send V P M; cheap – jeep V; we're – year P M;
burn – churn V P M;

Identify the pairs of words that have cognates in their onsets.

zoo – sue   get – kit   beg – peg   vine – fine
tent – dent   thigh – thy   cheap – jeep

Exercise 20-E:

badge – batch V; have – half V; caught – cough P M;
sing – sin P; hard – heart V; laugh – lass P; force – fort M;
paid – page P M; cord – cork V P; mouth – mouse P;
peace – peas V; leg – ledge V; bought – ball P;
bows – bowl M; have – hatch V P M; rag – rail P M;
plaid – plan M; fourth – fort V; dug – duck V;
fell – fetch V P M; lab – laugh V us – of M;

Identify the pairs of words that have cognates in their codas.

badge – batch	have – half	hard – heart
peace – peas	dug – duck	

Exercise 20-F: gone, bugged, phone, coin; rings, strength, beige, there/their; cow, close, clothes, cheek; shout, hawk, crowd, cloth; to/too/two, noose, shine, clothe; them, off, tube, height; growl, think, black, booth; shin, ones, tooth, live; price, odd, shape, match; shell, just, look, house; cash, bathe, thank, shot; yell, huge, wrap, has; song, thrill, jail, lost; spoon, urge, yet, shop; jet, doubt, chalk, cute; oink, ouch, meets, raced

Exercise 20-G

thee	ð	the	ð	same
though	ð	thought	θ	different
there	ð	thine	ð	same
these	ð	thesis	θ	different
filthy	θ	feather	ð	different
either	ð	ether	θ	different
mother	ð	father	ð	same
soothe	ð	south	θ	different
both	θ	bother	ð	different
that	ð	thaw	θ	different
together	ð	leather	ð	same
that	ð	than	ð	same
north	θ	south	θ	same
faith	θ	breathe	ð	different
thaw	θ	author	θ	same
soothing	ð	loathing	ð	same
Thursday	θ	thousand	θ	same
lethal	θ	leather	ð	different
thin	θ	thine	ð	different
south	θ	soothe	ð	different
nothing	θ	feather	ð	different
breathy	θ	breathe	ð	different
think	θ	thick	θ	same

breath	θ	cloth	θ	same
thin	θ	think	θ	same
author	θ	mother	ð	different
together	ð	birthday	θ	different
thereafter	ð	theater	θ	different

Exercise 20-H: either, leather /ð/; smooth, wreathe /ð/; sympathy, authentic /θ/; theater, ethanol /θ/; thought, lethal /θ/; mother, worthy /ð/; thunder, mathematics /θ/; thirsty, thumb /θ/; thousand, thin /θ/; third, faithful /θ/; altogether, teethe /ð/; clothe, therefore /ð/; think, cathedral /θ/; farther, father /ð/; lather, enthusiast /ð/; thermos, Thursday /θ/; thick, thaw /θ/; bother, brother /ð/; neither, though /ð/; thieves, theater /θ/; thousand, ethanol /θ/; thou, soothing /ð/; Othello, thick /θ/; worthy, bathing /ð/; thumb, thing /θ/; gothic, thermometer /θ/; loathe, this /ð/

Exercise 20-I: puree, cue, ~~fluke~~, use, ~~joy~~, ~~beau~~, beauty, volume, fusion, puny; human, cube, few, ~~dew~~, view; cure, bureau, fury, ~~furry~~, figure; ~~Figaro~~, ambulance, million, refuse, unit; ~~under~~, uvula, tortilla, yo yo, senior; ~~curl~~, behavior, accuse, ~~eye~~, excuse; onion, ~~pretty~~, ~~convene~~, convenient, yell; familiar, popular, ~~fool~~, huge, ~~ugly~~; value, ~~mission~~, tissue, ~~cruel~~, fuel

Exercise 20-J

/ŋ/	/ŋg/	/ŋk/
bang	anger	anchor
hang	bungalow	chunk
spring	English	wrinkle
long	stronger	chunky
strong	fungus	Lincoln
young	anguish	conquer
king	shingle	tank
savings	jungle	donkey
_____	longer	tinkle
_____	_____	shrink
_____	_____	bronco
_____	_____	_____

/nk/	/ŋθ/	/ndʒ/
pancake	wavelength	ranger
encode	fullstrength	strange
concur	_____	danger
_____	_____	engine
_____	_____	ginger
_____	_____	dangerous

/ŋk/	/ŋθ/	/ndʒ/
_____	_____	lounger
_____	_____	sponge
_____	_____	hinge
_____	_____	arrange

Exercise 20-K: /p/; /æ/; /tʃ/; patch; /b/, batch; /dʒ/, badge; /ʃ/, bash; /m/, mash

Exercise 20-L: /v/; /e/; /s/; vase; /fes/, face; /fez/, phase; /pez/, pays; /poz/, pose; /pɔz/, pause

Exercise 20-M

Voiceless palatal fricative + high back tense rounded vowel + voiceless alveolar stop-plosive	
/ʃut/	Describe the change
/ʃuz/	What changed in the coda? **Voicing& Manner**
/tʃuz/	What changed in the onset? **Manner**
/tʃud/	What changed? **Manner**
/rud/	What changed? **Voicing & Manner**
/rum/	What changed? **Place & Manner**
/zum/	What changed? **Place & Manner**

Exercise 20-N

Voiceless labiodental fricative + high front tense unrounded vowel + voiceless alveolar stop-plosive /fit/ = feet

Word in Orthography	Word in Phonetic Symbols	State the Change__ changed to __	Describe the Change
fit	/fɪt/	/i/→/ɪ/	**Tongue Tension**
foot	/fʊt/	/ɪ/→/ʊ/	**Tongue Advance-ment, lip rounding**
food	/fud/	/ʊ/→/u/ /t/→/d/	**Tongue Tension Voicing**
feud	/fjud/	C → CC+ /j/	**Addition of the voiced palatal glide**

Voiceless labiodental fricative + high front tense unrounded vowel + voiceless alveolar stop-plosive /fit/ = feet

Word in Orthography	Word in Phonetic Symbols	State the Change__ changed to __	Describe the Change
fuel	/fjul/	/d/→/l/	**Manner**
fool	/ful/	CC → C - /j/	**Deletion of the voiced palatal glide**
full	/fʊl/	/u/→/ʊ/	**Tongue Tension**
pull	/pʊl/	/f/→/p/	**Place & Manner**
push	/pʊʃ/	/l/→/ʃ/	**Voicing, Place, & Manner**

Exercise 20-O

Word	Trans-cription	How Many Phonemes?	What Is the First Sound?	What Is the Last Sound?
thrill	/θrɪl/	4	/θ/	/l/
does	/dʌz/	3	/d/	/z/
sawed	/sɔd/	3	/s/	/d/
spoke	/spok/	4	/s/	/k/
saws	/sɔz/	3	/s/	/z/
sauce	/sɔs/	3	/s/	/s/
ring	/rɪŋ/	3	/r/	/ŋ/
showed	/ʃod/	3	/ʃ/	/d/
thought	/θɔt/	3	/θ/	/t/
shirt	/ʃɝt/	3	/ʃ/	/t/
year	/jɪɚ/	2	/j/	/ɪɚ/
straight	/stret/	5	/s/	/t/
mixed	/mɪkst/	5	/m/	/t/
bathe	/beð/	3	/b/	/ð/
joint	/dʒɔɪnt/	4	/dʒ/	/t/
though	/ðo/	2	/ð/	/o/
sheer	/ʃɪɚ/	2	/ʃ/	/ɪɚ/
laughed	/læft/	4	/l/	/t/
know	/no/	2	/n/	/o/
fox	/faks/	4	/f/	/s/
shrink	/ʃrɪŋk/	5	/ʃ/	/k/
numb	/nʌm/	3	/n/	/m/

Word	Trans-cription	How Many Phonemes?	What Is the First Sound?	What Is the Last Sound?
square	/skwɛɚ/	4	/s/	/ɛɚ/
change	/tʃendʒ/	4	/tʃ/	/dʒ/
chew	/tʃu/	2	/tʃ/	/u/
cheese	/tʃiz/	3	/tʃ/	/z/
jay	/dʒe/	2	/dʒ/	/e/
snitch	/snɪtʃ/	4	/s/	/tʃ/
cash	/kæʃ/	3	/k/	/ʃ/
boy	/bɔɪ/	2	/b/	/ɔɪ/
fresh	/frɛʃ/	4	/f/	/ʃ/
gnawed	/nɔd/	3	/n/	/d/
thing	/θɪŋ/	3	/θ/	/ŋ/
clear	/klɪɚ/	3	/k/	/ɪɚ/
wow	/waʊ/	3	/w/	/aʊ/
real	/ril/	3	/r/	/l/
binge	/bɪndʒ/	4	/b/	/dʒ/

Exercise 20-P

j o y f̄ u l	t i n̄ k e r	t a l̄ k
k n o w n̄	c l ī m b	s u n̄ḡ
a u t ū m n	s h o u l̄d̄	v i s̄ i o n
t h o u g h t̄	k n i g h t̄	f r e̅ s h
c h o o s̄e̅	k i t̄c̄h̄ e n	s t a̅r̄ t
p a t̄c̄h̄ w o r k	s h r ī n k	n u m̄b̄
s h o c̄k̄ s	s o o t̄h̄e̅	p s y c̄h̄e̅
r o u ḡh̄	s q ū a r e	n a p̄ k i n
u n l̄ e s s	g n a w e̅d̄	t h o r n̄
b a t̄h̄e̅	s c r̄ i p t	s h r ī m p
c h u r c̄h̄	c h o r d̄	g l o̅w̄

Exercise 20-Q

Voiced sound: owl, bold, that, my
No coda: how, far, joy, blow
Voiceless sound: far, him, shine
Back tense vowel: boot, juice, most
Front vowels: beet, bit, bat, bait
Velar nasal: thank, tongue, sphinx
Not simple syllables: green, friend, think
Four or more phonemes: train

Bilabial sound: pop, farm, me
Low vowel: gnat, hot, cot
Not onset: all, honor, own, oh
Mid vowel: mate, mutt, note, nerd
Fricative: who, cell, vast, psych
Diphthong: buy, cow, voice, rhyme, house
Sonorant for coda: spin, spell, comb
Consonant sequence: graph, most, box, basket, skill
Affricate: junior, chair, strange

Exercise 20-R

Less	Graphemes than phonemes in the English language
Less	Allographs for the sound /h/ than for /f/
More	Consonants than vowels
More	Controlled r diphthongs than non-phonemic diphthongs
More	Unrounded vowels than rounded
Less	Tense vowels than lax
More	High vowels than low
More	Obstruents than sonorants
More	Voiced consonants than voiceless
More	Fricatives than stridents

Exercise 20-S: affricates, nasals, liquids, stop-plosives, glides, fricatives, approximants, sibilants

CHAPTER 21

Exercise 21-A: stung /ʌ/; strong /ɔ/; thing /ɪ/; slang /æ/; pong /ɔ/; length /ɛ/; bank /æ/; hung /ʌ/; cling /ɪ/; gang /æ/; tongs /ɔ/; tongue /ʌ/; junk /ʌ/; sings /ɪ/; think /ɪ/; hang /æ/

Exercise 21-B: bring /ŋ/; Jenga /ŋg/; blanks /ŋks/; morning /ŋ/; stronger /ŋg/; bongo /ŋg/; links /ŋks/; kangaroo /ŋg/; mink /ŋk/; gang /ŋ/; dangle /ŋg/; wrong /ŋ/; rancor /ŋk/; England /ŋg/; thinker /ŋk/

Exercise 21-C

Transcribed correctly: /strɛnθ/, /tæŋ/, /dɪpɪŋ/, /θæŋk/, /strɔŋ/, /sɪŋ/, /tʌŋ/, /lɔŋgɚ/
Transcribed incorrectly: /piŋ/, /rɛŋk/, /stiŋk/, /drepɪŋ/

Exercise 21-D: /æŋgɚ/, /sɪŋɚ/, /tæŋgo/; /hʌŋgɚ/, /præŋk/, /kɪŋ/; /dɛndʒɚ/, /ɪŋglɪʃ/, /klæŋ/; /kɪŋdəm/, /æŋgəl/, /bæŋkɚ/; /mɪŋgəl/, /dʒɪndʒɚ/, /sevɪŋz/; /lɔŋgɚ/, /fɪŋgɚ/, /spʌndʒ/; /ɪŋglənd/, /strɛnθən/, /jʌŋ/; /dʒʌŋgəl/, /sprɪŋ/, /rʌnɪŋ/

Exercise 21-E

Plurals

/sæk/ → /sæks/; /bɔl/ → /bɔlz/; /pɪn/ → /pɪnz/; /kʌp/ → /kʌps/; /rʌb/ → /rʌbz/; /kaɚ/ → /kaɚz/; /bɔɪ/ → /bɔɪz/; /wɝd/ → /wɝdz/; /pis/ → /pisəz/; /bræntʃ/ → /bræntʃəz/; /tæks/ → /tæksəz/; /dɪʃ/ → /dɪʃəz/

Third-Person Regular Tense (e.g., I go, you go, he goes)

/rʌb/ → /rʌbz/; /pʊt/ → /pʊts/; /raɪd/ → /raɪdz/; /tap/ → /taps/; /lʊk/ → /lʊks/; /rʌn/ → /rʌnz/; /tɔs/ → /tɔsəz/; /wɪʃ/ → /wɪʃəz/; /gɛs/ → /gɛsəz/

Past Tense

/stap/ → /stapt/; /rab/ → /rabd/; /nak/ → /nakt/; /pil/ → /pild/; /pʊʃ/ → /pʊʃt/; /kɔf/ → /kɔft/; /lɪv/ → /lɪvd/; /mʌntʃ/ → /mʌntʃt/; /trit/ → /tritəd/; /mɛlt/ → /mɛltəd/; /tred/ → /tredəd/

Exercise 21-F: yells /jɛlz/; stayed /sted/; typed /taɪpt/; hugs /hʌgz/; clapped /klæpt/; sings /sɪŋz/; lands /lændz/; tossed /tɔst/; toes /toz/; boys /bɔɪz/; etched /ɛtʃt/; facts /fæks/; climbed /klaɪmd/; grows /groz/; clowns /klaʊnz/; shrinks /ʃrɪŋks/; lengths /lɛŋθs/; dimes /daɪmz/; brains /brenz/; aimed /emd/; counts /kaʊnts/; tensed /tɛnst/; moaned /mond/; turns /tɝnz/; guided /gaɪdəd/; started /staɚtəd/; wishes /wɪʃəz/; guesses /gɛsəz/

Exercise 21-G

humid	/hjuməd/	plow	/plaʊ/	bowl	/bol/
Cuba	/kjubə/	toy	/tɔɪ/	cube	/kjub/
few	/fju/	whose	/huz/	cow	/kaʊ/
snowing	/snowɪŋ/	chewy	/tʃuwɪ/	enjoy	/ɛndʒɔɪ/
once	/wʌns/	destroy	/dɪstrɔɪ/	view	/vju/
cutest	/kjutəst/	future	/fjutʃɚ/	cure	/kjɝ/
humor	/hjumɚ/	own	/on/	sewer	/sowɚ/
employer	/ɛmplɔɪjɚ/	employ	/ɛmplɔɪ/	fumes	/fjumz/
thy	/ðaɪ/	myth	/mɪθ/	quilt	/kwɪlt/

Exercise 21-H

Transcribed correctly	scene	shirt	
	what	tucked	
	those	gleam	
	dish	down	
	fox	grown	
	health		
Transcribed incorrectly	done	/dʌn/	
	noise	/nɔɪz/	

how	/haʊ/
use	/juz/
cheat	/tʃit/
yawn	/jɔn/ or /jan/
calm	/kalm/ or /kɔlm/
teeth	/tiθ/
knead	/nid/
couch	/kaʊtʃ/
juice	/dʒus/
stormed	/stɔɚmd/
paint	/pent/
first	/fɝst/
pears	/pɛɚz/
who	/hu/

Exercise 21-I

Transcribed correctly	plums	them	pitch
Transcribed incorrectly	though		/ðo/
	rise		/raɪz/
	cough		/kɔf/
	rang		/ræŋ/
	wow		/waʊ/
	judge		/dʒʌdʒ/
	wink		/wɪŋk/
	booth		/buθ/
	spiced		/spaɪst/
	cows		/kaʊz/
	think		/θɪŋk/
	joy		/dʒɔɪ/

Exercise 21-J: shopping, healthy, public, withered; squinted, jammed, valued, igloo; jealous, ponder, gentle, thoughtful; pleasure, mistake, amused, surface; lucky, morning, kernel, cocoon; supported, millionaire, impatient, privacy; comical, equation, discover, ballerina; obligation, signature, fantastic, quality

CHAPTER 22

Exercise 22-A: instant, ~~between~~, brother; ~~engage~~, hydrant, recent; ~~diving~~, instead, above; boxer, fighter, ~~enough~~;

virus, illness, ~~disease~~; succeed, ~~table~~, erase; ~~button~~, pretend, debrief; liquid, sizzle, ~~away~~; bacon, ~~upon~~, open; ~~summer~~, survive, salute; balloon, trapeze, ~~comma~~; focus, ~~aware~~, silent; ~~assume~~, problem, traffic; ~~follow~~, contain, secure; declare, patrol, ~~scarlet~~

Exercise 22-B: /bʌzɪŋ/; /fɔlɪŋ/; /læstɪŋ/; /baɪkɪŋ/; /klaʊnɪŋ/; /kɝlɪŋ/ /fɛnsɪŋ/; /stɪŋɪŋ/; /mitɪŋ/; /bolɪŋ/; /tʃɑ˞mɪŋ/; /rʌnɪŋ/ /draɪvɪŋ/ /bʌksɪŋ/; /klæpɪŋ/; /fraʊnɪŋ/; /taɪpɪŋ/; /puʃɪŋ/; /pʌntʃɪŋ/; /sɝvɪŋ/; /dɑdʒɪŋ/; /tʌtʃɪŋ;/ /dʒʌmpɪŋ/; /jatɪŋ/; /staɪlɪŋ/; /lʊkɪŋ/; /onɪŋ/; /juzɪŋ/

Exercise 22-C

Transcribed with /ɪ/ as the final sound: hungry, crazy, kindly, funky, groovy, baby, truly, really, freely, handy, sunny, daily, simply, fully, shyly

Other sound is final sound of the word or not an /ɪ/ sound: monkey, cry, turkey, hockey, cowboy, rely, enjoy, play, unify

Exercise 22-D: /krezɪ/; /stɪkɪ/; /sɔftlɪ/; /dʒɛntlɪ/; /mʌnθlɪ/; /pɪkɪ/; /dʒʌmpɪ/; /tʃɪlɪ/; /graʊtʃɪ/; /kwɪklɪ/; /frɛndlɪ/; /nɔɪzɪ/; /kɝlɪ/; /grisɪ/; /bɔsɪ/; /slolɪ/; /skwikɪ/; /krʌmblɪ/

Exercise 22-E

First-Syllable Stress: stories, person, thirsty, sisters, writing, harvest, partner, fairly, feather, purple, yellow, nervous, foolish, fifty, member

Second-Syllable Stress: pollute, amaze, compare, extreme, afford, disturb, patrol

Exercise 22-F: /ʌndɚ/, /ɔθɚ/, /læðɚ/, /brʌðɚ/; /bɑðɚ/, /mɝdɚ/, /sʌmɚ/, /æŋkɚ/, /watɚ/, /manstɚ/, /θʌndɚ/, /ʃʌdɚ/; /ʃutɚ/, /æŋgɚ/, /rɪŋɚ/, /blʌʃɚ/, /ʌʃɚ/, /mɪstɚ/, /bɛtɚ/, /læðɚ/

Exercise 22-G: /vɪʒən/ /ɛksɛptəns/ /laɪkəbəl/ /mjutənt/; /mɪʃən/ /wʌndrəs/ /ækʃən/ /gɔɚdʒəs/; /moʃən/ /sɝvənt/ /straɪdənt/ /dʒʌdʒmənt/; /vɝʒən/ /kənfjuʒən/ /neʃən/ /kəmoʃən/

Exercise 22-H: /əbaɪd/ /əbaʊnd/ /əbrʌpt/ /əfred/; /əbjuz/ /əkaʊnt/ /əkjuz/ /əlon/; /əkwaɪɚ/ /ədʒɝn/ /əfɔɚd/ /əwe/; /əvɔɪd/ /əbaʊt/ /əbʌv/ /əlaʊ/; /ənɔɪ /əʃɚ/ /əkrɔs/ /əmɪd/

Exercise 22-I: /sɝkəl/ /dʒɝnəl/ /kɝnəl/ /tebəl/; /θɝməl/ /bʌkəl/ /nʌkəl/ /kændəl/; /stʌmbəl/ /nɪkəl/ /dʒʌŋgəl/ /pɪstəl/; /æŋgəl/ /ʃɪŋgəl/ /kɝnəl/ /trʌbəl/

Exercise 22-J

ɝ ə	ʌ ə	ə ɝ
colonel	dozen	avert
mural	fungus	allure
surface	muscle	secure
courage	stumbled	

ɝ ə	ʌ ə	ə ɝ
person	bubble	
turnip	troubled	
nervous	budget	
urgent	junction	
serpent		
journal		

ə ʌ	ɝ ɚ	ʌ ɚ
convulse	merger	culture
combust	murmur	hunger
annul	worker	bummer
succumb	nurture	sculpture
among	further	muffler
		usher
		thunder

Exercise 22-K

Group A:

First-Syllable Stress: easy, Egypt, eagle, either, even

Second-Syllable Stress: elect, eclipse, elite, erupt, emote, enough, equate

Group B:

First-Syllable Stress: omen, open, oboe, ogre, okra, odor

Second-Syllable Stress: obey, oblique, obese, overt, oblige, oppress

Group C:

First-Syllable Stress: inner, infant, instant, inches, insect, index

Second-Syllable Stress: infer, involve, indeed, intrude, inflict, instead

Group D:

Second-Syllable Stress: around, avenge, afraid, adore, amass, alike, achieve, aloof, abuse, adapt, avoid, anoint, atone, arise, astound

Exercise 22-L

success	1	**2**	pleasant	**1**	2	relief	1	**2**
debate	1	**2**	couple	**1**	2	urgent	**1**	2
create	1	**2**	embrace	1	**2**	decay	1	**2**
enough	1	**2**	gallop	**1**	2	thunder	**1**	2
mother	**1**	2	culture	**1**	2	journal	**1**	2
believe	1	**2**	purpose	**1**	2	perturb	1	**2**
easel	**1**	2	ideal	1	**2**	intend	1	**2**
leather	**1**	2	heavy	**1**	2	agree	1	**2**

Exercise 22-M

Transcribed correctly: region, neutral, mother, motion, thinker. Changes needed for alone /əlon/; couple /kʌpəl/; judgement /dʒʌdʒmənt/; nickels /nɪkəlz/; thunder /θʌndɚ/; quarters /kwɔˑtɚz/; fingers /fɪŋgɚz/; papers /pepɚz/; running /rʌnɪŋ/

Exercise 22-N: balloon, manage, honest; mistake, treasure, guitar; govern, herbal, convulse

Exercise 22-O: assist /əsɪst/; pertain /pɚten/; lucky /lʌkɪ/; happen /hæpən/; siphon; /saɪfən/; provoke /prəvok/; western /wɛstɚn/; language /læŋgwədʒ/; stagnant /stægnənt/; loser /luzɚ/; unsure /ənʃɝ/; twenty /twɛntɪ/

Exercise 22-P: af ter noon /æftɚˑnun/; bas ke tball /bæskətbɔl/; book keep er /bʊkipɚ/; busi ness man /bɪznəsmæn/; candle stick /kændəlstɪk/; hamburg er /hæmbɝˑgɚ/; com mon place /kamənples/; fin ger print /fɪŋgɚprɪnt/; fur ther more /fɝˑðɚˑmɔˑ/; gin ger bread /dʒɪndʒɚbrɛd/; o ther wise /ʌðɚwaɪz/; su mmer time /sʌmɚˑtaɪm/; ne verthe less (has 2) /nɛvɚˑðəlɛs/

Exercise 22-Q

❶ ○ ○ ○	○ ❷ ○ ○	○ ○ ❸ ○
/jutɔ/	/rodaɪlənd/	/mæsətʃusɪts/
/dɛləwɛɚ/	/mantænə/	/kæləfɔˑnjə/
/tɛksəs/	/wɪskansən/	/saʊθdəkotə/
/dʒɔɚˑdʒə/	/vɚˑmant/	/okləhomə/
/kænzəs/	/kəntʌki/	/kalərado/
/aɚˑkænsɔ/	/nudʒɝˑzi/	/ɛɚˑəzonə/
/mɪʃəgən/	/vɚˑdʒɪnjə/	/pɛnsəlvenjə/
/ɔɚˑəgən/	/nuhæmpʃɚ/	/ɪndiænə/
/flɔɚˑədə/	/ohaɪjo/	/mɪsəsɪpi/
/waʃɪŋtən/	/kənɛtəkət/	/tɛnəsi/
/mɛɚˑələnd/	/numɛksəko/	/ɪlənɔɪ/
/aɪdəho/	/waɪjomɪŋ/	/mɪnəsotə/
/aɪəwə/	/həwaɪi/	
	/məzɝˑi/	
	/əlæskə/	
	/nəvædə/	
	/nəbræskə/	

Exercise 22-R

surrounded	2 /sɚˑaʊnded/ 2 /səraʊndəd/	daffodil	1 /dæfodɪl/	India	1 /ɪndiə/ /ɪndijə/
example	2 /ɛgzæmpəl/	pharyngeal	2 /fərɪndʒəl/	ebony	1 /ɛbənɪ/
outrageous	2 / aʊtredʒəs/	misery	1 /mɪzɚˑɪ/ 1 /mɪzərɪ/	caribou	1 /kɛɚˑəbu/
clavicle	1 / klævəkəl/	stupendous	2 /stupɛndəs/	discover	2 /dɪskʌvɚ/
bananas	2 / bənænəz/	clarinet	3 /klɛɚˑənɛt/ 3 /klɛrənɛt/	violin	1 /vaɪəlɪn/
creative	2 / krietəv /	plantation	2 /plænteʃən/	asterisk	1 /æstɚˑɪsk/
persona	2 /pɚˑsonə/	spectacle	1 /spɛktəkəl/	terrified	1 /tɛɚˑəfaɪd/
distinctive	2 / dəstɪŋktəv/ 2 / dəstɪŋktɪv/	calendar	1 / kæləndɚ/	subscription	2 /səbskrɪpʃən/
expertise	3 /ɛkspɚˑtis/	magical	1 / mædʒəkəl/	majestic	2 /mədʒɛstɪk/
magenta	2 /mədʒɛntə/	arabesque	3 /ɛɚˑəbɛsk/	foundation	2 /faʊndeʃən/
assessment	2 /əsɛsmənt/	phonetics	2 /fənɛtɪks/		

The impact of morphophonemic changes on stress and vowel/consonant changes.

-ity Major stress is always on the syllable before the suffix.
ethnic /ɛθnɪk/; ethnicity /ɛθnɪsətɪ/ /ɪtɪ/; public /pʌblɪk/; publicity /pəblɪsətɪ/ /ɪtɪ/; solemn /saləm/; solemnity /səlɛmnətɪ/ /ɪtɪ/; divine /dəvaɪn/; divinity /dəvɪnətɪ/; similar /sɪmələ-/; similarity /sɪmɛlɛə-ətɪ/ /ɪtɪ/; abnormal /æbnɔə-məl/; abnormality /æbnɔə-mælətɪ/; sensitive /sɛnsətɪv/; sensitivity /sɛnsətɪvətɪ/

-ic Major stress is always on the syllable before the suffix.
athlete /æθlit/; athletic /æθlɛtɪk/ /ək/; magnet /mægnət/; magnetic; /mægnɛtɪk/ /ək/; chaos /keas/; chaotic /keatɪk/ /ək/; melody /mɛlədɪ/; melodic /məladɪk/ /ək/; nomad /nomæd/; nomadic /nomædɪk/ /ək/

-ical Major stress on syllable before the suffix
history /hɪstɔə-ɪ/; historical /hɪstɔə-ɪkəl/ /əkəl/; hysterics /hɪstɛə-ɪks/; hysterical /hɪstɛə-ɪkəl/ /əkəl/; politics /palətɪks/; political /pəlɪtəkəl/ /əkəl/

-tion/-sion Major stress always on syllable before the -tion/-sion
locate /loket/; location /lokeʃən/; invite /ɪnvaɪt/; invitation /ɪnvəteʃən/; create /kriet/; creation /krieʃən/; devote /dəvot/; devotion /dəvoʃən/; celebrate /sɛləbret/; celebration /sɛləbreʃən/; separate /sɛpəret/; separation /sɛpəreʃən/

What consonant changes did you notice in this group of words when the suffix –tion was added?
/t/ → /ʃ/
decide /dəsaɪd/; decision /dəsɪʒən/; invade /ɪnved/; invasion /ɪnveʒən/; divide /dəvaɪd/; division /dəvɪʒən/; collide /kəlaɪd/; collision /kəlɪʒən/; conclude /kənklud/; conclusion /kənkluʒən/

What consonant changes did you notice in this group of words when the suffix –sion was added?
/d/ → /ʒ/
fuse /fjuz/; fusion /fjuʒən/; revise /revaɪz/; revision /rəvɪʒən/; televise /tɛləvaɪz/; television /tɛləvɪʒən/; immerse /ɪmɝs/; immersion /ɪmɝʒən/; confuse /kənfjuz/; confusion /kənfjuʒən/

What consonant changes did you notice in this group of words when the suffix –sion was added?
/z/ → /ʒ/

Exercise 22-S

detain /dəten/	detention /dətɛnʃən/
gene /dʒin/	genetic /dʒənɛtɪk/

ignite /ɪgnaɪt/		ignition /ɪgnɪʃən/
exclaim /ɛksklem/		exclamation /ɛkskləmeʃən/
partial /paə-ʃəl/		partition /paə-tɪʃən/
substance /sʌbstəns/		substantial /səbstænʃəl/
stable /stebəl/	stability /stəbɪlətɪ/	stabilizer /stebəlaɪzə-/
apply /əplaɪ/	applicable /æplɪkəbəl/	application /æplɪkeʃən/
local /lokəl/	location /lokeʃən/	locality /lokælətɪ/
confide /kənfaɪd/	confident /kanfədənt/	confidential /kanfedɛnʃəl/
receive /rəsiv/	receptor /rəsɛptə-/	reception /rəsɛpʃən/
vocal /vokəl/	vocalic /vokælək/	vocalize /vokəlaɪz/
brief /brif/	brevity /brɛvətɪ/	abbreviate /əbriviet/
vision /vɪʒən/	revise /rəvaɪz/	visionary /vɪʒənɛə-ɪ/
sign /saɪn/	signal /sɪgnəl/	signify /sɪgnəfaɪ/
diction /dɪkʃən/	indicate /ɪndəket/	contradict /kantrədɪkt/
social /soʃəl/	associate /əsosiet/	association /əsosieʃən/
legal /ligəl/	illegal /ɪligəl/	legality /ləgælətɪ/
recite /rəsaɪt/	citation /saɪteʃən/	recitation /rɛsəteʃən/
impose /ɪmpoz/	imposter /ɪmpastə-/	imposition /ɪmpəzɪʃən/
fate /fet/	fatal /fetəl/	fatality /fətælətɪ/
elastic /əlæstɪk/	elasticity /əlæstɪsɪtɪ/	elasticize /əlæstəsaɪz/

Exercise 22-T: forced /fɔə-st/; newspaper /nuzpepə-/; thirsty /θɝstɪ/; yawning /jɔnɪŋ/; angel /endʒəl/; bounced /baʊnst/; thank you /θæŋkju/; Asian /eʒən/; stings /stɪŋz/; hungry /hʌŋgrɪ/; adorn /ədɔrn/; butcher /bʊtʃə-/; drinks /drɪŋks/; onion /ʌnjən/; delicacy /dɛləkəsɪ/; disruption /dɪsrʌpʃən/; domestic /dəmɛstək/; sequence /sikwəns/; awkward /ɔkwə-d/; musicbox /mjuzɪkbaks/; commander /kəmændə-/; thereafter /ðɛə-æftə-/; dangerous /dendʒərəs/; icecubes /aɪskjubz/; gangster /gæŋstə-/; cucumber /kjukəmbə-/; betrayed /bətred/; unworthy /ənwɝðɪ/; reached /ritʃt/; phonology /fənaləddʒɪ/; articulation /aə-tɪkjəleʃən/; underneath /ʌndə-niθ/; excellent /ɛksələnt/; computer /kəmpjutə-/; thinking /θɪŋkɪŋ/; sixteenth /sɪkstinθ/; classify /klæsəfaɪ/; sympathy /sɪmpəθɪ/; examine /ɛgzæmɪn/; indication /ɪndəkeʃən/; positive /pazɪtɪv/; accidentally /æksɪdɛntəlɪ/; exchange /ɛkstʃendʒ/; handful /hændfʊl/; luscious /lʌʃəs/; phonemes /fonimz/

Exercise 22-U

● ○ ○	○ ❷ ○	○ ○ ❸
comedy /kamədɪ/	unusual /ənjuʒəwəl/ /ənjuʒwəl/	diagnosis /daɪəgnosəs/

generator /dʒɛnɚ-etɚ/	romantic /roʊmæntɪk/	definition /dɛfənɪʃən/
dominance /damənəns/	attendant /ətɛndənt/	imitation /ɪməteʃən/
useful /jusfəl/	agility /ədʒɪlətɪ/	population /papjəleʃən/
iodine /aɪədaɪn/	debate /dəbet/	Mississippi /mɪsəsɪpi/
awful /ɔfəl/	election /əlɛkʃən/	constitution /kanstətuʃən/
essence /ɛsəns/	vacation /vəkeʃən/	
camera /kæmrə/	reluctant /rəlʌktənt/	
average /ævrədʒ/	expecting /ɛkspɛktɪŋ/	
never /nɛvɚ/	October /aktobɚ/	
	uncommon /ənkamən/	
	banana /bənænə/	
	unstable /ənstebəl/	
	ignore /ɪgnɔɚ/	

Exercise 22-V

Syllable Stress

1		instrument	/ɪnstrəmənt/
1		famous	/feməs/
1		after	/æftɚ/
	2	opponent	/əponənt/
1		learning	/lɝnɪŋ/
1		study	/stʌdɪ/
1		calendar	/kæləndɚ/
1		server	/sɝvɚ/
1		industry	/ɪndəstrɪ/
1		certain	/sɝtən/
1		partner	/paɚtnɚ/
1		cultural	/kʌltʃərəl/

1		country	/kʌntrɪ/
	2	division	/dəvɪʒən/
1		telephone	/tɛləfon/
1		Canada	/kænədə/
	2	occurrence	/əkɝəns/
1		personal	/pɝsənəl/
	2	condition	/kəndɪʃən/
	2	commercial	/kəmɝʃəl/
	2	commencement	/kəmɛnsmənt/
	2	processional	/prosɛʃənəl/
	2	humanity	/hjumænətɪ/
1		magnify	/mægnəfaɪ/
	2	assure	/əʃɝ/
	2	prediction	/prədɪkʃən/
	2	construction	/kənstrʌkʃən/

Exercise 22-W: /sɝvəs/, /gresfəl/; /nɔtɪ/, /ətʃivɚ/; /bʌbəl/, /lɛvəld/; /əgɛn/, /damənoz/; /gɪgəld/, /prɪzənɚ/; /plɛzəntriz/, /æbsəns/, /kansoləbəl/, /gɔɚdʒəs/; /səfɪʃənt/, /səfɪʃənsɪ/; /ɛntrəns/, /rəlaɪəbəl/; /prəvɛnʃən/, /rɛvəluʃən/; /pɚsɪstəns/, /kənvin/; /paɚʃəl/, /kənvɛnʃən/; /brɪljənt/, /momənt/; /brɪljəns/, /momɛntəs/; /rɛzədənt/, /kɚedʒəs/; /dəbetəbəl/, /kɝədʒ/; /vaɪbreʃən/, /kənvinjənt/; /trævlɚ/, /dɪfrəns/; /vaɪlənt/, /vɛndʒəns/; /ɪmprəvaɪz/, /aɚkətɛkt/; /dəsɛmbɚ/, /eprəl/; /frikwəntlɪ/, /θɔtfəl/; /tɛstɪŋ/, /æθlɛtɪk/; /næʃənælətɪ/, /næʃənəl/; /əlɛktrɪsətɪ/, /əlɛktrɪk/; /kənfjuʒən/, /ənebəl/; /brʌðɚ/, /sɝkəs/; /ɪnkʌmplɪʃən/, /ɪmbæləns/; /kəntɛndɚ/, /kəmɪtɪ/; /ɪmpasəbəl/, /əbʌndənt/; /əfɛɚ/, /səspɪʃən/; /kəmpænjən/, /baɪsɪkəl/; /əmjuzmənt/, /əsɝʃən/; /sɪləbəl/, /krɪtəkəl/; /ɛmpəθɪ/, /mjuzɪʃən/

Exercise 22-X: phonics, enjoy, stallion, ahead; glancing, myself, strengthen, tango; major, compound, climate, yellow; measure, amnesia, volume, famous; union, poison, survivor, lawful; yesterday, connection, treasure, away; junior, chocolate, pollution, lovely; beyond, lengthen, ownership, model; fingers, athlete, across, outer; teacher, flower, telephone, often; unfasten, written, quota, shallow; center, pacify, disqualified, closet; shoestring, dinosaur, compassion, laughter; university, liquid, anguish, bandaid

AUDIO CD KEY FOR TRANSCRIPTION PRACTICE

Set 1: 1. /e/ 2. /ɑ/ 3. /i/ 4. /ʊ/ 5. /æ/ 6. /u/ 7. /ɪ/ 8. /ɔ/ 9. /ɛ/ 10. /o/

Set 2: 1. /vo/ 2. /hʊ/ 3. /sæ/ 4. /ke/ 5. /bɪ/ 6. /ip/ 7. /ɔm/ 8. /ɛp/ 9. /ut/ 10. /ɑg/

Set 3: 1. /us/ 2. /gi/ 3. /ko/ 4. /ɛv/ 5. /ʊp/ 6. /ef/ 7. /læ/ 8. /zɑ/ 9. /tɪ/ 10. /ɔz/

Set 4: 1. /sɝt/ 2. /hʌp/ 3. /tog/ 4. /huk/ 5. /zæb/ 6. /fos/ 7. /wɛk/ 8. /gɝm/ 9. /lʌz/ 10. /hep/

Set 5: 1. /maʊ/ 2. /lɔɪ/ 3. /faɪ/ 4. /ɔɪp/ 5. /aʊd/ 6. /aɪk/ 7. /dɔɪb/ 8. /saʊt/ 9. /zaɪg/ 10. /hɔɪm/

Set 6: 1. /hʌz/ 2. /mɛb/ 3. /daʊp/ 4. /lug/ 5. /kaɪp/ 6. /nɝt/ 7. /wem/ 8. /zof/ 9. /ris/ 10. /sæf/

Set 7: 1. /ɑɚd/ 2. /kɪɚ/ 3. /ɛɚt/ 4. /zɔɚ/ 5. /dɪɚn/ 6. /lɔɚp/ 7. /fɑɚb/ 8. /tʊɚv/ 9. /pɛɚf/ 10. /mɪɚz/
Note: /r/ can replace each /ɚ/ symbol; e.g., 1. /ɑɚd/ or /ɑrd/

Set 8: 1. /aɪb/ 2. /mɝ/ 3. /nʌv/ 4. /hɛp/ 5. /suf/ 6. /gɛɚd/ or /gɛrd/ 7. /bɔɪm/ 8. /lot/ 9. /hɪɚk/ or /hɪrk/ 10. /paʊz/

Set 9: 1. /tʊb/ 2. /gɛp/ 3. /dok/ 4. /kaɪd/ 5. /taʊg/ 6. /gæt/ 7. /tɔɪp/ 8. /kɪɚd/ or /kɪrd/ 9. /tɔɚb/ or /tɔrb/ 10. /dup/

Set 10: 1. /zɛɚ/ or /zɛr/ 2. /sɪtʃ/ 3. /fæʃ/ 4. /hɪɚv/ or /hɪrv/ 5. /tʃis/ 6. /θuz/ 7. /dʒof/ 8. /heð/ 9. /fɝdʒ/ 10. /ʃaʊs/

Set 11: 1. /faʊm/ 2. /dʒʊt/ 3. /hɪɚʃ/ or /hɪrʃ/ 4. /dʌʒ/ 5. /pus/ 6. /vɔɪn/ 7. /tʃæk/ 8. /peʃ/ 9. /soθ/ 10. /gaɪð/

Set 12: 1. /mʌn/ 2. /lɪŋ/ 3. /jem/ 4. /nɔɪl/ 5. /wɛm/ 6. /wæŋ/ 7. /jaɪm/ 8. /laʊn/ 9. /lɝl/ 10. /rɪn/

Set 13: 1. /klɝ/ 2. /staʊ/ 3. /skɪɚ/ or /skɪr/ 4. /twe/ 5. /plɚ/ or /plɔr/ 6. /snaɪð/ 7. /plɪf/ 8. /græp/ 9. /smɑθ/ 10. /swɪt/

Set 14: 1. /ɔɪps/ 2. /ʌlf/ 3. /æntʃ/ 4. /opt/ 5. /aʊsp/ 6. /vuks/ 7. /nɛft/ 8. /dʒɔɚmd/ or /dʒɔrmd/ 9. /rɑps/ 10. /tʃaɪst/

Set 15: 1 /plæsk/ 2. /spondʒ/ 3. /flɪŋk/ 4. /ʃlumd/ 5. /blɔɪts/ 6. /staɪmp/ 7. /kwosk/ 8. /grɑŋk/ 9. /klɝsp/ 10. /smʌzd/

Index